The Darlings of Downing Street

The psychosexual drama of power

Also by Garry O'Connor

Biography
The Pursuit of Perfection: A Life of Maggie Teyte
Ralph Richardson: An Actor's Life
Darlings of the Gods: One Year in the Lives of Laurence Olivier and
Vivien Leigh
Olivier: In Celebration (editor)
Sean O'Casey: A Life
William Shakespeare: A Life
Alec Guinness: Master of Disguise
The Secret Woman: A Life of Peggy Ashcroft
William Shakespeare: A Popular Life
Paul Scofield: The Biography
Alec Guinness, the Unknown: A Life
Universal Father: A Life of Pope John Paul II

Fiction
Darlings of the Gods (novel)
Campion's Ghost: The Sacred and Profane Memories of John Donne,
Poet
Chaucer's Triumph

Drama
Different Circumstances
Dialogue between Friends

Theatre and cinema studies
Le Théâtre en Grande-Bretagne
French Theatre Today
The Mahabharata: Peter Brook's Epic in the Making

The Darlings of Downing Street

The psychosexual drama of power

Garry O'Connor

POLITICO'S

First published in Great Britain 2007 by
Politico's Publishing, an imprint of
Methuen & Co. Ltd
11–12 Buckingham Gate
London
SW1E 6LB

1

Copyright © Garry O'Connor 2007

Garry O'Connor has asserted his right under the Copyright, Designs and Patents Act 1988 to be identified as the author of this work.

A CIP catalogue record for this book is available from the British Library.

ISBN 978-1-84275-202-9

Typeset by SX Composing DTP, Rayleigh, Essex
Printed and bound in Great Britain by Biddles Ltd, King's Lynn, Norfolk

Contents

A political speech, a piece of assertive propaganda, a plan for a new society or a philosophical system can all be built with apparent harmony even on an error, or a lie; and what has been hidden or distorted will not be immediately apparent.

Alexander Solzhenitsyn, 'One Word of Truth'

Nemo iudex in sua casa.

Latin proverb

Preface

The ten years of Tony and Cherie Blair's tenure of Downing Street have shifted all of us, myself included, from being relative outsiders to the workings of power, to the status of privileged insiders. The revolution brought about by the internet in the global and instant dissemination of facts, opinions, rumours and propaganda has added to the endless availability of material to draw on. More crucially, the torrent of leaks, supplemented by the unchecked flow of often premature memoirs and diaries, with an effect mainly indescribable in the boredom and sense of dreary self-righteousness they induce, has extended the reservoir of sources on which one can draw to almost limitless horizons.

Writing this book is, to some degree, the same as with all books: an effort to extricate myself from the subject, and moor my frail craft – such as it is, and if not shipwrecked – to terra firma. But the process has also been an exhilarating voyage of discovery, and for that I must thank all concerned. I can only hope that for some it might serve as a warning, as well as laying down a few precepts to be followed by anyone who might want to enter politics. 'Abandon all hope, you who enter here!' wrote Dante over the entrance to Inferno: I might add, for anyone thinking of entering Downing Street, 'Be warned. It's not a talent contest. It's never going to be rites-of-passage fiction, and end with a beautiful epiphany, or an awards ceremony.'

I have tried to keep to a chronology as far as possible. I have hardly touched on recent issues such as the outcome of the cash-for-honours police investigation. The arrest of the ultimate power in the land might make the perfect ending to the book, but I have no crystal ball, nor would I wish this on him or on anyone.

My involvement in writing a life of the previous Pope landed me, purely by chance, in Rome in February 2003, just prior to the Iraqi war, when

Tony and Cherie Blair were visiting the Vatican. From here, grounded in the religious aspect of their mingled yarn of politics and personal life, sprouted my interest in writing this book, and some of its source material. But this was not all: as I began, my own experience in struggling with the lives of actors, and bringing works of imagination to biographical scrutiny and investigation, seemed to be appropriate.

By the end I must confess to a certain confusion as to where my own political beliefs lie, as if, in trying to draw a map, some of the contours have become seriously blurred. What I can say is that we have far too rosy a notion of the virtues of power, inflate the image of those who have it or struggle for it to indescribably absurd proportions, and hold an exaggerated belief in its omnipotence. It would be better to have much lower expectations all round and operate, say, with the circumspection of E. M. Forster in his *Two Cheers for Democracy*.

Finally, reflecting what is by now probably the general feeling, I know that politics and the government of one of the great countries in the world should never have become the drama or Aristotelian clash of personalities such as I attempt to narrate, in direct contrast to the dreary blind alley of its endless new 'reforms' and restrictions. In different or better circumstances I would never have written such a book. I fear that the contagion and implication in seeing it as drama or a compelling narrative, as have – unhappily – many of the participants, has spread to me, which is not as it really should be. I can only end by pleading for my shortcomings in this respect, as I am a writer and not a politician or an economist. This book is not intended to be a definitive history or biography, and among the sources for this book there are many that I have preferred for various reasons to leave anonymous. So I have to pass also on the conventional formality of listing those to whom I have spoken. This has at any rate by now become something of a wasteful and unnecessary routine, serving little more than to bolster what can be viewed as a rather spurious form of authority. Here I must ask for the reader's indulgence, and possibly risk the scorn of the scholar.

But even so I express my profound gratitude to those who have talked to me, pointed me in the direction of new material, or given me ideas I would never have thought of myself, and otherwise contributed in a host of different ways, not least, several of them, in reading through the chapters in draft.

Inevitably such a work as this is bound to be a patchwork or mosaic of many different minds and much conflicting observation, so I must insist that all faults as may occur be laid squarely at my door. The perspective or *trompe l'oeil* I provide is entirely my responsibility, as is the interpretation of the material, and neither is to be attributed to anyone else. I also warmly thank all those who have had to suffer the proximity of this writer in the throes of writing and publishing this particular book, the staff of Politico's for its careful, rapid and efficient production, and especially Alan Gordon Walker and Jonathan Wadman for their scrupulous comments and editing, as well as Christopher Sinclair-Stevenson and David Montagu-Smith for their comments, and Samantha Hill for processing my drafts.

May 2007

Introduction

This is a joint biography of Cherie and Tony Blair seen from the perspective of how each has behaved as the mimetic, or imitative, double of the other, and acted out roles for themselves as if in a mirror. From the start the theatrical component is important. In the cases of both, their family and educational backgrounds, their deprivations and heritage of family emotions prepared them for a life of style – or deliberate lack of style – and impersonation rather than substance and depth.

Cherie and Tony have excelled in the present-day culture of politics as a performance art, showing all the arts and traits of showbusiness personalities, while their lives, and the exercise of their power, have been dramatic and suspenseful to a degree probably unsurpassed by any other leader, or leaders, of this country. In this respect it can be called a love story unlike any other.

Tony and Cherie, especially in the early years in Downing Street, exercised and enjoyed, if not exploited, prime ministerial power as a duo, as a dyad of joint rule. A dyad is an atom, radical or element that has the combining power of two elements. Cherie and Tony have consulted together on virtually every issue, and while Tony has been the executor, on most occasions the performer, Cherie has always been visible in the foreground, the adviser and enabler. Since they first met in 1976 each has been the mimetic double of the other, while mutual narcissism has been an important aspect of their lives together. Their mentors for this have been primarily Hillary and Bill Clinton, the American presidential pair, whom Cherie and Tony have worshipped and imitated so far as they have been able to. A story about the Clintons illustrates one fundamental aspect of their own '*égoïsme à deux*', and also provides a clue to how Cherie and Tony relate to each other.

The Clintons are on the road together and pull into a petrol station.

Hillary points to the attendant and says to Bill, 'I used to date that guy.' Bill laughs and says, 'If you'd married him you'd be stuck here instead of being married to the President of the United States.' 'No,' says Hillary, 'if I'd married him, *he'd* be President.'

This book is therefore an account of personalities, and the comic and tragic relationships Cherie and Tony have formed not only with one another, but also with others. It attempts to show how, driven by very personal ambitions, each personality reflects, is affected by and reacts upon the other, and how this has crucially affected the governing of the United Kingdom. Cherie has been incorporated into Tony's years in Downing Street as an integral part of them, and often it has been difficult to define where one of them ends and the other begins, or how they have differed, as on occasions they undeniably have, while ostensibly remaining inseparable. It may be controversial to call them Margaret Thatcher's children and true heirs, but they are the inheritors of the culture that elected them and the chosen favourites of the New Labour party, which at first rapturously applauded them, and continued to support them for two further terms of government.

To those who voted for them in 1997 it was quite evident from the start that they were a double act, so the public and media at large, too, must bear responsibility for encouraging them to fulfil their deep, if well-disguised, personal needs in the exercise of power. Now, as they leave No. 10, and while their influence is still paramount, is the time to relate from within if possible, amid the frantic pace and pressure of their lives in Downing Street, what has driven them – and even why they have been so driven. By personalities, Tony Blair prophesied with a strange, unforeseen accuracy, his own government would eventually be brought down.

It is, as the number of representations we have seen on film, on stage, on television, in the press and the huge volume of widely disseminated response to it shows, a fascinating if unsettling story of deceit and illusion as well as of hope and expectation. It is also a profoundly disturbing tragedy in which, to some extent or other, the whole of mankind has shared.

A note on mimetic desire

'Mimetic' means addicted to or pertaining to imitation. *Mimesis* is the title of Eric Auerbach's seminal work on the representation of reality in Western literature. Mimetic desire, mimetic envy and mimetic rivalry are driving, or motivational, forces of imitation. Shakespeare understood mimetic doubles and mimetic desire better than anyone, and his plays and poems illustrate the dramatic use to which he put his understanding. He defines mimetic desire in such phrases as 'love that stood upon the choice of friends', 'love by one another's eyes' or 'love by hearsay'. That we imitate others in dress, mannerisms, facial expression, speech, body language, artistic creation and so on is undisputed, but we ignore the fundamental aspects of desire and envy which not only create our dramas of personal life, but also carry us into another dimension, that of power and politics. The mimetic desire we have for what others have unites us as long as we can share what we desire, but when we cannot we become the worst of enemies. The rivalry which ensues is then identifiable as a fundamental source of human conflicts, in particular in the struggle to obtain power and keep it. The theory applies just as much to nations as to individuals.

As for mimetic envy, we repress our awareness of it in ourselves. Primitive cultures have feared and repressed envy so much that they have no word for it, while we maintain a silence about envy today, which we feel ashamed to own, while secretly encouraging it in every aspect of our lives. For more on the mimetic theory in general and applied to politics see Appendix 2; I am also indebted to René Girard's exposition in *Things Hidden since the Foundation of the World* and *A Theater of Envy*.

J. K. Galbraith wrote of politics in mediaeval times, 'In such a world politics are embodied in personal affections, or in personal jealousies and hatreds.' Nothing could be more applicable than this to the government of the United Kingdom over the past ten years, while in charge has been the man whom Jack Straw, one of the two longest-serving members of the Cabinet, has called 'a master of ambiguity'. For greater accuracy we might change his wording to 'two masters of ambiguity'.

Part I

1953–1994

1

Seafield Follies

Take my advice, d'Artagnan, when you're in trouble, hide it. Silence is the only refuge of the unhappy. Don't let others into the secrets of your heart; prying folk feed on your fears as the vampires feed on human blood.

Alexandre Dumas, *The Three Musketeers*

Tarquin, the name copied from Laurence Olivier's firstborn son, would have been Cherie Booth's first name had she been born a boy. 'I come from a theatrical family,' says Cherie; 'our home was always revolving around performing and singing.'

Tarquin, the last tyrant of Rome, driven from the city by the republican Brutus's ancestors, tried in vain to recapture it. The other more infamous Tarquin, his son, features as the celebrated ravisher in Shakespeare's *The Rape of Lucrece*. With such a name Cherie Blair might well have become Prime Minister instead of Tony Blair, her husband.

But as well as acting there was a combustible political element in the Booth genes: while Tony Booth, Cherie's father, was once the president of Equity, the actors' union, his great-grandfather was the uncle of John Wilkes Booth, the actor who assassinated Abraham Lincoln. This makes Cherie a first cousin of the assassin four times removed.

Cherie's mother, Gale Smith – as an aspiring young actress she had changed her name from Joyce to Gale – married Tony Booth at Marylebone Register Office six months before Cherie was born. Gale's mother, Hannah, had dark hair and dark eyes like Cherie, and her father, Cyril, a miner, wrote poetry and later took an external degree from

Nottingham University. In his seventies he worked as a night watchman.

As Gale's nine months of pregnancy came to an end she and Tony Booth were staying in Leigh, an old textile town in Lancashire. Gale gave birth to Cherie on Thursday 23 September 1954 in Ward 3 of nearby Bury's Fairfield Hospital. She weighed 13 pounds, possibly a testimony to Gale's solid maternal metabolism and secure expectations of motherhood as she sat in the stalls of Bury's Hippodrome, knitting away at baby clothes and keeping a critical eye on the work of Tony, who was the Fortescue Repertory Company's stage manager, as well as bit part player.

Cherie's body weight at birth was more than twice that of her first son, Euan, who in January 1984 checked in at 5 pounds 10 ounces; by this time Gale's Tony – who earlier called himself grandly Anthony Howard-Booth, had become a household celebrity as the 'Scouse git', son-in-law and sparring partner of Warren Mitchell in *Till Death Us Do Part*, a mixture of comic knockabout and cynical scurrility. By now, too, Tony was in his own word a 'crumpeteer', a serial womaniser who had long deserted Gale. His current lover was Pat Phoenix of *Coronation Street* fame; so famous were they both, with Booth's additional credential as a cult left-wing figure and hell-raiser, that in 1982 Tony Blair, a completely unknown parliamentary candidate up for election in Beaconsfield, a safe Tory seat, promised his constituents that the illustrious pair would come and canvass for him.

The night before Cherie's birth, as she had passed the date expected, Gale drank castor oil to avoid being induced. The night following Cherie's birth, when the Fortescue Company performed *The Chinese Bungalow*, Tony came forward in front of the curtain and announced the arrival of his daughter, Cherie, saying the words of an old music hall song, which was her name's source: 'Cherie, I love you so, that's my desire.'

So began the extraordinary journey which was to culminate in the heady White House celebration given by Bill and Hillary Clinton for Cherie and Tony in 1998, when Stevie Wonder crooned 'My Cherie Amour'. Here, not surprisingly, Cherie appeared full of awe, star struck and overwhelmed by the glamour, and one might be forgiven for concluding that this was a life spent more in showbusiness than in politics. But in 1999, in a speech to a theatrical charity, Cherie declared she wasn't too happy with her name, although 'it could have been worse,' she said, citing the possibility of Tarquin had she been male. That she wasn't too pleased had by now become a characteristic response.

*

At the time of Cherie's birth Gale and Tony lived in a Victorian house on Walmesley Road, Leigh, but were, at least from what Cherie has said, 'passing through'. She named the play her father was in not as *The Chinese Bungalow* but as *White Cargo*: race and colour were there in the very beginning. 'I started life as the daughter of someone,' she said of herself, a touch self-pityingly in July 1994, 'now I am the wife of someone, and I'll probably end up as the mother of someone.' But Tony Booth, born in October 1931, was so much more than just 'someone'. At this time characterised as a 'noisy, political animal', red hot, almost a communist, he found a wife and daughter cramped his style and quickly became the absent, ever-strolling player.

Descended from an Irish immigrant family which settled near Liverpool's dockside where there was work, Tony Booth's paternal grandfather had been a pacifist imprisoned in the First World War, but had left prison to join up as a non-combatant stretcher-bearer. He was gassed at Mons but survived. Tony's other grandfather, too, had a history of army service, then deserted, changing his name to avoid discovery. When it comes to Cherie's future relation to war this background is important, for maybe it shows where her instincts lie. Tony's father, George Henry Booth, was a merchant seaman, the chief steward's writer, away at sea for long periods, but clearly an organised and literate man to hold such a position. George had talent as an amateur pianist, and would sing, 'Thank Heaven for Little Girls' to his granddaughter, so here too was an artistic streak. But George had lost his balance and pitched headlong into a ship's hold, which broke his pelvis and crippled him (an accident similar to that which killed the father of David Blunkett, Tony Blair's first Education Secretary, who fell into a vat of boiling water at the East Midlands Gas Board and died), so he remained largely an invalid for the latter part of his life. Much to his granddaughter's disapproval he smoked untipped Senior Service and died when Cherie was eleven or twelve. Curiously enough Tony, the worse for drink and a chain-smoker, locked out of his house in 1979 by Susie Smith, mother of two of his daughters, tried to frighten the family with an explosion to let him in, and fell on a drum of paraffin and set it alight, only just surviving.

George's wife, Vera, whom he had married in 1931, was a devout Roman Catholic. She had an Irish background too. They bought 15 Ferndale Road, a yellow-brick terraced house in a narrow street a few blocks from the Mersey estuary, and roughly halfway between the centres of Waterloo and Crosby, northern suburbs of Liverpool. It lay in a mainly Catholic area between the richer, long-established middle-class area of Blundells, where ship company directors and managers, and later professional people, lived and built houses, and the rougher parts of the Protestant suburb of Waterloo, where some of the kids ran around unwashed, owned no shoes and, as a former pupil of Cherie's school also brought up in Crosby says, 'were too poor to have underwear'.

The women in Crosby like Vera had great strength of character, as Catholics, they kept their families together and in order, and they showed their unity, for example, by congregating together to say the rosary with one leader calling the refrains – rather like the mantras and Eastern rituals to which Cherie was later to become attracted. They were deeply superstitious and intensely devoted to the Virgin Mary, to whose image, paradoxically, Cherie remained loyal and affectionate – or so she was to claim.

The Waterloo area, shared with or bordering on Crosby, was by no means a drab or unstimulating situation in which to be brought up. Liverpool in the 1950s still boasted productive dockyards and its mythology of maritime power with the great shipping lines – Blue Funnel, P&O, Cunard – stood in evidence everywhere. The closeness of the docks engendered a presence of working-class militancy. On the other hand the mass, compulsory for every Catholic family on a Sunday and still celebrated in Latin, opened windows into a mysterious spiritual world which brought another dimension to the developing imagination of every child, while strictly enforced religious observance of the rules gave discipline and order even to those who rebelled and felt it was backward and reactionary.

Number 15 Ferndale Road had three bedrooms. For Cherie's first two years both Gale and Tony were away working together, and it was left to Vera, aged fifty-one, a strong and resourceful woman, to look after the child. Tony made Gale pregnant a second time, which resulted in the birth of

Lyndsey when Cherie was two. The young family then moved to London for a year before Tony Booth consigned his wife, Cherie and his new daughter to be looked after in Liverpool while he went off to pursue his vagabond trade and his new amours.

When she grew up Lyndsey worked for Hackney Borough Council and later trained as a homeopath, joining the Lifesmart team run by Carole Caplin, Cherie's controversial friend and health adviser. During the MMR inoculation scare of 2001, when Tony and Cherie refused to confirm or deny whether their baby son, Leo, had had the injection, Lyndsey became involved in autism research.

Tony went on to give his eldest daughters six half-sisters from three more women, two of whom he married. Jenia, one of Cherie's half-sisters, took a PhD in psychology, exploring the explosive relationships between alcohol and aggressive behaviour – paternal issues perhaps cropping up here. Lauren, another half-sister, described as a 'loose cannon' and now quite well known as a journalist, became renowned for her criticism of Cherie and Tony Blair: for instance, in the *Daily Telegraph* in May 2001 she savaged her 'charming, Marmite sandwich-making brother-in-law', and later decried the presence of the entrepreneur and donor millionaires at Tony Blair's last Labour Party conference in 2006 who 'sneeringly called ordinary delegates the "Dolcis Shoe set"'.

*

Tony Booth had first attended the late Victorian St Edmund's School, named after St Edmund of Canterbury, which stood next to the big ugly brick Catholic church only minutes away from Cherie's house. Here Tony developed a precocious love of literature, naming Gibbon's *Decline and Fall of the Roman Empire* and novels by Dostoevsky as favourites; he, like Cherie, had a retentive memory and a quick, clever, grammar school mind. St Edmund's, run by Irish Christian Brothers, was warmly Christocentric: for example, every day lessons would stop at midday to observe the Angelus, while on Wednesday the whole school went to Latin benediction. On Friday they would process round the statues in church.

As a child Cherie went to the same primary school as her father. It was a very friendly place, according to a former pupil who reacted against the 'weird mysticism' of the Latin mass, while J. B. Sweeney, the head, 'ran a tight ship, would strap both girls and boys if he needed to, but was very fair'. His ambition, in which he succeeded with boys and girls who passed the eleven-plus and got into the local Catholic grammar schools, was to see his pupils achieve entrance into Oxbridge.

On Saturday morning once she had reached seven, Cherie would line up with other pupils to go to confession, and would be absolved in Latin from her sins. For children observed not attending mass on Sunday, the priest would call round after a week or two at the house, and, in a friendly way, point this out. 'I didn't see you at mass. Is anything the matter?' She went on to join the Brownies, and later the Guides, recalling a 'motherly, sweet lady' who was Brown Owl – 'I did all the badges,' she says, but not camping on their annual holidays, or if so, never gaining much affection, as most did, for the 'great outdoors'. This was to emerge later in the widespread hostility she showed towards the countryside and countryside pursuits, and endless anecdotes about her aversion to pets, especially the corgis belonging to Queen Elizabeth II. The Guides' nitty-gritty of tying knots and turning off main stopcocks did not appear to make a deep impression either. ('Now that we live in No. 10 we don't know how to turn off the main tap because that would turn off the taps for the whole house,' she told a BBC 2 reporter in January 2007.) She gave up the Guides aged fourteen or fifteen, 'when boys are more interesting'.

The nuns at Seafield Convent, to which Cherie progressed when she left St Edmund's, were not, as a former pupil recalls, exactly sympathetic, but were 'of a sallow complexion' and could be vicious and vindictive; but they were 'careful not to be too hell-fire'. Notwithstanding, Cherie flourished academically in Crosby, as did pupils at Liverpool's other Catholic secondary schools; they would include people not exactly unnoticed for their ambition and pushiness, such as John Birt, the future entrepreneurial director-general of the BBC, who like Cherie were far from being disadvantaged. From the start, Cherie was in the top stream, led the second violins in the school orchestra, and was so bright that she was a year younger than the average class age. At home in a house crowded with relatives under Vera's watchful care, she had a tiny boxroom to herself at the back where she could study in private. At school she adhered to the strictly regimented dress code. This consisted of navy blue skirt or gymslip and white blouse, navy blue and light blue striped tie, with a navy cardigan, which also had a light blue stripe, and a blazer and a felt hat with a brim and elastic under the chin. If you were caught without your hat you were in trouble. Fawn socks, worn up to the knees in the winter, or thick wool tights completed the picture.

Cherie was noticeably reserved and quiet; she excelled at most subjects and acted in school plays. She played the leading role, the martyred saint Thomas à Becket, in T. S. Eliot's *Murder in the Cathedral,* in which her concentratedly quiet and convincing delivery of the Easter Day Sermon was much praised: 'A man by willing and contriving ways', she had to say, as Eliot contrasted the design of God with the ways of man, 'may become the ruler of men.' But the true martyr is 'he who has become the instrument of God, who has lost his will in the will of God, and who no longer desires anything for himself, not even the glory of being a martyr'.

She also shone as a debater, representing her school in contests, and as such attended the 1972 finals in Llandudno of a national debating competition. A boy, also a keen debater, from St Mary's, the brother foundation to Seafield, recalls:

> For us boys in a single sex school run by Irish Christian Brothers it was enormously exciting to have the girls around. Everyone fancied Cherie – but then we fancied virtually all the girls, driven mad as we were by adolescent hormones. But Cherie was exotic. She was considered the sexiest girl – it may be difficult to see now but she was very attractive and had the added interest of a TV actor father. I wasn't aware she went out with anyone from our school, however.

She confided that about this time she had the ambition to become the first woman Prime Minister of the United Kingdom.

The sense of Catholic exclusivity stayed with Cherie, who would travel if she could when at Downing Street with a mainly Catholic entourage. Overall there was rich diversity and a sense of superiority in Cherie's background, crowned or enhanced by a celebrity father who was a household name, but was also, according to the Crosby housewives, a rather raffish or dangerous heartthrob who, until Cherie was nine, was, in name but not in presence, Gale's husband and her father. But in their extended family they could draw on both material and spiritual resources, for example the use of a family caravan for picnics on the beach, or a cousin, Paul Thompson, who was a Catholic parish priest. But money, except for Tony Booth's bursts of generosity and occasional windfalls, was tight.

Far from fostering feelings of deprivation and poverty, although not by any means privileged, this highly focused Catholic education gave its recipients strong self-esteem and, in some cases, a powerful, even arrogant, feeling of moral superiority. Just as pupils at Eton College imbibed a tradition that they were special because they had been to Eton, so it was instilled in Seafield girls, 'You're superior because you're Catholic.' Another old pupil, the mother of the television presenter Anne Robinson, exemplified the tough ethic of superiority it instilled, if not the Catholicism.

The boys at St Mary's used to refer to the 'Proddy dogs' – there was much sectarian hostility still, even in the 1950s and 1960s, and Orange marches continued to function until they were stopped. A big 'dare' for Catholics used to be to dash in and out of a Protestant church without being caught. This cauldron of political emotion experienced at first hand by Cherie was to have a profound influence on the future Northern Ireland peace process. It also drove her towards a political rather than academic choice of university.

At sixteen Cherie echoed early an identification with her father's political and social beliefs. She made the unusual move of joining the local branch of the Labour Party and attending meetings. As her half-sister Lauren revealed in the *Mail on Sunday* in 2006:

> Despite his appearances at her childhood home . . . being only sporadic, our father Tony Booth, a passionate socialist, would have lectured Cherie on the same three elements that I had drilled into me. Our philosophical times tables (which we were able to say by rote) were: 1. No one, but no one, is better than anyone else by right of birth. 2. It's not what you know but whom you know (Tony Booth was acutely aware of having no contacts whatever when he first became an actor). And 3, as Polonius advises Laertes in *Hamlet*, 'To thine own self be true.'

For a girl to side with what was still a very male, working-class organisation hardly won Cherie much favour with the Seafield nuns; nor, when she passed her four A-levels with A grades, were they too keen on her ambition, stemming from her skill at debating, of becoming a lawyer and therefore studying for the Bar as opposed to taking Oxford entrance. But her presence at Labour Party functions predicates an original and unusual form of mind, for she was attracted to the Young Christian Workers movement, begun in France after the Second World War by Father Joseph Cardijn, a Belgian priest. This movement also had a powerful influence on the future Pope John Paul II. It may have partly accounted for the strong ambition Cherie cherished, when John Paul was elected in 1978, to meet the new Pope. She fulfilled this as Prime Minister's wife in very fraught circumstances in early spring 2003, on the eve of the Iraq war.

Serious and studious, Cherie was notably indifferent to glamour, with no more interest in clothes or make-up than the average bluestocking of that era. Her father carried for her the infamous trappings of the scurrilous 'Scouse git' he acted both on and off screen. The traumatic moment of her parents' splitting up had happened when she was nine and very vulnerable, so we might expect her to do all she could in her future to avoid celebrity and limelight.

But no. While at some level she was wounded by her father's absence and neglect (and shared the humiliation of her mother, who, while on paper still with a famous husband, worked in the Rawton Road chip shop, and later in another in St John's Road, to make ends meet), she also wanted to compete with him, and show off to him. Liverpool, too, while she was growing up, was humming and buzzing with a burgeoning pop culture, a taste for which she shared early with her future husband, whose worship of pop stars remained constant all his life:

> I met Paul McCartney a few weeks ago and he was a lovely guy, really down to earth. It was the first time I'd met him and I was thrilled, he was a total hero of mine. I did tell him that my wife, Cherie, used to keep his picture beside her bed. Paul said to me, 'Is it not there still?' and I had to tell him, 'No, she's got mine there now!'

The 'Liverpudlianisation' of Great Britain started early, not least in Cherie's soul, while one day she would be Chancellor of Liverpool John Moores University. Moreover, wherever she went Cherie carried her mother, Gale, with her; when she married in 1980 in Oxford, Gale lived and worked in Oxford. Later, on the singer-entertainer Des O'Connor's chat show in 1998, Tony joked that taking his mother-in-law on holiday was 'obligatory'. He went on to comment, 'My mother-in-law is my closest political adviser. She is the one person of absolute common sense.' To the very end of Cherie and Tony's years in Downing Street, Gale was on tap, ordering and receiving takeaways during an unfortunate last, and much-criticised, holiday in Florida in December 2006 with Robin Gibb of the Bee Gees and his wife. Downing Street was not so far away from the Rawton Road chippy.

2

Two Etons of the north

It's a feature of fiction that it can rarely be stretched far enough to capture the stupidities of real life. People don't always act in their own best interest ... politics are acted out on a stage in a way that demands the suspension of disbelief and any sense of moderation and ... can't be transported into real life without terrifying consequences.

Michael Dobbs, *First Lady*

No less '*bourré de complexes*' was Anthony Charles Lynton Blair, born on 6 May 1953 in Edinburgh. He has always contrived to make those 'complexes' vanish, as if by a conjuring trick, in order to convince everyone – and most of all himself – that he is just a decent, simple, straightforward guy. He is anything but this.

It is impossible for anyone to hide the influence of their past, their heritage of emotion, while concealed family secrets can menace behaviour and fulfilment in children as they grow up, and well into maturity. But concealed secrets also include unconsciously repressed or hidden pains or traumas, secrets possessed by a person he or she does not want to own, and equally does not want to confront, so true secrets and the feelings they might engender remain unarticulated, and therefore access to them is lost. These may come in time to play a great part in that person's life and conduct.

Perhaps this is a start to the answer why Tony Blair, as Prime Minister, has been so out of his depth, making decisions which, with consequences he never anticipated, no broadly based, well-grounded person would ever believe possible, yet was able to carry along with him for so long a trusting electorate and Labour Party. The *New Oxford Textbook of Psychiatry* defines the cognitive style of someone who suffers from what it terms a histrionic personality disorder as 'global, impressionistic and diffuse, and lack[ing] sharpness of detail'. Was this to become true of Tony Blair? If so, was it not also true of the millions who supported him? Leo Abse, for nearly thirty years Labour MP for Pontypool, but also an accomplished interpreter of psychoanalysis, believes Tony and Cherie confirm Freudian theory in an alarming and striking way, especially the truth and accuracy of this passage from Freud's *Token and Taboo*:

> We may safely assume that no generation is able to conceal any of its more important mental processes from its successor. For psychoanalysis has shown that everyone possesses in his unconscious mental activity an apparatus which enables him to interpret other people's reactions, that is, to undo the distortions which other people have imposed on the expression of their feelings. An unconscious understanding such as this of all the . . . dogmas left behind by the original relation to the father . . . make it possible for later generations to take over their heritage of emotion.

Abse, in an interview with me, emphasises what he calls Tony's 'transgenerational pathology', his heritage of emotion which explains that rootless, gypsy mentality and those superb mimetic skills which he has been able to develop on the political stage – at a time in history unlike any other for the advancement of those with histrionic talent – and how it all began with his grandparents. Tony himself admits the turbulent background: as he told Paddy Ashdown, the former Liberal Democrat leader, 'Of course, all my ancestors were Irish and pretty rabble-rousing at that.'

Hazel Corscadden, Tony's mother, born in County Donegal in 1923, lost her father at six months and moved to live in Glasgow after her mother, Sally, remarried to a butcher. Hazel was tall and good looking, as was Tony's father, Leo, also born in 1923, who was the illegitimate child of two strolling variety artistes, Charles Parsons (who had the stage name James Lynton) and Celia Ridgway, who at the time of Leo Blair's birth was married to someone else.

On tour in Glasgow the Parsons–Ridgeway pair befriended James Blair, a dockside rigger often out of work, and his wife, Mary, who had miscarried two babies. The variety artistes, in a way possibly similar to Cherie's father Tony in discarding his own children, persuaded the Blairs to foster the infant Leo on a temporary basis (in other words they dumped him), and when later they married they sought to reclaim little Leo as their own. As Leo said later (and reported by his son in Cape Town in 1999), despite being brought up in Glasgow in the 1930s, living in a crowded tenement with five or six families sharing a toilet, he stayed with the Blair couple. But when he was thirteen his blood parents, now married, sought his return. Mary barricaded herself in her tenement, threatening suicide if Leo was taken from her. She subsequently severed contact between him and his natural parents, although Leo hid letters and postcards in a biscuit box under his bed until the war (in which Hazel became a Wren and Leo a junior officer). Mary lied to the blood parents that he was missing, presumed dead.

Tony told an early biographer that he knew his father had been adopted 'but it was something Leo did not speak about and something the children didn't ask about'. But his grandfather, with that showbusiness heritage and the unstable touring life, lived on in shadow form in the grandson, in the middle names he had been given at his christening of 'Charles' and 'Lynton', presumably by Hazel and Leo in some kind of atonement for Leo's foster parents' severance of contact with his true parents.

It came to Tony as what he called 'a bombshell' when, during his bid to lead the Labour Party in 1994, a daily newspaper revealed the significance of his two middle names. It was extraordinary that neither he nor his elder brother, Bill – then aged 41 and 43 – nor Sarah, their younger sister, who also became, like her siblings, a lawyer, had ever registered curiosity about the Blair family history. Clearly history, the past, was taboo, a no-go area. There would soon be immediate, dramatic events to blot out that more distant family past. But for the moment more of Leo's earlier life should be considered before that stroke of monumental importance, which was, or so it has been widely claimed, not least by Tony, to shape Tony's future life.

Leo lost his foster father, James, when young and while Mary Blair was a lifelong communist, Leo, after serving as branch secretary of Govan's Scottish Young Communist League at the age of fifteen, and then finding his first job with the then highly popular *Daily Worker*, reacted fiercely against the class war of the epoch. He became a lifelong Conservative, ultimately aspiring to election as Tory MP for Hexham. Leo's progress showed in reverse the far more common pattern, the beneficiaries of a tough Jesuit education who became diehard Marxists. This strong contradictory element is all too evident in Tony's character. By day Leo slaved in the Edinburgh tax office, but by night he studied for a law degree and when he had gained his doctorate, moved with his family to Adelaide in Australia for three years, where he taught administrative law in the university. A lectureship in law at Durham University brought the Blair family back to Britain.

But Leo's self-help aspiration, beginning in the war years, which transformed his life and gave his children the opportunity of a privileged upbringing with attendance at top independent schools, never achieved what he so much wanted, to change from an outsider to an insider, in spite of his achievements, during Tony's first decade. Friends say he was a workaholic and a ladies' man, although not unfaithful to Hazel; while lecturing on law he also had a flourishing legal practice in Newcastle. As chairman of the Durham Conservative Association he acted as influential host to the visiting and local Tory grandees and councillors: his ambition was unstoppable.

Tony attended, first, the Durham Cathedral Chorister School, although not as a choirboy, but as a conventional quiet boy who worked at his lessons in an all-male environment 'tinged by a vague eroticism', as one former pupil described it. At home Leo, Tony's fellow pupils recall, among them the poet James Fenton, was a severe, forbidding barrister now with a thriving practice in Newcastle, while Hazel, who had after the war worked in Glasgow's national insurance office, managed the house. Leo was mainly the absent father, a powerful figure, who it must be noted was an outstanding communicator and self-publicist, often seen on local television. While Tony represents himself as a happily well-adjusted schoolboy, others have claimed this was just the façade. He was forever smiling at his teachers, outwardly compliant and fervently prayerful.

As revealed in canvassing at elections, Tony's 'autobiography', one might call it, of these early years denies his rootlessness, the rootlessness of the actor who is no one and yet everyone according to which script he holds in his hand. He claimed that, in his childhood, he had been influenced by the traditional socialism of the Durham miners, 'a feeling which has stayed with me ever since'. He gave an interview in 1996 to *Country Life* in which he asserted, 'I wouldn't live in a big city if I could help it. I would live in the country. I was brought up there, really.' The Blairs' house was in a suburban estate of private houses.

*

The irreversible blow fell on the Blair family on Friday 3 July 1964, when after returning from a dinner party at 2.30 a.m. Leo suffered a disabling stroke. It rendered him speechless and put him in hospital for months, during which Hazel guarded him and kept the children away, not allowing them sight of their father, full of fear and silent rage. Although Leo's fortunes were now reversed, he gradually, with Hazel's unremitting support, spoke again and in time returned to lecture at Durham University, although he was to remain but a shell of his former dynamic self.

Tony was a little over eleven. His tireless father, from whom he now felt more alienated than before, had been on the threshold of becoming an insider, and at his moment of arrest, of being cut off, it seems the son would carry both the stigma and the wound of being cast as, and feeling, an outsider while being in the thick of everything – therefore now the insider, with all the trappings and rewards of public life, but never quite integrated.

There is argument over the depth and importance of this formative episode, which reverberates with classic Freudian overtones. Did Tony squash and interiorise his grief over it? Did it act as a spur to fame and achievement? Tony himself called it 'one of the formative events of my life … After his illness my father transferred his ambitions to his kids. It imposed a certain discipline. I felt I couldn't let him down.' This may be so, but it must also have affected Tony's brother, Bill, a diligent scholar, a responsible decent boy who also worked hard and later achieved much. Bill has operated successfully the policy of keeping himself and his family away from the limelight, while Tony has made an exemption in his brother's case of the use of family for political ends.

Hazel's dedication to her ill husband, and then soon after to Tony's sister, Sarah, who at the age of eight fell victim to Still's disease, a form of arthritis, which kept her in hospital for the next two years, confirmed her unwavering constancy as a devoted spouse and mother. 'She was an absolute rock. I didn't see her break down, never once. When you think what she must have gone through . . . But she never exhibited any sign of it, so I owe her a very great debt.'

In spite of the financial constraints caused by illness, Tony followed his brother to Fettes, the expensive public boarding school in Edinburgh, and not to the local and popular Durham School, to which most pupils from the Chorister School progressed, and which locally had the sobriquet 'Eton of the North'. Fettes was also called this, but was by far the more snobbish rival. The thinking behind this choice was clear: Hazel had much to contend with, and to isolate Tony's schooling from home seemed a good idea, for formation of both intellect and character. Her stepfather, the butcher in Glasgow, helped pay the fees.

Today's public schools have possibly changed – in Tony's favourite word 'modernised' – but in his time there was still something about a top boarding school, which Cyril Connolly defined in *Enemies of Promise*: 'Were I to deduce anything from my feelings on leaving Eton, it might be called *The Theory of Permanent Adolescence*. It is the theory that the experience undergone by boys at the great public schools are so intense as to dominate their lives and to arrest their development.' The intense experience was there for Tony, but it was hidden and became subtly transformed.

Typically, Tony was to say he enjoyed Fettes and was happy there. Yet a daily newspaper in 1996 reported an escapade when as an unhappy new boarder he ran away from Fettes; arriving at Newcastle airport, he tried to stow away, he claimed, on a plane bound for the Bahamas. He related this also to Des O'Connor, and that the stewardess 'sussed' him out when they were about to take off, saying, 'I don't think I saw your boarding pass.' Leo Blair did confirm that Tony got as far as the airport, but not as far as the plane. And the airport never offered flights to the Bahamas.

He settled down for a while but after a year of good-natured promise and conformity, and reports now encouraging his all-round development, Tony, aged fourteen, again soured in his response to this estrangement from home life, and from then on never really fitted into the routines of the prestigious boarding school. Bill, his brother, still at Fettes, was conventional and fitted in well; Tony, as the younger sibling, had to strike out, not surprisingly, in a different direction – that of the subversive, the anti-hero.

There was by now a good cultural validation for this, with the Angry Young Man movement which had begun ten years earlier, the new power of rock music and everything else that went under the title of the 'Swinging Sixties'. Institutions such as Fettes, with teachers including Eric Anderson, tried to balance the traditional values with forward-looking, innovative ideas. Anderson in particular became popular with Tony, as he teetered on the edge of becoming the complete rebel. On the other hand Dr Ian McIntosh, the headmaster, made a firm distinction between the cynicism of *Private Eye* and *That Was the Week That Was*, and the satire of Gillray and Swift: the first sought to sneer then destroy instead of reform and validate truth. He spoke out one Founders Day for the overriding 'authority of truth . . . we ought to be sceptical with the scepticism of Socrates, not of David Frost'. McIntosh didn't mind being unpopular in his stand against the permissive society.

Anderson kept a bust of Sir Walter Scott in the hall of his house, and when the length of hair became the *casus belli* between authority and rebels, Scott's not exactly short back and sides was the measure to which the boys had to conform. One day McIntosh saw that Tony's luxuriant locks far exceeded the set criteria and straightaway marched him into the barber's nearby, standing over him as he had his mop chopped. In spite of charges of consorting with disreputable company and earning a lasting reputation for disruptiveness and a Macavity-like propensity for escaping the scene of the crime (Macavity in T. S. Eliot's collection *Old Possum's Book of Practical Cats* defied every human law, and even the law of gravity), all of which seemed predictable, even laudable, younger-brother behaviour, Tony enjoyed Anderson's housemastership of the most progressive Arniston House, which opened in September 1967. But Tony remained unsettled, even with Anderson, who was 'far more liberal and laid back than most teachers'. He became something of a troublemaker, prompting Anderson later to tell Roy Jenkins that if anything went wrong in Arniston's 'I expect it is A. C. L. Blair who is behind it again'. Blair's great talent, Anderson also said, was talking himself out of trouble. The teachers as a whole thought him very clever, smart, with the gift of the gab, but an 'annoying wee shite', as one recalled.

By the age of seventeen, when Anderson left to become head of Abingdon School, Tony and he had seriously fallen out in spite of the teacher's devoted attempts to channel Tony's talents into acting, and in particular arguing and debating in university-style tutorials. But Anderson refused to appoint Tony, now a senior boy, a house prefect, so he gained no early experience of being in a position of authority over others, while he was never a team captain in sports. Socially, outside school, Tony was popular and considered attractive. He befriended notably a fifteen-year-old girl called Angela, or Anji, Hunter at a house party in Forfar where both had been overnight guests. She was to become a close aide in the future (see Chapter 28).

As an upper sixth-former, in a different house regime, Tony's school career almost completely unravelled as he flouted the rules more, the culmination of his failure to adapt to the Fettes ethos and the company of the scions of Edinburgh's merchant classes. While he had during his first year run away from school and been brought back by Leo, now in the summer of 1971, caught exiting over the school wall to chat up local girls at the fish and chip shop (an eerie echo of his future mother-in-law's occupation) he was threatened by McIntosh with expulsion. Eric Anderson stepped in to recommend that he should be allowed to stay, and it was because of Anderson's intercession that Tony avoided this stigma. A compromise situation, worked out between the family and the school, enabled further confrontation between Tony and staff to be avoided. Tony's popularity with girls also saved him.

At this dangerous moment of threatened expulsion another girlfriend, Amanda Mackenzie Stuart, among the first sixth-form day pupils at the school, persuaded her father, Alexander Mackenzie Stuart (later to become the first UK judge at the European Court of Justice and ennobled as Baron Mackenzie-Stuart), to allow Tony to reside for the rest of his time at their Edinburgh home in Doune Terrace and finish his A-levels. The school agreed and Macavity was redeemed. But Tony lost out to a sixth-former from Glenalmond in his bid to win the affections of Amanda. His name was Charles Falconer, another Scottish lawyer's son who later in London became Tony's landlord and in time adviser and second Lord Chancellor in the Blair government.

Nominally responsible for his musical education, Michael Lester-Cribb, a talented pianist and composer outside the school, contradicted the pop idol future image of Tony, revealing that as 'a voluntary member of Fettes chapel choir [he] showed every sign of enjoying singing music from Palestrina to Stravinsky'. Lester-Cribb added that he accepted that for 'understandable political reasons Mr Blair now stresses he ran a pop group at Fettes'. Lester-Cribb cast Tony in his first ever stage role, that of the Little Monk in Jean Anouilh's *Becket*. The Little or Young Monk was a much more important role than it sounds, and was acted in the first London production by the young Ian Holm. In the play the Little Monk, a Saxon, has come over to France with Thomas à Becket to attempt to assassinate the Norman Henry II, but is caught with a knife hidden under his robe and quizzed by Becket, who holds the post of Chancellor of England. 'Did you imagine you could liberate your race single handed?' Becket asks him. 'No,' the Little Monk answers, but 'if I can kill one Norman first – just one, I don't want very much – one for one, that will seem fair and right for me.'

Becket's theme is the conflict between church and state, a theme President George Bush senior claimed occupied him mentally: asked once what he had thought about after being shot down over the Pacific in the Second World War while bobbing around in the ocean, Bush answered, 'The separation of church and state.'

Tony certainly benefited from the opportunity to show off his latent acting talent and subsequently distinguished himself in several bigger roles. It seemed he could find himself when acting someone else. In his last year he played Captain Stanhope, the hero of R. C. Sherriff's *Journey's End*, set in the trenches of the First World War. In this role he was able to smoke on stage, an enviable but illicit breaking of the school rules (ironically, the Scottish anti-smoking law passed in 2006 proscribes smoking even on stage in character during a performance: in the cause of realism you can swear, strip naked and even simulate same-sex intercourse, but you cannot smoke).

But it was the role of Marc Antony in *Julius Caesar* that offered a striking image of a future Tony Blair as Prime Minister. In playing it Tony came closer than in any other aspect of his school life to fulfilling himself – in fantasy, that is – but it also prefigured his future capacity to move crowds to passion. We might perhaps see something prophetic in this tall, good-looking, blue-eyed boy enjoying the spectacle of himself rousing and inspiring others to action in response to an act of terrorism: namely the murder of the 'tyrant' Caesar:

Domestic fury and fierce civil strife
Shall cumber all the parts of Italy;
Blood and destruction shall be so in use,
And dreadful objects so familiar,
That mothers shall but smile when they behold
Their infants quartered with the hands of war;
All pity chok'd with custom of fell deeds.

These lines are uncomfortably similar and parallel to what happened in Iraq as the result of an ill-considered deed, the removal of Saddam Hussein in 2003, and we now see them coming true night after night on television. They have rebounded graphically in irony on the sixth-former who once played his namesake's role.

But more, there is also later in this play Antony's cynical political opportunism, his seizure of the moment to obtain power. He deconstructs or distorts his adversary Brutus's character at his death in order to capture the political high ground, so that he, Antony, can win the kudos of praising 'honourable Brutus':

This was the noblest Roman of them all:
All the conspirators save only he,
Did what they did in envy of great Caesar;
His life was gentle, and the elements
So mix'd up in him that Nature might stand up
And say to all the world: 'This was a man!'

This was not strictly true: Brutus did envy Caesar, although through his own lack of self-knowledge rather than through crude, base ambition. In *Julius Caesar* there was political advice in plenty for anyone who cared to explore it. The play showed how the selfish embrace and enjoyment of power leads to self-destruction and ultimately eats itself up, but above all how naked ambition and mimetic rivalry hide behind false ethical debate. Here were valuable lessons to be learned by an aspiring politician.

Fettes's magazine commented on Tony's Antony that the college was 'very fortunate in having so experienced an actor as Blair for a central figure'. Something inside had taken off: the actor, the performer in front of an audience. Eric Anderson had never seen anyone change so much as when on stage: 'He lit up and became almost a different person.' To express this slightly differently, Tony, it seemed, could find himself when acting a figure of Antony's stature.

One swings up high and free by means of an immense pressure. 'Thus the celestial bodies soar through space by means of a great weight . . . the light soaring of faith is aided by a prodigious heaviness; the highest upswinging of hope is aided precisely by hardship and the pressure of adversity,' wrote Søren Kierkegaard. The prodigious heaviness was there, both at home and in his dislike of Fettes. The day-to-day discontent beneath the surface may well have stemmed from his father's stroke, his beleaguered mother; the dislike and the rebelliousness too, at school, could well have been a result of the strain of family illness, so that he was taking out on the school some of the tensions induced by that. But the release in acting was a revelation.

Tony's impulse to fly was to be explored more fully in the next year of his life.

3

Lines oblique

'Tis much that glass should be
As all-confessing, and through-shine as I . . .
But all such rules love's magic can undo
Here you see me, and I am you.

John Donne, 'A Valediction of My Name, in the Window'

The two mirror images converging on one another had not yet met. Cherie, ambitious and secretly nursing an ambition to become Prime Minister which she was also to voice later in her remark about being named Tarquin, escaped from the increasingly narrow confines of 15 Ferndale Road in September 1972. No gap year for her. A county major scholarship provided the means to study law at the London School of Economics, which also suited her by now pronounced left-wing leanings.

Her father, well on the way to begetting his eight daughters from various sources, had been mainly absent but a long-running presence on television. At one point during Cherie's childhood he had been entrenched in writing a novel in the front parlour where his grandfather had lain dead in an open coffin. His influence pervaded the Crosby home: the 'Scouse git' of *Till Death Us Do Part*, duplicated in the wild-man drinking and womanising antics of real life, cast a long shadow; there was always plenty of florid gossip. When he came home the local wives would 'shiver', as one said, with excitement.

Such was Tony Booth's celebrity that during Harold Wilson's premiership he was invited to Downing Street, the family's first deeply ominous contact with the fateful locality. He had drunk too much, arrived late and berated Wilson for having 'sold out on socialism'. Wilson, who had a Liverpool constituency, told him, 'Not tonight, Tony, this is a party, no time for politics.' Upping the ante of cheeky or obnoxious behaviour, Tony took the formally dressed Prime Minister of Luxembourg for a waiter, telling him to fill up his glass, whereupon he then drunkenly crashed into Harry Secombe, who told him off: 'For God's sake, boy, don't make a show of the profession in No. 10!'

'It's our house! It belongs to the people, doesn't it?' the sozzled actor riposted.

Marcia Williams, the *madame* of Wilson's kitchen Cabinet, decoyed him into a tour of the house, showing him the Cabinet Room. 'That's the place where you carve it all up between you,' he railed. She told him he was a rebel and left him. Later, Cherie boasted in *The Goldfish Bowl*, her book on Prime Ministers' spouses, that her father had been invited to No. 10 – but left out the lurid details. It has also been suggested that her father tried unsuccessfully to introduce his future son-in-law to cannabis, although outrage was now the rage.

Tony had a putative brush with the obscenity laws when he agreed to appear in Kenneth Tynan's *Oh! Calcutta!*, the erotic review performed by a nude cast. He confessed in his autobiography, *Stroll On*, that at rehearsals performed *au nature* with the voyeuristic Ken and his wife Kathleen avidly in attendance he kept getting erections. Tynan summoned John Mortimer, the celebrated barrister of anti-censorship causes, to determine whether this would be considered to constitute a breach of the Public Decency Act, but at the arrival of the celebrated barrister of anti-censorship causes, Tony lost his erection and during the subsequent run never had another.

The Liverpudlianisation of Great Britain proceeded apace, and there were no limits. Tony Blair's own particular hero, John Lennon, was no exception. Approached by Tynan to submit a sketch for *Oh! Calcutta!* – the subject of which they had agreed on, Lennon replied:

Dear Kenneth,

I know I won't get time to do anything about the wank show – you know the idea, four fellows wanking – giving each other images – descriptions – it should be ad-libbed anyway – they should even really wank which would be great! Every now and again somebody fucks it up by throwing in a Winston Churchill etc. hysterias & so on.

See you soon, luv, John (Kenneth Tynan papers, British Library)

('Wanker' was to become a favourite derogatory word in the New Labour vocabulary, applied notably by Alastair Campbell to journalists, and by Home Secretary John Reid to Jeremy Paxman.)

The mutual loyalty shared between Cherie and Liverpool should not be under-estimated. She would return in future to raise money for the St Peter and St Paul Hospice in Crosby, and give talks to more potentially hostile student audiences at John Moores University. 'She worked the crowds fantastically,' says an admirer of these charitable appearances. Liverpool took Cherie to its heart – unlike Cilla Black, who had turned her back on her hometown.

Tony Blair's own mimetic envy of his father-in-law appeared in the pro-Labour *Sun* two weeks before the 2005 election under the banner headline 'WHY SIZE MATTERS'. Tony and Cherie talked about their twenty-five years of faithful love, and how they worked to 'rekindle the spontaneity of their relationship while surrounded by security guards'. The *Sun*'s photographer asked Tony to take off his shirt to show his pectorals. Then he asked, 'So how fit are you, Tony?'

Cherie answered for him, 'Very!'

'What, at least five times a night?' asked the *Sun* man.

'At least. I can do it more depending on how I feel,' was Tony's answer. 'Are you always up for it?'

Cherie, in this unique joint interview, capped his boast: he was, indeed, 'always up for it'. 'Cherie says Tony needs a BIG one – a big majority!' shrieked the sub-headline. While the tacky claim of sexual athleticism was aimed at the *Sun* readership it betrayed their contempt for their own self-trumpeted rights of privacy. They had recently celebrated their twenty-fifth wedding anniversary with a private mass, organised by Cherie, during which they had renewed their vows. 'The event was a secret to all,' warbled the paper – until pimped for political gain. Of course, in the welter of morning-after condemnation of the sex talk by other papers ('Squidgygate-standard descent into smut and leer', 'toe-curling', 'jaw-dropping in its vulgarity') the

Sun put on an act of seeming mortified, but apart from the invocation of marital fidelity its story could have come straight out of *Stroll On*. The joint theatricality of the pair had now turned real.

Tony Booth's rampant exhibitionism, the uncouth language, the combined staginess and narcissism were to become a randomly operating undercurrent in Cherie's behaviour too – when she broke free from the respectable constraints of her upbringing – just as phallic display was a constant factor in Bill Clinton's behaviour. It was to find its future reflection in the 2003 tableau of Cherie being taught by Carole Caplin how to apply lipstick on the Downing Street marital bed. Tony Booth's cheeky outspokenness often became evident in Cherie's impromptu asides, her off-the-cuff explosions.

The most extraordinary of these was to occur during the Labour Party conference in September 2006, when after Gordon Brown's carefully crafted speech, Cherie stole the thunder, and captured the headlines next morning by commenting audibly as she walked past the Bloomberg Television reporter, 'What a liar that man is!' This was deliberate, of course, in spite of her denials she ever said it, and the excuses that it was a 'Cherie gaffe'. But was it not instead a true 'Scouse git' or 'scallie' comment? How Booth senior must have jumped for joy: it was surely a brilliant stroke of upstaging, and he couldn't have done better himself.

'At least', Tony Blair wittily defused the subsequent outcry, 'I know she's not going to run away with the bloke next door.'

4

The Shake 'n' Vac sheen of pop music

Italian PM Silvio Berlusconi, 70, a former cruise ship crooner, launches a second album of love songs tomorrow.

Daily Mail, 2004

If Cherie's first year away from Liverpool saw her focused intently on legal studies which brought her academic distinction, Tony's engagement in Peter-Pan-itis, pursuing his dreams as a wannabe rock star, saw him making an early start on the path of mimetic envy.

There was about this time, significantly, a change in the world of so-called culture when originality, that very rare quality, was, in the huge explosion of the music industry, abandoned in favour of repeating a brand. The messy detritus of early pop music, its intriguing freshness and radical disobedience, was being cosmetised and coaxed into the big markets, gathered and fed into the tentacular growth of global capitalisation. This, translated into Blair terms, meant he didn't aspire to be something entirely new, he merely wanted to be like his idol, in this case Mick Jagger. So with his hair long and unkempt, and looking remarkably like Cherie with the same wide-mouthed grin, he joined the ever-swelling ranks of the derivative and the deferential, gyrating to the sounds of his home-made guitar called Clarence while mouthing 'Honky Tonk Woman' and 'Brown Sugar'. His rebelliousness stayed well within the limits of the tame, protected gestures of the privileged. The Fettes schoolboy gang he led now became the pop group, while 'dare and bravura' were swapped for a cool, sexual androgyny. Both these could be seen in the distorting mirrors of time as prototypes for a kitchen Cabinet, or 'Tony's cronies' as later they were to become known.

In 1995 Tony said, 'Rock music is the absolute love of my life' – this at the moment when those mummified spectres of once-worshipped youth such as Cliff Richard and Mick Jagger, and of course Paul McCartney, were capitalising on and prolonging the eternal Peter Pan myth with the kinds of enhancement of voice and face that technology could bring (all three were later knighted by Tony). 'Among millions of others I'm a huge fan,' he said of U2's Bono in 2006, on whom he conferred an honorary knighthood. The Irish pop star retaliated, calling him 'the Lennon and McCartney of global development'.

This boyishness, sexual insubordination and temporary rebelliousness typified Tony in his gap year when, in west London, he staged concerts without much success, notably one at the Queen Alexandra Hall in Kensington, when he filled only 100 of the 2,000 seats. But the Peter-Pan-itis, and the orientation towards rock stardom with its sexual implications, was to offer the media a temptation to underline the connection between sex and politics. *Tony Blair: Rock Star*, the docu-drama shown on Channel 4 in early 2006 when the fictional Blair character strips off his white leather lace-up trousers and ruffle-collar shirt, showed him in a sexually submissive role with suggested fellatio performed on him by a girl, and later in bed, lying underneath his partner. As the naked girl descends on his pectorals he says, 'We don't have to do this!' The real if unintended point perhaps being made here was that sex and politics were bedfellows.

*

One of Cherie's Marie-Antoinette comments is that she would have worked in a shop had she not had a grant to go to university. The effect of Cherie's law degree on English history may be a good subject for future postgraduate study, but it could never have been achieved had the law on student top-up fees passed by her husband's government been in force at the time. Tony Booth was unlikely to have coughed up the fees, and she may well have taken up her parents' profession instead. But on her arrival at the London School of Economics she found she already belonged to the aristocracy of celebrity culture. The progeny of celebrities at educational establishments enjoy the status of minor celebrities in their own right, especially if they are related to a raffish, good-looking sitcom star. The Tony Blair in the docu-drama *The Deal* (Granada, 2003), seeing an *EastEnders* actress come into the Granita restaurant, urges the Gordon Brown character to chat her up as she has the real power – he points out that thirteen and a half million viewers watch her programme four times a week.

At the LSE Tony Booth had left-wing credentials, while the baggage of his ill treatment of his children was left behind in Liverpool. As Cherie's fellow student John Carr confirmed, she was the celebrity, and with the other students she could enjoy this without the stigma of her father's disreputable behaviour.

Women students at the LSE drank deep of the new feminist outpourings that dominated the bookshop counters. Germaine Greer and Betty Friedan had their paler English counterparts while at a more sensational sexual level Erica Jong led a host of writers devoured hungrily by young women eager to express their own sexuality. There was not only a new impetus for women to achieve distinction and equal opportunity in the workplace, but also a radical rethink of the relationship between men and women on the emotional and domestic fronts. In a nutshell, sex was no longer just sex, it became sexual politics, and just as sex became politicised, so, almost in the same breath, did politics become sexualised. Gender became a burning issue. The wonder woman who revolutionised British politics at this time was another lawyer. At least, law was her second degree – her first being chemistry.

Margaret Thatcher, the dutiful daughter of a shopkeeper turned politician, a measurable comparison of humble origin to the devout daughter of a left-wing celebrity actor, was the unpopular minister for education in the Heath Conservative government of 1970–4. By abolishing free school milk, and initiating a decline in school children's healthy bone development, she had acquired the sobriquet 'Thatcher milk-snatcher'. She had also signed over thousands of grammar schools, similar to the one attended by Cherie, into the new comprehensive secondary school system.

Thatcher was never far off being the centre of attention while Cherie studied law at the LSE, and as such was a mesmerising love–hate object. For Cherie, as for most young women who aspired to become high flyers and engage in politics, Thatcher may have been a right-wing Tory, but first of all she was a woman. Heath's government fell in 1974, but the following year Thatcher became Tory leader in opposition. Here was a woman who seized the demoralised Tory party by the scruff of its neck and placed herself firmly in charge of it.

Now, as she entered her final year as a law student, Cherie worked hard, hoping to get a good result, and surpassed fellow students both male and female by obtaining a first in her finals. The next year, 1976, she took the Bar finals and on the day she went to see the results pinned up she looked first at the list near the middle, feeling she had done well but not all that well. 'Some chap standing near me,' she told a friend, 'who had a double first from Oxbridge, was convinced he would be top. He looked straight at the head of the list for his name, but couldn't find it.' But here was Cherie's name. 'He was miffed to see', added the friend, 'Cherie had beaten everyone, passing out top in the country.'

Cherie, twenty-two and fully qualified, decided to become an employment lawyer. She maintained loyalty to her family Catholic faith, still went to mass, but by now leaned towards liberal as opposed to traditional Catholic teaching. She had, as was very common to many highly intelligent, professional women, the ability to be high powered and focused on a problem in her role as a barrister, yet at the same time to attach herself to far more way-out, even weird, beliefs. A management psychologist points out that this condition, fairly common among successful women managers, is known as schizotypal. Someone with this personality disorder in its mild form is 'often deficient in accurately sensing social cues or affective signals from others. Although they can interact with people when necessary, they often prefer not to.' Other features of 'this complex and chronic condition', according to the *New Oxford Textbook of Psychiatry*, include 'magical thinking', a form of thought disorder, and resorting to 'techniques to facilitate stress reduction (e.g. relaxation techniques, exercise, yoga and meditation)'. The benefit of these techniques may be countered by unusual appearance, and an oddness or eccentricity which is 'often ego syntonic (i.e. they are not experienced as problems)'. It sounds a very common disorder of the times.

Margaret Thatcher had opened a way forward for women like Cherie, whatever the widely opposed beliefs she might hold. But Thatcherism and the 'Blairism' of the distant future, now only in early conceptual form, were beginning to converge before Cherie met Tony, and before Thatcher became Prime Minister. Personality was turning into the key factor in winning a general election. So aware of this did Thatcher become, having won two successive elections in 1979 and 1983, that she declared in August 1986 to the *Daily Telegraph* that she was 'willing to respond to media interest whatever the situation'. Personality was perceived as the key to political success: 'Her run up a Cornwall beach being pulled along by a borrowed dog delighted her party managers.'

When Tony came to power in May 1997 it was the borrowed dog that had taken charge, pulled by hidden hands, but guided largely by clever Cherie's Thatcher-like brain.

5

Longings sublime

I prefer the company of peasants because they have not been sufficiently educated to reason incorrectly.

Michel de Montaigne

If Margaret Thatcher fuelled Cherie's political ambitions, no such stirring was visible in Tony's Oxford days, where, at St John's College, he passed what might be termed a desultory three years studying law. Tony distinguished himself at Oxford, as a future Prime Minister, by what he did not do; basically he did not do much: not being president of the Oxford Union, not becoming a leading actor, which he surely could have done, nor even joining the Oxford Labour Club. He appeared in a few undergraduate revues, happy, as someone said of him, when he could create his own (highly simplified) characters, but he eschewed formal roles. He dabbled slightly in politics, but seemed more interested in theory than in playing a role.

The received view is that Tony did not much like being up at Oxford. Indeed, he said so himself. The peripheral activities, his appearance as a would-be star leading a public school rock band called Ugly Rumours, enveloped 'in the imagery of the archetypical pre-pubescent nasty little boy . . . accompanied by a display of serious gyrating all designed to emphasise the essential androgyny of the singer', have all exhaustively been explored.

Tony did join the posh college wining and dining set known as the Archery Dining Club, and was photographed in an inebriated state making an obscene gesture with his right hand. Peregrine Shannock, a fellow member, pictures a bizarre circumstance: in a third-floor room, Tony, dressed for tennis and on his way to play, pulls down his shorts for simulated if not complete flashing for the benefit of the young female typing pool of Morrell, Peel and Gamlen, a firm of solicitors over the road in St Giles (he may have been wearing a jock strap, for Shannock stood behind him and couldn't see properly). 'Here you go, girls,' Shannock reports him as saying, but the girls never noticed him.

'Ah yes, Ugly Rumours,' Tony ruminates on his fiftieth birthday, 'those days were great. Every so often I feel I should graduate to classical music, properly. But the truth is, I'm more likely to listen to rock music. I listen to what the kids play.' He had girlfriends, though none too serious; he gave parties; he smoked, but not too seriously. Unusually for an undergraduate in that era, he found a Christian spiritual mentor, who helped him to contain an inner restlessness. This was Peter Thomson, a 36-year-old ordained Anglican who had studied theology and who led him to confirmation.

Thomson, an Australian, preached friendship; 'all meaningful action is for the sake of friendship,' he said, quoting the 'Boy Scout' theme of the Scottish philosopher John Macmurray, whose influence on Tony will be considered below. But any thoughtful psychologist or sensible parent will point out the danger that 'preaching sweetness, light and pure friendship ensures – since sex and aggression will always hit back and wage incessant guerrilla wars – that discords swell into a deafening cacophony.'

Tony told John Sopel, an early biographer, that he found the Labour Club 'a complete turn-off . . . I could not be bothered with that'. The reason was that student politics wasn't 'practical enough for him', even less so the ambitious political aspirations of students, for he 'loathed the falseness and pretentiousness and wanted no part in the affectations of would-be Prime Ministers'.

The common diagnosis that the rocker/rapper was in revolt, regarding women as the architect of conventional life, and therefore 'still on the run from Mother' may seem far fetched. But that imaginative space filled by Tony Blair as Mick Jagger brought relief, at least, from a new trial, his mother's illness, an awareness of which encroached on his whole career at Oxford.

When Blair was still in the upper sixth at Fettes, Hazel fell gravely ill. They diagnosed cancer of the throat. The strain of caring for both husband and daughter had taken its toll. But, as with Leo's earlier background, much of her deterioration remained hidden from Tony during his time at Oxford.

Over three years Hazel received treatment but she downplayed it and, as Tony said later, he never realised how serious it was. Concealment and cover-up again played an important part in his family life. In June 1975, just after completing his finals, Tony returned to Durham, to be told by his father, 'I'm afraid Mum's a lot more ill than we thought.' Tony answered, 'She's not going to die, is she?' Leo said, 'Yes, she is.' She would only last a few days.

*

Tony visited every day, noticing how terribly she had aged until on 28 June 1975 she died. She was fifty-two and the profound protective instinct she awoke in Tony at this juncture never weakened and was to be transferred only a year later onto someone else. He had called his mother the 'cement' of his life, and her death removed from Tony the flexibility and ongoing change that might have come with continued contact with this stoical and dutiful woman who had met family adversity with complete unselfishness. 'Cement' was his word, but not a very happy or organic one. Her death, which he felt very deeply, was in more ways than one tragic.

Cement conveys a hard and inflexible monotony. Cement is also cold. Hazel's death at such an early age cemented her importance over Tony, especially in her example of resilience, and also perhaps that switched-off, abstracted quality many have noticed of not being quite there. Political power is, as the late Anthony Storr, the influential psychiatrist and writer who explored power in several of his books, said, the aim and compensation for those who have not achieved a credible reality and identity for themselves in their years of growing up. Storr believed that few if any leading politicians have a normal pathology. Or, more simply, as Fleur Adcock expressed it:

If [Blair] were to ask me out for a meal,
how would I feel?
Would I grovel and kneel,
Aflame with atavistic socialist zeal?

No, I'm sorry, he doesn't appeal:
He's not quite real.

35

Hazel's resilience becomes central to Tony and Cherie's narrative: her death, Tony said, 'strangely galvanised me'. The choice of words: 'galvanise', like 'modernise', is not a particularly happy word either.

*

Thomson, the 'spellbinding' priest, said of Tony's Oxford days that 'his life lacked purpose and direction' and that 'I don't think he really knew what he was doing there'. Later Tony complained bitterly to Roy Jenkins that he should have read history instead of 'boring' jurisprudence. But had he done this he would never have met Cherie; it's hard to believe he ever liked history: as John Mortimer says of both of them, 'They don't like history. They don't like the past.'

At Oxford Tony came under another strong influence. 'If you really want to understand what I'm about,' he said in his *cri de coeur* upon election as Labour's leader in 1994, 'you have to look at a guy called John Macmurray. It's all there.'

During the time I was writing this book the frequent buzz I heard was that a Scottish mafia now ran the United Kingdom: but my heart sank much more when I learned that, born in Edinburgh, and attending a Scottish public school, with Scottish money paying for his education, Tony's main influence in life should be a minor and mediocre Scottish philosopher. (For the reader's benefit, as a proud mixture of Italian, Irish and English blood, I also had one Scottish grandfather called Tate.) Tony is identified in most people's minds as a 'southerner', but in many ways he is still a Scotsman: while there is no accent, that short, sharp, prevaricating tone he has increasingly come to adopt in answering questions has a Scottish ring. All the social engineering and moral relativity in the world will not change what W. B. Yeats called 'the two eternities' – those of race and soul, the tribal and the spiritual.

Why did Tony not tackle some serious theological or philosophical thinker – Socrates, perhaps, who might have taught him to question himself, Descartes, Francis Bacon, Montaigne, all of whom could have developed in him the necessary cognitive recognition between subjective and objective truths? Or what about the philosophers of the Scottish Enlightenment such as David Hume, James Burnett and Adam Smith, and by extension the writers James Boswell, Robert Burns, and Walter Scott, who had a good deal of common sense? But John Macmurray? Macmurray was at best a mediocre but reassuring philosopher-cum-theologian whose level of debate and rigorous thinking was roughly that of the self-help therapeutic books churned out in prolific numbers during the last decades of the twentieth century. Tony went to visit him in Edinburgh in 1974 but by then Macmurray, then eighty-six, was too frail to see him and died shortly after.

> When two friends quarrel [wrote Macmurray] and are estranged each blames the other for the bad relations between them. Or, to put it otherwise, if my motivation is negative then I appear to myself as an isolated individual who must act for himself and achieve whatever he can by his individual efforts, in a world which cares nothing for success or failure. Yet in reality, my isolation is self-isolation, a withdrawal from relationships through fear of the other. This attitude which expresses the experience of frustration and despair is nothing but the sophisticated adult version of the attitude of the child whose mother refuses to give him what he wants. Its unsophisticated formula is 'nobody loves me'.

Now no one would find anything particular to object to in this, of course; it is perfectly sound and ordinary, the mental equivalent of steamed pudding and custard: comfort mental food, and as such just the sort of thing that the 'me-me-me' stars such as Lennon and McCartney, and Madonna, ought to take to heart.

Macmurray was very sceptical of politics:

> If we track the state to its lair, what shall we find? Merely a collection of over-worked and worried gentlemen, not at all unlike ourselves, doing their best to keep the machinery of government working as well as may be, and hard put to it to keep up appearances. They are, like ourselves, subject to the illusion of power. If we expect them to work miracles, we flatter them, and tempt them to think they are supermen . . . Those of them who are wise enough to know their limitations, and to be immune to the gross adulation of their fellows, will resign; and government will be carried on only by megalomaniacs.

In a curious way Blair, by his later refusal to resign, was to fulfil

Macmurray's gloomy prophecy in reverse. But it was in the convoluted, and yet very intimate, advice that Macmurray extended to the 23-year-old student when it came to personal relations that spoke to him most directly. Macmurray offered Tony a kind of woolly reassuring formula which married, in a sentimental way, religious belief and personal commitment. It was so woolly it could be adapted to more or less any situation, any marriage – or even running a government:

> If we isolate one pair as the unit of personal community we can discover the basic structure of community as such. The relation between them is positively motivated in each. Each then is heterocentric; the centre of interest is in the other not himself. The other is the centre of value. For himself he has no value in himself, but only for the other; consequently he cares for himself only for the sake of the other.
>
> If [a pair's] relationship to the other is negative . . . this will destroy the realisation of the exclusive relationship itself. To be fully positive, therefore, the relation . . . must be inclusive and without limits. Only so can it be a community of persons. The self-realisation of any individual person is only fully achieved if he is positively motivated towards every other person with whom he is in relation.
>
> We can therefore formulate the inherent ideal of the personal. It is a universal community of persons in which each cares for all the others and no one for himself . . . if the negative motive could finally and completely be subordinated to the positive, in all personal activity, the redemptive function of religion would be complete; and only its central activity would remain. Religion would then be simply the celebration of community – of the fellowship of all things in God.

This was in a marginally more sophisticated form the 1960s philosophy of Liverpool: 'Make love, not war', but softer, more gradual, more unemotionally put, and not so graphically sexual as Lennon and Yoko Ono adorning their album covers in the nude. The tameness, the undifferentiated love, the soap opera culture of universal sameness, were to become a powerful tool in Tony's developing persona, and just as he was to deny the conflict in himself, so he was to disavow opposition and challenge.

6

Boy meets girl, so what?

The reason that lovers never weary each other is because they are always talking about themselves.

François de la Rochefoucauld

The paths of Cherie Booth and Tony Blair collided in 1976. In that instant, which in time was to deepen as each came to know the other more, Cherie and Tony recognised in one another in every possible angle the potential for fulfilling their future individual needs and ambitions.

In the stuffy world of legal practices native cunning and greedy opportunism stand out far more visibly than romantic good looks, natural charm or a hesitant, public-school set of manners. Tony excelled at once in attracting both men and women. He was at once the catch for all the eligible, striving young female lawyers who were, because of their tunnel vision and intense ambition, more likely to fall for something that had the image of the very opposite yet also was ambitious and possessed acuity of a very special kind.

Tony, first and foremost, in a world increasingly ready to capitulate to image, was Romeo: but Romeo with a darkness, that of two family tragedies. He was only twenty-three and looked every inch a lover, but a lover fey and foredoomed. He had classic flexible features, clear blue eyes and was strikingly tall. He moved, with his intermittent but quite serious acting experience, in a gracious manner, but he gesticulated with imaginative gestures. Above all he gave the feeling he had hidden depths of passion and a profound family grief. He was both Romeo and Hamlet.

There is reference to him seeing Cherie too, in her legal robes and wig as junior counsel in court, as Portia, *The Merchant of Venice*'s level-headed barrister who, conscious of her own intrinsic worth as opposed to outward riches, knows the world is 'still deceived by ornament' and hides the 'counterfeit' picture she challenges her suitors to find in a 'casket of meagre lead'. But Cherie was more than that. She had the brain of Portia, but a much more impulsive and complicated nature.

Like most very young couples they fell in love at first sight, but she, it would seem, more at first sight than he. 'The type of human being we prefer reveals the contour of our heart,' wrote José Ortega y Gasset; in their case at an instinctive unconscious level they recognised the remarkable and extraordinary symmetry of their family backgrounds.

What causes the rush of good feeling we call romantic love? Both Cherie and Tony had been hurt and to some extent sought an escapist form of relationship that would compensate for this. Psychopharmacologists, if one is inclined to listen to the widespread biochemical cant of the twenty-first century, say that lovers are literally high on drugs – natural hormones and chemicals which flood their bodies with a sense of well-being. Dr Michael R. Liebowitz, associate professor of clinical psychiatry at Columbia University, goes into rhapsodies about how falling in love releases in the brain endorphins and enkephalins, natural narcotics which enhance a person's sense of security and comfort. Liebowitz takes the idea one step further and suggests that the mystical experience of 'oneness' that lovers undergo may be caused by an increase in the production of the neuro-transmitter serotonin. Louann Brizendine in *The Female Brain* is more blunt: 'The basic drive for romantic attachment', she writes, 'is hardwired in the brain.'

The forced rekindling of Tony and Cherie's wooing period for the cameras and tabloid columns in the later years provided an echo of what, from 1976 until the time of their marriage in 1980, was positive and exuberant: folded scraps of paper on which had been written, ' "Tony loves Cherie", drawings of a little stick man and a little stick woman and loads of kisses,' revealed Cherie. 'It's not a very expensive gesture, but I think it's very romantic.' We have a sense of that earlier spontaneous attraction both felt to each other which they revived in mystic, esoteric ceremonies during their Downing Street years. In 2001 Cherie and Tony partook of a rebirthing experience on a Mexican Riviera summer holiday when together, to the sound of Mayan hymns, they immersed themselves in a temazcal steam bath and smeared their bodies with watermelon and papaya. To revive the classic symptoms of early love is by this time perhaps rather embarrassing, for it, says Brizendine, like drugs such as ecstasy 'trigger[s] the brain's reward circuit' and switches off 'the normal wariness towards strangers'.

Tony had passed only low down on the list when, on leaving Oxford, he sat the Bar exams (there are no grades) in which Cherie had so luminously shone; but this disadvantage apart, evidenced at once in his deferential attitude to her sharper intellectual grasp, each appeared at that fortunate moment to fill more than adequately the other's desire to love and be loved. Cherie, with this romantic love kindled in her by Tony, might have shown herself the more passionate of the pair, yet scientists cannot explain what exactly causes the release of these potent chemicals, or what especially causes them to diminish. It is also seems likely that Cherie, who had severed her family bond in Liverpool in a quick, decisive way when she came to London, felt her sexual appetite awakened by Tony. She at the same time stimulated in Tony a lifelong desire to 'keep' his Cherie as a romantic image – with the even stronger social intention of preserving her as a wife of extraordinary status value and earning power.

Cherie was also a watching, observing, analytical person who saw in Tony her security. As an attractive man, handsome like her father but reliable, he was able to reinvent the image of the male for her, and cancel out her father. In the exciting new mode of feminism, where women were men's 'equals' and could be like them in every way, she was out to see how she could profit from, in one sense perhaps steal from him, everything that was useful to her. And why not? Rogue though he was, she still sought Tony Booth's affirmation and his admiration.

Both lawyers, Cherie and Tony looked to find the ideal of him or herself in the other, but at the same time loving what he or she would like to be, as well as searching for the partner who, like the adoring mother, was once part of him or her. The attraction was strongly romantic and was to remain so: 'I know we've just met, but somehow I feel as if I already know you' must have been how they felt: at ease with each other, a comfortable resonance, the phenomenon of recognition – 'Even though we've only been seeing each other for a short while, I can't remember when I didn't know you.' Their relationship had no temporal or rational boundaries: 'When I'm with you I no longer feel alone. I feel whole, complete.' In Cherie's yearning eyes towards Tony in the many photographs, one can see only too easily her desire to recover and restore a lost unity, but also her fascination with the sight of her own image. This was one of existing in a fantasy of ideal love, clinging as in 'poor-little-me wife' to her alpha male husband. This was far from the reality, for to pretend she was shy was nonsense. In 1985 in a cabaret turn she shimmies on a Hammersmith stage to sing a number dressed in pink and yellow with spiked hair in her attempt to be Siouxsie Sioux.

A definitive need in both was to be monogamous, he to find a rock-like mother substitute, she from a hunger to cancel out Tony Booth, to show she was superior and provide someone with what her father had never provided for her mother. This sense of being reunified and made whole goes back to the Greek myth described in Plato's *Symposium* of one larger hermaphrodite being split in half, in other words 'I love you so much I can't live without you'. Tony says he found her 'unusual and interesting' but that does not tell us much.

But in their romanticism, their merging together, they also possibly failed to discover, young as they were, their own uniqueness, to find out what and who they really were. 'To the unconscious, being in an intimate love relationship is very much like being an infant in the arms of your mother' (Liebowitz). There is the same illusion of safety and security, the same total absorption. So they had to rely on each other (and this became evident in both of them) and remain cemented to one another within a set of very complicated needs. Neither experimented or even in the short term became attached to anyone else – Cherie in an unguarded moment let it be known, 'Not all the people I went out with were particularly religious but it was one of the things that Tony and I had in common from the beginning.' They stuck to what was essentially a narcissistic image. Each urged the other on with this, as well as themselves, to heroic achievement. This was the central and most important aspect of their burgeoning love for each other. It was based upon love for oneself – or, expressed in another way, the image one found of oneself in the other person. If she became the mother rock he needed, for her Tony was the 'cement' – she actually used this word too – to hold their life together.

The term 'narcissism' comes from Narcissus, the figure in Greek mythology who fell in love with his own image in the mirror-lake. O. Fenichel, in *The Psychoanalytic Theories of Neurosis* (1945), calls the narcissist 'the Don Juan of achievement', while Ernest Jones, the English Freudian, describes the God complex and how the grandiosity that accompanies it covers an underlying feeling of inferiority and a diffuse and aimless inner identity. However much people might disagree with Freud, it is undeniable that his pioneering definitions of narcissism in *Narcissism* (the libidinal investment of the ego or self, in contrast to the libidinal investment of significant others), caused by high parental expectation and harsh criticism, and the corresponding effects of negative narcissism – anger and resentment, laden with vengeful wishes, or resorting to delusion as a reaction to injured self-esteem – are both acute and potentially applicable to Cherie and Tony in the future. Freud's opening description crystallised the 'narcissistic personality as a disorder derived from a pathological integration of a grandiose self as a defence against unbearable aggressive conflicts, particularly around primitive envy'.

In the year they met, 1,002 people in England and Wales were called to the Bar and of these 890 were men and 112 women; but in the new climate, a different kind of global warming, the old stereotypes of male and female identities were melting down fast, with the male becoming feminised, the female masculinised. Sexual roles were changing. In the eyes of those who met them Cherie and Tony shared their lives in what was an innovative equality, and as such were an exemplary couple.

Tony now lived as a lodger in the Wandsworth house owned by Charles Falconer, who was the same age and whom he had known since his schooldays in Edinburgh. Falconer, cleverer and much richer than Blair, with a taste for the high life, had a photographic memory, one of his skills being that he could recall the names of the B-sides of almost every single hit in the 1960s and early 1970s. He joined the crowd of many brains that Tony had begun recruiting for his ambition – this surely must list among one of his greatest talents – to do his thinking for him, and Tony worked hard alongside this new intimate of Crown Office Row in the Inner Temple, and quickly foresaw what he would become – a lightning decision-maker and man of will.

Another 'brain', this time 'the size of a planet' in Tony's words, who, the other way round, actually recruited Tony although in the long term the positions would be reversed, was Derry Irvine, twelve years older than him. When both of the pair had applied (typically Cherie had been the first) to join Michael Sherrard's chambers as a pupil in 1976, Irvine's choice as a senior figure in the chambers of Tony, as well as and after Cherie, made Cherie unhappy – he had been supposed to take on one, not two, new pupils. Subsequently when the pupilage was over, and in spite of having the poorer academic record of the two, Tony's outstanding powers of self-presentation impressed him more. It was Tony who was, with Irvine in charge on the *primus inter pares* principle, chosen to remain, and Irvine often appointed him as his junior over the next years. Cherie, who lacked social skills and could appear intense, also had problems with her body image, an important factor in courtroom appearances.

When questioned about how Tony had been picked over Cherie, Irvine avoided the issue of how much he had been involved. 'They are an extremely able couple. She chose toward the end of her pupilage to accept an offer from another chambers. I was not the head of chambers. She decided to take a bird in the hand. She had to calculate what was best for her.' Derry already had one woman and according to Cherie, believed that she, not Tony, was destined for politics.

On the surface, at least, Cherie should have been the better choice to be taken on permanently. But Tony had attraction without that brooding cleverness. Derry Irvine rang his friend Michael Beloff, without success, then George Carman QC, who gave Cherie a tenancy. These chambers were headed by David MacNeil, while Benet Hytner, father of Nicholas Hytner, present director of the Royal National Theatre, was a senior member; he remembers Cherie with deep affection. When in an amicable split Carman left MacNeil, Cherie went with him. Carman had a reputation, like Tony Booth, as a drinker and womaniser, revealed in his son Dominic's biography, *No Ordinary Life*. Cherie told Dominic in the course of writing his book that his father, like herself a Catholic, was 'not always larger than life, and could be subdued at times'.

Tony settled into law work, and moved with Irvine when in 1981 he left Sherrard to become head of chambers at 11 King's Bench Walk. Irvine praised unstintingly his 'beautiful, easy' manner in court and his charm outside, and furthered his career. He even went so far as to laud Tony later, in 1995, as 'a brilliant lawyer, a complete natural', who had the ability to 'sift through a mass of material, define the issues and come up with answers'. But it may be that Irvine showed, like Tony, what's called 'headline intelligence', which is a common feature of pathological narcissism: as the *Oxford Textbook of Psychiatry* puts it, 'Narcissists may be articulate and excellent lecturers, but their knowledge is often shallow and exhibitionistic.' Irvine's praise does seem rather excessive, as Tony, while always hard-working, has been known to be somewhat impatient with if not neglectful of detail, and to rely on others for its supply. But by 1995 Tony was party leader, 'one step away from the big one', and 'when you're in government all of a sudden you have friends everywhere'. His main skill, demonstrated early, was, while desperate to cover up his own uncertainty, to bring together the people who would engineer his progress. Of these Irvine was the first.

Cherie was none too happy, letting on, 'It didn't please me at all, because I was assured I would be the only one' (to remain at Crown Office Row). However, envy on Cherie's part did not stand in the way of the relationship developing, for in the theory of mimetic desire envy impels you to possess its object. This was undoubtedly the case here. Irvine took the pair out to dinner at Luigi's in Covent Garden as a conciliatory move. Some time later Tony said, 'I can still remember it. It was the longest lunch I've ever had. Cherie and I were still there in the evening and ended up having dinner too. Derry tactfully made his excuses in the middle of the afternoon, but I can't say that I noticed him going.' He added about Cherie, 'I thought, and still think, she was one of the most unusual and interesting people I've met. I was attracted to her looks of course, but also she was so different. She's a one-off, unusual and totally her own person' (quoted in Linda McDougall, *Cherie: The Perfect Life of Mrs Blair*).

There is a feeling in that 'of course' that a compliment about looks was de rigueur. About Tony as her right choice Cherie still needed convincing. 'She wasn't quite sure whether I was what she was looking for,' he said.

7

A marriage of equals

The business of a biographer is often to pass over those performances and incidents which produce vulgar greatness, to lead the thoughts into domestic privacies and display the minute details of daily life.

Samuel Johnson

Euan Uglow, the artist, was forty-four years old, with quite a reputation for bedding his nubile models. His studio was in the basement of a house in Clapham, where he measured out with plumblines and floor markings his placings of the young women who would pose for him, often in the nude, over periods as long as five years.

One such student, a pupil in legal chambers, arrived here sometime in 1976. She pulled at the bell chain to gain entry into the redbrick house with chequered tiles and introduced herself to the artist. He led her downstairs and here she stripped and put on a plain blue denim dress, well opened at the front, to confront the artist about whom one of his models said, 'There was something in the way he looked at me with piercing eyes.'

The painting Uglow did of Cherie, titled *Striding Nude, Blue Dress*, was never properly finished: painted in right profile, with left leg forward, bare breasted with a modest show of pubic hair – demure by Lucien Freud standards – Cherie was, according to Georgia Georgallas, Uglow's fellow artist, model and mistress, 'quite proud of posing'. She had the instincts of a young Helen Mirren, say, who had no inhibitions about taking off her clothes. She was introduced to the artist by Derry Irvine, who collected Uglow's paintings. 'I know she wouldn't do it for the money,' says Georgallas, although it was likely that Irvine, aware of Cherie's lack of funds, took the view that this would help her financially. 'Cherie wouldn't be embarrassed by it – she's not the type to be embarrassed.'

She posed for some months but broke off to visit America, and once she returned and had started seeing Tony she dropped the posing. She remained proud of the painting, which in 2006 appeared on an art gallery website, but Tony, according to a New Labour figure, 'rather prudishly didn't want the world to see his wife nude when he was a rising star in the party'. They liked the name Euan, and when their first son was born in 1984 they gave him the artist's name.

Meantime Cherie was sharing a flat in Fulham with Maggie Rae, a left-wing lawyer who was to become a media divorce specialist and to marry Alan Howarth, secretary of the Parliamentary Labour Party. Lauren Booth recalls her dressed like a hippie, with bangles and beads, coming round with Tony to baby-sit while her parents had a night out. Their ambition, with a widening network of friends and colleagues cultivated with this end in view, as well as personal reasons, kept the couple together until permanence loomed in the shape of Tony's proposal. They were on a holiday together in Tuscany in the summer of 1977. He explained his decision: 'I'd come to the complete conviction [can convictions be half-hearted?] in my own mind [where else do convictions take place?] that this was the person I wanted to marry. I was very nervous. Then, quite near the end of the fortnight, I thought: Right, it's now or never.'

The engagement lasted until March 1980, when they married in the chapel of St John's College, Oxford. Cherie wore a cream dress she picked up in a Liberty sale, while Tony, as he had promised her, had smoked his last ever cigarette before the ceremony. In lieu of Tony Booth, who had now left *Till Death Us Do Part* and nearly incinerated himself in the fire he started, Derry Irvine gave away the bride. Leo, having suffered a second stroke, was also absent. About this time Irvine ribbed Tony for two articles published in the right-wing *Spectator*, one called 'Second-Class Justice', the other 'Where Interest Should Prevail', written in a mundane style without anything much fresh to say.

Surprisingly, Cherie consented to a Church of England wedding, conducted by Anthony Phillips, St John's chaplain, who commented that both were 'so devout in their Christianity'. To marry in a Protestant church

Cherie had to obtain permission from her bishop, otherwise in canon law the marriage would be invalid and she would be banned from taking the sacraments. Her cousin, Father Paul Thompson, took part in the service, as did her bishop. Cherie's ever-present mother, Gale, who was Protestant, was there: she now lived in Oxford and worked in the John Lewis store, overlooking Bonn Square. The Rev. Phillips said in his address, invoking Proverbs, chapter 30:

> There be three things which are too wonderful for me, yea, four which I know what.
>
> The way of the eagle in the air; the way of a serpent upon a rock; the way of a ship in the midst of the sea; and the way of a man with a maid.

This last was possibly not so wondrous or mysterious, for his 'way of a man with a maid' was pre-eminently the shared ambition to enter politics as soon as possible and climb to the top of the greasy pole. The matchmaker Irvine, who described himself at the wedding reception as the 'Blair Cupid', was also the political go-between. Did he realise Cupid was blind?

*

By now, which was significant for Cherie, Margaret Thatcher had become the first ever woman Prime Minister. The country had been taken over by what Freud described as the dark continent of woman, throwing into confusion and turmoil the serried and hitherto closed ranks of male ministers who shifted uneasily on the Tory front bench, giving the lady more than usual berth either side, and plotted behind her back.

Beatrix Campbell in *Iron Ladies*, published eight years after Thatcher came to power, described how she had 'edited' the woman out of her life:

> Her body language is womanly – as she speaks at party conferences she tilts her head in that gesture which is placatory but superior, her stride is stiff from the waist down, she makes her point in the mannered tilt of her shoulders and her bosom, which manoeuvres sexuality into vision. Her gender is unmistake-able, her power is manifest, but her sexuality . . . ?

We were witnessing another birth – that of the influence of body language, a new claptrap of interpretation and a gift to the visual media. But Thatcher had set her own and very different trap into which the aspirant woman politician would inevitably fall:

> Thatcher is a model neither of traditional femininity nor feminism, but something else altogether – she embodies female power which unites patriarchal and feminine discourses. She has brought qualities of ruggedness and ruthlessness to femininity which perhaps only men hadn't noticed before in women. She has not feminised politics, however, but she has offered feminine endorsements to patriarchal power and principles. (Campbell)

The psychologist Erich Fromm wrote, 'When men and women become equal, they cease to be different'; Margaret Thatcher famously trumpeted, taking a line from Sophocles, 'Once a woman is made equal to a man she becomes his superior.' To the future male Prime Minister, would the Downing Street wife offer unconditional support – as Denis Thatcher did to Margaret – or would she desire to exercise her power and principles in her own right, follow her own career and stalwartly assert her equality?

8

The very basis of civilised society

It is always the best policy to tell the truth, unless, of course, you are
an exceptionally good liar.

Jerome K. Jerome

The law had become as never before a hotbed of ruthless political ambition,
and in the early married life of Cherie and Tony competition was rife in
chambers such as Derry Irvine's. Irvine had already stood and failed to
secure election as Labour candidate for Hendon North in 1970 and
Aberdare in 1974, but he did not stand in the way of his protégé's intention
to become a candidate at the by-election caused by the death of the sitting
Tory member in Beaconsfield in 1982. In the meantime Cherie unsuccessfully applied for the Labour candidature at the Crosby by-election to fight
the defecting Shirley Williams.

Cherie and Tony made a pact: the other would support whoever got
ahead first in the bid to obtain a parliamentary seat. This was equality with
a vengeance, but was it ever likely to be carried out to the letter? When
Cherie was briefly in front, at the snap general election called by Margaret
Thatcher in June 1983 after victory in the Falklands War, Tony had no seat
to fight, while Cherie was chosen for Thanet North, a safe Conservative seat
she had little chance of winning. Tony turned up to campaign beside her but
his intrusion was held to be bumptious; only a year older than Cherie he was
never likely to become the ideal spouse of a candidate. His role definitely was
not that of her supportive Denis Thatcher.

Luckily, having been warned wisely by Irvine not to fight Beaconsfield a
second time, Tony heard he had been selected for the safe Labour seat of

Sedgefield, in the north-east of England. This sealed Cherie's political fate: upon hearing of Tony's selection she whooped for joy, but later, and after she had come a poor third at Thanet, she displayed a churlish reaction to being relegated to a back seat, insisting that it was 'pure chance' Tony succeeded before her. She was now cast, with her far superior salary as a flourishing barrister, as the main family breadwinner: 'Now I am the wife of someone,' she expressed in her resentment.

But they conceived their first child during that self-same election campaign, and Euan was born in January 1984, to be followed by Nicholas (December 1985) and Kathryn (March 1988). They conceived all three children in early summer months.

They could hardly complain, as Cherie did, of poverty. Still under thirty, both of them had up to now led a charmed existence, the material deprivations of their respective childhoods relatively minor and in the past. At first they bought a flat in Hackney and, in 1986, a house in Islington. Cherie paid for a succession of nannies and they holidayed, together with socialist friends of their very politically active set, in Italy and France; they soon now owned a second home, Myrobella, a Victorian detached house in Sedgefield, where they spent many weekends among Tony's constituents. Life was fast, exciting and stressful, and they argued openly: 'They are close enough and secure enough to have a testy relationship and to fight with each other in the company of others,' an insider commented, and this would confirm Cherie was definitely in control. Stories circulated of her slagging off everyone in the shadow Cabinet, Gordon Brown in particular, while Tony 'shrugs and smiles'. Later she was to tell the *Times*, 'My husband says – and heaven forbid he ever disagrees – I'm a bolshie Scouser.'

But there were clouds looming, clouds of unreason and mendacity. There was Cherie's superior air and manner, her contempt for shop-girls and inferiors in the chambers; she was bossy, even with her own step-family and increasingly with politicians and journalists, either charming if they adhered to her value system or abrupt and dismissive if they broke it. For instance, her dismissal of Stephen Fry when, outside in the corridor at an awards ceremony, he offered her a cigarette shocked him. 'She didn't even say, "Thank you." She said, "Absolutely not!" . . . We sent all the Puritans over to America.' There developed also, as she and Tony became better off, her greater insistence on her 'deprived' childhood, which signalled a hypocrisy which was to become an *idée fixe* and almost a passion. And how could she have said, speaking on the same platform as the unworldly Tony Benn at Thanet, that he had 'inspired' her in her 'quest for socialism'? What nonsense. Married to an American millionairess, Benn had sent his son Hilary to follow his own path to Westminster School before switching him to the showpiece comprehensive Holland Park. Opportunism and narcissism made odd bedfellows.

In a hastily typed curriculum under the pressure of last-minute selection for Sedgefield in 1983 Tony stated that he had 'written for' the *Guardian*, while he also said Cherie's law work could 'transfer' to the north. Both statements were inaccurate, but even more remarkable were the rather stunning omissions that he had been to school at Fettes and as a barrister in London handled employers' briefs and engaged in corporate litigation. Minor peccadilloes these may have been, judicious selective pruning of the truth, but they were the thin end of the wedge. 'The ethos of the Bar', says a barrister, 'is based on truth.' In criminal law every defending counsel will assume his client is innocent unless the client tells him otherwise.

9

The Socialist Republic of Islington

I will go root away
The noisome weeds which without profit suck
The soil's fertility from wholesome flowers.

William Shakespeare, *Richard II*

Surprisingly, in June 2003, just as Tony was beginning to reap the whirlwind from the Iraq war and still, in spite of greater and greater desperation from him and George W. Bush to find the weapons of mass destruction (WMDs), the glossy Night and Day supplement of the *Mail on Sunday* lauded Cherie to the skies.

King Magnus, in George Bernard Shaw's political extravaganza *The Apple Cart*, asks, 'Is it not curious how people idealise their rulers? The old divine theory worked because there is a divine spark in all of us, and the stupidest or worst monarch or minister, if not wholly god, is a bit of a god – an attempt at a god – however little the bit and unsuccessful the attempt.' This now had rubbed off on Cherie. No. 10 mustered a pack of high-flying women to kindle her divine spark and divert attention from the beleaguered Tony. So, against an acreage of glamour pictures, as airbrushed as a Boeing 747, a number of elite women gave their views to counter the malicious reports in the papers about Cherie ('gossip made tedious by morality'), aimed mainly at getting at Tony through her.

'She can't really defend herself,' expostulated an owner of gourmet food stores, one of Cherie's friends; 'maybe I'm American, but it seems to me nobody in this country wants anyone to get ahead.' Cheek to cheek with Cherie in a lookalike pose, Geri Halliwell purred, 'Hey, this chick is down to earth.' 'She has a very fine intellect,' said Esther Rantzen, a connoisseur of the power of thought, while Sarah Ferguson, another powerful mind, chipped in, 'She's a very impressive multi-tasker.' Cate Haste, wife of the ennobled Melvyn Bragg, the broadcaster, shareholder of the former London Weekend Television and an early donor to Labour Party funds, commented on her 'Liverpudlian directness and wit' and – at this time she was working on the book with Cherie about Prime Ministers' spouses – raised the question, 'Does she have a right to privacy?'

Haste answered it herself: 'There's now this sense that the PM's spouse is somehow public property, whereas in fact Cherie guards her privacy very carefully.' (And yet was writing a book about PMs' spouses?) She had also, the American CEO of Burberry revealed, invited all the Burberry PAs and store assistants to a No. 10 reception – presumably not making remarks to them such as 'I would have worked in a shop if . . . '.

This fulsome fare reached an ecstatic high when Sally Greene, a Labour Party supporter and owner of the Old Vic Theatre, said, 'Whenever she's criticised, I'm sure Tony comforts her.' Further, 'they are still madly in love', 'no airs and graces' – and, to cap it all, what a fantastic contrast Cherie made with Margaret Thatcher. Greene and her husband had been invited to Downing Street a couple of times during the Thatcher regime 'and I always found them so pompous', unlike Tony and Cherie, who shared their ideas with everybody. 'They listen to other people's thoughts and they want to hear about things from your point of view.'

There was a brief flirtation with reality, away from what might have been Alastair Campbell's A-list of Cherie-damage-limitation celebrities, when two female colleagues and friends gave their views. Barrister X said, 'She's not a particularly organised person – well, not in a conventional sense. She can be a bit scatty – always shouting for things.' She also commented on the Downing Street flat looking 'like a jumble sale'. Barrister Y, an Islington neighbour, worked in Matrix Chambers, to which Cherie moved from George Carman's, now concentrating on cases to make the workplace 'more family friendly'. She told how she worked with Cherie on a number of race and discrimination cases, taking one to the Court of Appeal, 'successfully arguing that mobility clauses in contracts of employment discriminate against women. She is a formidable advocate.' She, too, failed to recognise the Cherie as portrayed in the press; as she said, 'Virtual reality Cherie is nothing like the real thing.'

Another former younger colleague of her chambers contradicts the pristine image, saying how she could be rude and bossy to those ranked below her, and high handed in her use of flunkeys socially – while even her half-sister Lauren had found herself summoned at a dinner to her by an unknown intermediary: 'Mrs Blair will see you now.'

Undoubtedly she was odd, and to many what drove her was a mystery, exhibiting as she did the 'many faces of Eve' – on the one hand a courageous, dedicated, focused lawyer, a multi-tasking, devoted mother in intention (and often in practice, but not always); on the other hand a figure at whom columnists aimed scurrilous demonology: white witch, wicked witch, shark in the goldfish bowl, Lady Macbeth and so on.

But between the years of 1986 and 1994, until Tony became party leader, she had a dual role in life which she fulfilled completely: a model career woman, earning a high income as a barrister and supporting her MP husband, and a mother sharing with him and successive nannies and childcarers the domestic duties of looking after her three small children. Here was the cosy Islington pond in which she swam easily and effortlessly, and she was never out of reach of comfort or dry land. These were, for her, Tony and their family, halcyon days, or so Cherie says, yet was there really a limit to her ambitions?

*

Cherie already had a severe problem, which from the glamorous pictures in the *Mail on Sunday* spread in 2003 any reader would have deemed impossible. In 1986, recently gentrified from humbler origins than N1, Cherie wore the Islington uniform of a Jill Tweedie or Polly Toynbee, *Guardian* contributors at a time when the makeover team Trinny and Susannah were not even a gleam in a TV executive's eye. Tony and Cherie were in a moneyed, post-hippie set who had acquired by early middle age enviable lifestyles but, as Paul Scott says in *Tony & Cherie*, had 'never come by the barest understanding of the visual. The result was an expensive and messy metropolitan melange.'

They were as yet unmade-over: Cherie's hair was styled into 'an unflattering spike at the front [and] a mullet at the back', and she displayed bushy eyebrows and a 'gawky self-consciousness' which, bewigged, confident and sure of her brief, she never had in court as advocate in her Portia image. Accompanying Tony on a visit to China in 1998 she would explain, as she set up a mock court for Chinese law students to understand British trial by jury, the importance of ritual dress: 'I myself', she told them, 'am occasionally seen in wig and gown.' Tony said of her during this trip, 'She was always a better lawyer than I was.'

Here she acted the role model, one of a new and powerful breed who amazingly juggled many roles, the 'schizotypal woman', but one who, as her detractors were later to charge, was growing compartmentalised in her mind to such a degree that there could be a labile disconnectedness as she went from one persona to another.

Without the reassurance of an adoring father, Cherie had not grown up confident in her own body. Her body language shows deprivation: it was 'asymmetrical, ungrammatical':

> Her tenseness and humourlessness, her curious atactic mien, her much remarked upon public holding hands with Blair, her rapturous gazing at, and kissing of, her husband at conferences, are outward symptoms of much painful insecurity. At best her early bruising can lead her to champion causes like Refuge, the charity that provides accommodation for battered women; and she speaks out in favour of the Labour document 'Peace at Home', advocating a national helpline for women victims of irresponsible violent partners. But less benign public consequences can stem from her early bitter experiences. (Leo Abse, *The Man Who Lost His Smile*)

This may sound harsh, but it contains more than a grain of truth. Tony was streets ahead in well-adjusted sociability, but rather blinded by his own charismatic image. Had Tony been more different from Cherie he might have been more of a visual mentor for her. But he was curiously unobservant of her (to judge by the way she dressed). What did this signify?

She, on the other hand, was streets ahead in employment law, and while he was the MP he became for the first time her imitative double, taking up the cause of the employee underdog. Before he was elected for Sedgefield, he espoused union opposition against Margaret Thatcher's animus to crush organised labour; in February 1980, writing an attack in the *New Statesman* on plans by Jim Prior, the employment secretary, to curtail the unions' legal immunity. 'These proposals are not moderate. They are a concerted attempt to destroy the effectiveness of industrial action.' Calling himself 'barrister' Anthony Blair (November 1981) he lambasted Thatcher's law against secondary picketing as 'a draconian limitation on effective industrial action which involves anyone but the industrial parties'. Then, as elected MP, he duplicated Cherie's long-held belief in nuclear disarmament and withdrawal from the European Union, and while Shirley Williams and David Owen had resigned from Labour in 1981 over those very issues, he mocked the Social Democratic Party, which Owen continued to lead after the formation of the Liberal Democrats, as 'the political wing of Sainsbury's' (*London Review of Books*, October 1987). The retail baron David Sainsbury, later ennobled and made a minister in Blair's government, supported the SDP but was already a Labour party donor and would go on to donate £2 million to New Labour. Tony wrote:

> The 'free' market does not distribute fairly or efficiently . . . There is a tremendous danger – to which Dr Owen has succumbed – in believing that 'Thatcherism' is now somehow invincible and that all the rest of us can do is debate alternatives within its framework. The fundamental error of Dr Owen has been to surrender to Mrs Thatcher's philosophy and say that power can only be devolved through the market. The 1990s will not see the continuing triumph of the market, but its failure.

Brave words. The very opposite happened. It is perhaps not quite enough to defend Tony on the basis that he changed his ideas. More possibly to the point is that he picked up this idea to gain influence by denouncing Owen's defection. But by any standards, it is a remarkably stupid piece of reasoning.

The impact he increasingly made was from his speeches in the House of Commons. In an age other than our own Tony might well have been dismissed as a handsome and charming gadfly, a politician of enormous charisma but little substance, but as he moved up the Labour shadow pecking order, assimilating the support and advice of abler aides and researchers, again marshalling those who would engineer his progress, his outward-seeming substance grew and grew. And whatever personality faults Cherie had, she had formidable weight as a lawyer, which underpinned his more feckless skills.

They operated as a duo. They would often be seen seated and huddled together in the corridors or reception rooms of power, ignoring the passing flow of underlings: the striker and head coach, leading actor and director, discussing tactics and the next great performance.

10

Cassandra prophesies

> Narcissistic grandiosity is often masked by opposing tendencies (false
> modesty, social aloofness, and a pretended attempt for status).
> Pathological lying is frequent.
>
> *New Oxford Textbook of Psychiatry*

He needed her there. It seemed, too, when it came down to a matter of detail
that Cherie was much sharper. Tony was always prepared to listen and to do
what he was told. Leo Abse told me, 'She gives him the authentication', and
further, 'Tony and Cherie's intactness, their worship of one another depends
on constantly having a reflection . . . embracing him she is embracing
herself.'

Abse recalls an episode in 1984, early in Blair's parliamentary career. The
Labour MP introduced reforms and modification to the 1979 Matrimonial
and Family Proceedings Act, called the Divorce Reform Bill, which did just
as in the description – make divorce possible if over a set period the marriage
had already broken down. These reforms sought to rectify the injustices
caused by the first law, especially in the apportioning of incomes. After the
second reading of the Bill the Labour whips put Tony on the committee to
consider it in detail. Abse's first sight and chat with him is revealing of the
inner man:

> I was puzzled for a moment by the ambiguity of his mien. There was such
> dissonance between the athletic build of this clear-blue-eyed, six-foot-tall,
> good-looking man with classic broad shoulders tapering down to a narrow
> waist and the essential sinuosity within his bearing, which became more

pronounced as it was accompanied by an over-ready winsome little boy smile. That night, when I told my wife, which was my habit, the day's gossip in the House, I mentioned – as she reminded me some years later – that an intelligent young rock star had joined our committee. I had evidently believed myself to have picked up Blair's vibes; the androgynous quality.

Tony opposed Abse's Bill, which dealt with custodial problems, easing the pain of break-up by allowing the marital separation to become cleaner; and Abse found Tony's coolness to any implementation of the Bill's provisions, which were complicated and 'to which I had given so much thought and so long striven', presumptuous. 'Unpleasantly carefully', with a sweet smile, Blair avoided confrontation with Abse on the committee, going so far only on one occasion to suggest 'with respect, that the honourable Member for Torfaen had gone slightly over the top in some of his rhetoric'.

Blair hated the principle of the clean break and wanted Abse's Bill changed so that, in the words he used in the House of Commons when he came to speak in the debate on the Bill, 'marriage should be viewed as a common endeavour, in a broader sense, as opposed to pounds, shillings and pence', saying also 'that principle shuffles off the lifelong responsibilities of marriage and brings a change in the marriage contract by permitting an easier clean break even where the parties may not consent'. During this involvement was noted 'his talent to combine pronouncements of unexpected banality with a distaste to anchor them in the sordid details of legislation'. The implication for Abse was that Tony (and behind him the devoutly Catholic Cherie) had a strong need to avoid confrontational situations and strove to place himself and his politics 'in a conflict-free zone'.

A veteran politician who declined ministerial office, Abse had already seen at close quarters the misplaced optimism of Harold Wilson, his Walter Mitty fantasies and above all his outstanding ability as a practitioner to turn false consensus into an art form. Here was another set of the Wilsonian articles of denying the existence of contradiction. Already Tony was displaying the prejudices of his principles 'when he wished to have in statutory form an idealised mutuality and an avoidance of acknowledgement of strife, a wish that reflected his essential mode of thought: all difference of views should be minimised'.

When Abse came later, in Tony's company, to mention his early participation in that committee he found that Tony denied all knowledge of it and had forgotten everything about it. Ah, Abse sighed during our meeting, 'Art is long, politics is short,' – and then the most significant statement he made in my presence: 'The worst fate to befall a politician is to have a political wife.'

A further clash – at one remove this time – which Abse reports to me took place in 1999, when he wrote in the *New Statesman* that Tony's aggressive enthusiasm for armed intervention in the Balkans came from a displacement, a 'desire to obtain release from all that suppressed and unreleased aggression he felt towards his father as a child'. There was nothing defamatory in the article, Abse says, but instead of the *Statesman* printing it straightaway, a staff member informed him that Leo, Tony's father, had been taken seriously ill, and that therefore the editor believed it would be tasteless to publish such an article when Tony might lose his father. They would hold it over for the time being. Abse then promptly checked up on Leo Blair, whom he found to be in rude health, having just returned from holiday in Ireland. He found out Downing Street had read the article, shown to them by the *Statesman*, and intervened.

'They kill off the father,' Abse summarises in 2006, but 'Tony's fears are much greater than those of a hostile press . . . I could see the disaster he was going to become.' The fears resided deep within the man, and were of himself.

11

Conviction becomes a selling point

Beliefs are like possessions, and convictions are simply more valued possessions which allow an individual to passionately [*sic*] work toward either large-scale or individual completion of goals, projects, wishes and desire.

Dr Robert P. Abelson, quoted by Anthony Robbins in
Awaken the Giant Within

The Blair duo reached their first peak of power when the Labour Party chose Tony as their leader in the summer of 1994, just after John Smith's death from a sudden heart attack. But paradoxically, where Tony had got into bad trouble at Fettes as leader of the wrong gang of rebels and misbehavers, now he got lucky. The odd thing is that this now much more sophisticated gang was just as anti the Labour establishment as Blair's first gang was against the hidebound public school ethos.

Like the boys in *If . . .*, Lindsay Anderson's 1968 film about an English public school, they were to go the whole way in their anti-establishment riot and gun down the teachers. With hindsight it is difficult to separate the members of what came to be known as 'the Team', 'P5' or 'Political Five', the inner core of five men – Tony, Gordon Brown, Philip Gould, Peter Mandelson and Alastair Campbell – and to say that without one or another Tony would never have come to power. Each was indispensable to what was to become the most extraordinary political coup in British history.

But first of all there was the transformation of society and politics at almost every level between the mid-1980s, when Blair and his team began their coherent rise through the then disordered ranks and muddled thinking of Labour politics, and the late 1990s, when New Labour came to power. To touch briefly on the causes: among them were the mainstreaming of the earlier, elite permissiveness, which now reached into all levels of society and especially into the prouder, more humble working base of society; the rise of the global village mentality through the internet; the speeding up of all communication; the crumbling of the Eastern communist empire; the spread, as a result, of now unfettered capitalism and the market economy. The new freedoms saw few limits, especially in the storage of data and fast access to it, with the impact this had on the centralisation of political power. Debate died, or rather mud-slinging took the place of serious debate. The fact that Alastair Campbell could rise so high and come to hold such influence is the most palpable evidence of that extraordinary change, and in many ways defines it.

Campbell was three years younger than Tony, the son of a vet, a Scot who would as a young man wear his Campbell of Argyll tartan and play the bagpipes, and enjoy a legendary spell as a 'crumpeteer' and even as a gigolo. He wrote this up for the pornographic magazine *Forum* both in factual accounts and in fictional form. As a modern languages student in France, in his third year at Gonville and Caius College, Cambridge, he encountered women 'the majority of whom were rich, beautiful and in love with sex', for example one Madame Rinaudo: when still finding his feet in a strange country, he wrote in *Forum* magazine, 'we were halfway through a bowl of marinated mussels when it became transparent that Mme Rinaudo had a more than purely personal interest in me'. Another, from Nice University, 'in return for a handful of orgasms, helped me to write my thesis on Racine and Corneille' (could anything be a greater contrast?).

Campbell disavowed the truth of these escapades, saying he had made them up, but it would seem that the two-way mirror between truth and fiction, between reality and lies, in this powerful young man's psyche and mind would never leave him – right up to the point of 'sexed-up' dossiers – and at the same time, he tossed a liberal sprinkling of sexual and scatological metaphor over everything with which he came into contact. 'Time to sexy up those bits on the economy,' says Eddie, the character based on Campbell in Alistair Beaton's *Feelgood* (2001); and, at another point, 'Fucking euro. It's not exactly the Viagra of politics, is it? You try bringing the press to orgasm with a two-hour debate on convergence criteria.'

Eddie wants to wreck a female journalist. 'Get me all you can on that idiot woman,' he tells his assistant. 'You know, does she fuck dogs, has she had a sex-change op, has she ever been on holiday to Cuba, etcetera, etcetera. I want the full dustbin on her. Enough to give the red-tops a hard-on.' This was good fiction, but where do truth and fiction cross? Public life had crossed over, especially in the way all non-sexual relationships were becoming sexualised, a symptom of the histrionic personality disorder. The minor players, the press aides and policy advisers were set too, in their own behaviour and language, to adopt the histrionic traits of their leaders and mentors.

Campbell had been a master Machiavel of dustbin journalism years earlier on the *Mirror*, where, for example, in a sensational lead story he implied that Cliff Richard was gay: 'The man who has lived with pop star Cliff Richard for nineteen years, denied yesterday that they are lovers.' He was skilled at what Michael Dobbs in *First Lady* calls 'insinuation wrapped in gossip and then boiled in tittle-tattle'. He outed Martina Navratilova and Judy Nelson as a couple during Wimbledon in 1984: they hit back with the accolade 'scum', the same word he would employ for journalists as poacher turned No. 10 gamekeeper.

As Campbell graduated through bouts of heavy Fleet Street bingeing when that was still the culture – on a not untypical day 'fifteen pints of beer, half a bottle of scotch, four bottles of wine' – he weathered a serious nervous breakdown while working for the short-lived newspaper *Today* but then, unlike Cherie's father, Tony, firmly put 'crumpeteering' behind him to emerge as a fearsome, Cromwellian figure, a puritan enforcer whose main weapon still remained his 'bully-boy swearing capers'.

He also fell in love with Fiona Millar. She became the updated version of the common-law wife now known antiseptically as 'partner' and they had three children. In spite of repeated exhortations to do so by Cherie Blair, they refused to marry. Fiona, an attractive ash blonde with a strong and personable character, was the daughter of the *Express* journalist Bob Millar. Scottish in origin, like Campbell, 'The Millars were a distinctive Labour type: civilised, decent, politically active in north London', according to Peter Oborne and Simon Walters, Campbell's biographers. 'The existence of people like them was one of the reasons that Labour survived as a political party during the convulsions of the early 1980s. They had nothing to do with the arid and destructive infighting of the period, belonging to an older, wiser, more profound and warmer version of socialism.'

Thereafter Campbell became as ferocious a teetotaller as he had been a riotous and uninhibited Cavalier drinker and soul of any party, and his Damascene conversion led him to dedicate himself, both as the *Mirror's* political editor and in his new-found role as Neil Kinnock's spin-doctor, to gaining power by the compelling use of fact or fiction. 'We only do truth' was his battle cry – 'truth' meaning the force of conviction behind any statement made. Tony recognised in Campbell a significant reflex of his own personality: the Blair upholder about whom a High Court judge had once said 'not a witness in whom I could feel 100 per cent confidence' was just about to get into his stride.

A further addition to this inner core of policy-makers, Patricia Hewitt, collaborated with Philip Gould on the magazine *Renewal.* She had served Kinnock since 1983. She had always been greedy for power at all costs, and wielded a formidable armoury of positivism in order to achieve this. Roy Hattersley and Neil Kinnock had been racing against each other for leadership of the Labour Party (and Hattersley had just lost), when both men were lining up together for pictures outside the Grand Hotel in Brighton. 'Oh, I had a letter', said Kinnock, 'from Miss Hewitt, saying how much she hoped I would win, and how keen she was to serve me.' 'Funny,' responded Hattersley, 'I had from her an identical letter backing me.' She became Kinnock's press secretary and was at once entangled with the victim culture, first banging the anti-press drum: 'Neil was being abused in the press, it was disgusting.' Hewitt, together with Fiona Millar, Tessa Jowell and Cherie, composed the Team's outer circle, its filters and insulation, its female as well as its feminist endorsement. And of course Cherie was an integral part of the dyadic centrepiece, the fusion of two minds directed to a common purpose.

12

Where there's death there's hope

> One of these men is *genius* to the other:
> And so of these, which is the natural man,
> And which the spirit? Who deciphers them?
>
> William Shakespeare, *Comedy of Errors*

Peter Mandelson, born on 21 October 1953, perhaps most perfectly exemplifies the description of the shadowy, shifting human and political identity that was to become central to the seizure of power by New Labour in 1994.

Again, his slippery personality was to become an echo of Tony's own. The disturbed homosexual who is at odds with his sexual orientation in many ways was to reflect the cool heterosexual who was at odds with his deep-rooted aggression. Each unconsciously saw and felt the other was hiding something, a formula for solidarity – but only up to a point.

As the grandson of Herbert Morrison, a member of Churchill's wartime Cabinet, later deputy leader of the Labour Party and a member of Attlee's Cabinet, Peter Mandelson had status and statesman-like potential enjoyed by none of the Team. Half Jewish on his father's side, he was born in Hampstead Garden Suburb the same year as Tony, but unlike his future leader he was a left-wing, progressive atheist. Disclosed on *Newsnight* in October 1998 by Matthew Parris, Mandelson's homosexuality, a BBC spokesman immediately claimed, was not appropriate subject for news 'on grounds of personal privacy', and the BBC then refused to refer to such matters.

As by this time Mandelson had been for thirteen years New Labour's most active spin-doctor, the press seized upon the news with undisguised glee. That the master manipulator who was obsessive about secrecy had been caught in his own web was one way of looking at it. Another way was that of gay rights campaigners such as Peter Tatchell, who advocated openness and could not understand why Mandelson denied his sexual orientation. As the Labour MP Chris Smith, who later became Culture Secretary, showed, it was no big deal in politics any more to be gay.

One of Mandelson's friends, Steve Wakeham, claimed that he had even managed to get back into the closet. 'He is living as if it is still the 1950s . . . I think he has no emotional life.' Another gay acquaintance speculated that 'his gayness drives his personality. He tries to exploit his personality where he can, where he hopes it can curry favours.' But he did not confide in others: 'He never confirms he is gay, unless he absolutely knows who it is. He is fiercely discreet about who he sleeps with. He is paranoid about the press turning him over.'

From these statements and from his own inscrutable demeanour, dry wit and constant air of superiority, as if aware of his political pedigree, Mandelson came to be dubbed the 'Prince of Darkness', although '*éminence grise*' might be the more suitable expression. Mandelson was a plotter and a planner; and there was no one better suited to Michel de Montaigne's description of the ambiguous figure in Elizabethan cloak-and-dagger politics that was to become typical again in Cherie and Tony's years in Downing Street: 'When we have penetrated through the deceptive exterior of appearance and imagine we have come to the real man, a new uncertainty arises. For what is the real man?'

Tony recognised in Mandelson a rebel at heart who wanted to tear down the old system and put something new in its place. As he himself had done, Mandelson rebelled at Hendon County Grammar School, hating the hierarchical rules, although some of his contemporaries said he felt this was a result of him being passed over in his desire to be made head boy. He later confessed, 'I was a rebel at school and with the others rebelled against the prefect system. It was a terribly hierarchical sort of old-style grammar school. We got petitions up and led protests. Our old headmaster got up in assembly and denounced me and my chief collaborator as industrial militants who were pulling apart the fabric of the school community.'

Pulling apart the fabric was his metier, so he was appointed Labour's director of campaigns and communications, aged 32, in October 1985. Subsequently in command of Neil Kinnock's failed attempt to win power at the 1987 election, he gained prestige and power rather than opprobrium, while a year later, during Margaret Thatcher's third term, he began to promote Tony and Gordon Brown, coaching both in presentation. Before Kinnock's second defeat in 1992 led to his resignation, Mandelson had wanted a political career of his own, and a seat in Parliament, for which he worked hard and now won, becoming the member for Hartlepool. Asked what he would try to save if his house was on fire, he answered his Hartlepool United scarf. An insider at last rather than an outsider, he continued to coach and mentor Brown and Blair under the new leader, John Smith.

Meantime, Tony and Gordon Brown had been neck and neck in their rise in the shadow ranks. The MP for Dunfermline East had been elected, like Tony, in 1983. Within weeks of each other they made their maiden speeches, both revealing that considerable difference which in the long run would make them more effective colleagues than if they had been mirror images of each other. Tony, defining his awkwardness, said he 'called' himself a socialist 'not through a text book which has caught my intellectual fancy, nor through unthinking tradition', but because as a virtue he preferred cooperation to confrontation. Brown demonstrated that tradition could be thoughtful and challenging by claiming mass employment could produce mass poverty; in the style that became his hallmark, he delivered an onslaught of statistics. With Robin Cook, Labour MP for Edinburgh Central, Brown published *Scotland: The Real Divide* later that year, but while in the following year Tony was appointed junior Treasury spokesman, Brown, having refused a post he considered demeaning, had to wait to the end of 1985 to be made Trade and Industry spokesman.

Subsequently Kinnock promoted Brown to shadow Chief Secretary to the Treasury, by which time Tony was City and Consumer Affairs spokesman, and following this shadow Energy Secretary. The post of shadow Employment Secretary was next for Tony, matched by Trade and Industry for Gordon. When the changeover came with Kinnock's resignation, which also released Alastair Campbell and Fiona Millar from their willing and devoted bondage to Neil and Glenys, Blair and Brown, ever more impressive in their articulate and combative opposition to John Major's government, were rewarded with the respective posts of Shadow Home Secretary and Chancellor. Here they both remained for nearly two years as they carved out their careers, with Mandelson sharpening their public faces.

One well-concealed event of a personal nature happened to Tony at the time, or thereabouts, of John Smith's first heart attack in October 1988. As Tony told David Blunkett in October 2003 when he was rushed into hospital with heart trouble, he had himself had an intermittent heart murmur for fifteen years. This dates its first occurrence back to 1988. President Clinton also unguardedly let slip in 1997 that Tony had confided to him he suffered minor heart trouble. It seemed to happen when he got into over-work mode – as it had with his father, Leo. Was this to be taken as a premonition, a prophetic blip, or even a symbiotic response, to what was to happen on 12 May 1994, when Smith, the Labour leader on whom everyone placed the highest hopes of becoming premier, suffered a massive heart attack, and died?

While Tony revealed to friends or visitors to Richmond Terrace that his reading tastes were *Treasure Island*, the magical Catholic fantasy *The Lord of the Rings*, Jeeves novels or, more to the practical point – as noticed by an aide in his Islington drawing room – *Middle Class Dreams*, Gordon Brown was the intellectual heavyweight, well read in the seminal literature of his early years. He expressed admiration at the Cheltenham Literary Festival in 2003 for Albert Camus's *The Outsider* and works by Jean-Paul Sartre and George Orwell, who was perhaps the most level-headed socialist of his time (his political essays should be made compulsory reading for aspiring politicians of all parties).

'Tell me who influences you and I'll tell you who you are,' said Jean-Louis Barrault, France's greatest twentieth-century actor: Brown's stated favourites were Tolstoy, who had a vision of history, and Dickens, who had a sharp eye for social justice, but more importantly for lies and hypocrisy. Brown had a taste for poetry too, in particular Shelley and Wordsworth. As the son of a Scottish Presbyterian minister with whom he ever identifies – on a visit to the Vatican in 2007 he presented Pope Benedict XVI with a copy of his sermons – Brown was also well grounded in the Bible, which he described at the same Cheltenham Literary Festival as 'incredibly important to me' (Tony, too, claims he keeps the Bible beside his bed). In practical manoeuvring he was well earthed in politics, a master of networks yet with a depth underpinned by a good academic mind and years of hard theoretical study.

When Fiona Millar visited Gordon in 1985 in Edinburgh to write a *Sunday Times* profile, she found he lived in improbable squalor: his flat had not been cleaned or tidied for years. 'Brimming with character' was how she evaded the issue of showing female approbation. 'The overall impression is very much a bachelor pad.' At the end of their interview Millar wanted a picture and sent Brown out of the room to change from his forbidding dark suit; she was amazed to realise on his return that, having donned a more casual tie, he had no clothes apart from these working suits.

Brown seriously had not given his appeal to women any high priority; in his long bachelordom he had a history of relationships with girlfriends which led to nothing. As a climax to these he went out for five years with Princess Margarita, daughter of the exiled King of Romania, but the common view held that Gordon represented a very old, very male school of politics, preferring the committee room to the bedroom. As Princess Margarita said when they parted, 'It was a very solid and romantic story. I never stopped loving him, but one day it didn't seem right any more. It was politics, politics, politics, and I needed nurturing.'

But Brown, early on, did embark on marriage, a kind of asexual political marriage which was to become one of the most extraordinary features of Tony's ten-year rule, both in its success and its fallings out. In their first years in the Commons, Tony and Gordon shared an office. The wide-eyed amateur was closeted with the able strategist and from Gordon Tony acquired his political education. This was how he learned everything he needed to know. But it seemed that Tony had also learned at an early age or knew instinctively that supreme political trick employed centuries before by Lord Burghley with Elizabeth I: namely, as he advised young courtiers, 'overcome her with yielding'. This was of course in old-fashioned times the way wives and mistresses controlled their men. And this is what Tony did with the formidable and intellectually superior Gordon, praising him as such but knowing that in the end he held the highest trumps in his own hand: married and with children, he appeared unequivocal in his maleness, his procreative capacity proven. As most voters lived in the south, in manner and accent he appealed as a southerner. He acted with ease and confidence before the cameras.

It became, notwithstanding, a 'marriage', the word Tony used to describe the closeness of their relationship. 'When you're with them together, you find them finishing each other's sentences,' a woman close to both said. They were, it seemed, destined to wield great power together, but in the moments immediately after John Smith's death, it was not altogether clear who would lead the other. There is much to be said for the early receipt of scars, as long as they are not disabling; Brown had plenty and was a well-seasoned, veteran politician, but in the eyes of their main sponsor, the Mephistophelian Peter, both were golden boys flourishing under his watchful, ever jealous eye. But Brown believed he was Smith's legitimate heir.

*

In the summer of 1993 Alastair Campbell and Fiona Millar, together with Philip Gould and his wife Gail Rebuck, shared a villa in Majorca, where they were later joined by Mandelson, who agreed, much to everyone's surprise, that he would support Gordon Brown – assuming, that is, they could cast off the ponderous and unsuccessful leadership of John Smith.

Gould was the architect of Labour's unity in discarding its left-wing values. He argued the obvious, namely that an election campaign should have one aim and one aim only: to influence people to vote for Labour, and that understanding and judging the mood of voters was the key to this. From a short spell helping Bill Clinton's electoral campaign in 1992 he advocated the tactic of the huge, last-minute effort: 'It's the last week that counts. Forget the plaudits, concentrate on the smears; fear builds slowly, and only shows in the vote; tax and trust are the only issues that matter.'

The big-picture man, careless of what others thought of him, Gould returned from Arkansas with a suitcase full of new strategy ploys to win elections, use of 'instant rebuttal' and 'war rooms', which were to revolutionise Labour's electioneering conduct. 'Content' was to be abandoned; 'process' was all-important instead. With Gould as Mandelson's deputy, but soon to be much more than that, the Labour Party was able to jettison doctrine and tradition in favour of 'values' and a market-driven mindset. Gould believed from the start that Blair's own values were an important asset, while Campbell, in an attempt to dissuade Mandelson from supporting Brown, claimed he was 'insecure and will just be the same if he becomes leader'. Later Campbell claimed that Brown was 'seriously flawed', while Gould supported Campbell's charge, saying Brown was by turns 'brilliant and barmy'. Mandelson hit back with conviction and what most likely, if exaggerated, was the truth: 'Tony is just a little boy and knows nothing about the Labour Party. Gordon's a proper grown-up politician.'

During this period prior to the death of John Smith, Tony had grown restless and downhearted and thought of chucking in a career doomed to perpetual opposition. Cherie functioned in her Lady Macbeth role of screwing up her husband's courage to the sticking place – the first instance of her ever being compared to Lady Macbeth by a Tory MP happened at this time – and conceived a dislike for Brown which never left her. Was it merely that she feared him being chosen as leader instead of Tony?

Her distrust went back to an earlier time, when in 1992 Brown had tipped Tony as a future Prime Minister, but then added those two deadly words 'after me'. But deeper than this there had grown a psychosexual rivalry between Cherie and Gordon. More profound than their sibling competitiveness (and both Tony and Gordon were middle sons – as was Mandelson) there was a compatibility of different, complementary qualities in Tony and Gordon which made them a perfect match as partners. Cherie, whether consciously or not, became jealous of this.

It seemed that this pair, as well as Mandelson and Campbell – four young men of a similar age – had the unassuaged, immature lust to squabble and then kiss to make up. They jostled and jockeyed for position, fought one another for attention in the eyes of others as if each was eager to win the biggest role or be kingmaker and dominator of the one who landed the ultimate job. It may of course be this that unsettled Cherie in her nascent distrust for Brown: what really she saw reflected in Tony was herself in that position.

As for what Cherie thought of Mandelson, it is significant that in Paul Routledge's biography of him there is not a single mention of Cherie. Was the reason, simply, that as far as she was concerned he was 'a blind spot'? While he was not 'one of us', he wielded some sort of superior influence over

Tony. And so the double acts multiplied: Blair with Blair, Blair with Campbell, Blair with Mandelson, Blair with Brown. And they would go on multiplying with the artless, or artfully concealing, giveaways – as when Tony says of Mandelson, 'He's a straightforward sort of guy.' Tony would show himself, as Mandelson sums him up in 2007 in a phrase corresponding to all seven of William Empson's *Seven Types of Ambiguity*, 'overwhelmingly successful in matching himself against the integrity bar'.

Tony. A man of doubles, of doppelgängers, other selves. An amazing histrionic personality. An actor.

13

Rabbit and two glasses of white wine

There's always been an understanding between us that I'm the one.

Gordon Brown in *The Deal*, Channel 4

John Smith's sudden death in his mid-fifties at breakfast time in his Barbican flat provides a cameo of the thick-skinned, fast-moving double act of Blair and Blair.

Cherie, shocked but aware of the implications, left her chambers and grabbed a taxi to meet Tony at Heathrow; Tony cut short a campaigning tour in the north of Scotland to return to London. He had found time before he caught the plane at Dyce airport, Aberdeen, to do the Marc Antony peroration over Brutus's body for the cameras. 'He had the extraordinary combination of strength and authority, humour and humanity. I think the whole country will feel his loss.' Minus one or two, including himself that is, feeling (potentially) that 'the mantle of office falls on his shoulders'. He called Gordon Brown, who was deeply affected and emotional, and arranged to meet.

'If it is done when done, 'tis well it were done quickly.' Brown, although more Scottish than Blair, sadly lacked his Lady Macbeth, but Cherie, excessively animated, spurred Tony on to use his assets to make sure Gordon wouldn't be able to steal a march on him. Chief of these were the 'normal' family-man credentials – her, and their three children; at her urging and with her assent Michael Brunson, ITN's political editor, interviewed the pair at 1 Richmond Terrace.

Cherie became sufficiently relaxed to admit quite openly that she was indeed looking forward to the prospect of life at 10 Downing Street, should it ever happen. Even as she was uttering the words I could sense Tony Blair's considerable unease that his wife appeared to be mentally measuring up the curtains for the Prime Ministerial flat, before he had even been elected leader of the Labour Party.

I begged for one last shot inside their home, and with considerable reluctance they agreed. It turned out to be just what we wanted. Their son Euan, as well as being good at football, also turned out to be rather good at playing the piano, though all requests to Tony Blair himself to remind us of his prowess on the guitar fell on deaf ears. In the street outside, however, as we prepared to leave, he could no longer contain his anxieties about the whole operation, and especially about the interview with Cherie. He quietly suggested a deal – that we should use the pictures of Euan at the piano in return for not using Cherie's remarks about Number 10. (Michael Brunson, *A Ringside Seat*)

Brunson claimed Cherie's admission was innocuous. But was it? Using the child as a political shield was a foretaste of things to come.

In the immediate aftermath of John Smith's death, the plotting and manoeuvring gathered pace, as hasty and tactless as Hamlet's mother's remarriage after the murder of his father. Brown was perhaps in deeper mourning for Smith than Tony, for he was considered the more rightful son and heir of Smith. ('They say he's the son I've never had,' Smith had been quoted as saying; also Smith told Roy Hattersley, the deputy leader, that when he vacated the leadership he expected Brown to prevail in the end.) Brown genuinely grieved over Smith's death. He regretted that Smith had taken little heed of the signs of ill health, wining and dining indulgently, as he had for example with John and Penny Mortimer at the Ivy just a day or so before, when he had been up very late. Smith had been much feted and loved. Many believed he would have made a great Prime Minister, and with Blair and Brown serving under him in the most important offices of state, time would have revealed which was the better minister of the two. When Mandelson visited Brown he found him absorbed in penning a heartfelt obituary for the *Mirror*; he was also deeply occupied in the 'New Labour' task of laying the ghost of the Labour reputation as the 'tax and spend' party, but socially he was well out of focus in the popularity market. His old friend and mentor's death could not have come at a worse time. But he still believed he would win the leadership contest.

Marc Antony Blair was on a high. Death always, as he was to prove again and again in the future, gave him an historic moment. He seized the 'tide in the affairs of men', and while Smith's body was still warm, Alastair Campbell unsportingly and to Brown's disgust began to brief against Brown. Tony became the acceptable and charming 'face' of the coup, which was really the work of the Team.

But there was one waverer: Mandelson, who had promised, or strongly hinted, that he was backing Brown, and as master strategist had the casting vote: he had already fixed Brown in the public mind as 'the biggest intellectual force and strategic thinker the party has'. Brown had only to throw himself into a last week of 'intensive campaign', as Philip Gould had advised Bill Clinton, and he could win. The two had agreed not to stand against each other, so one had to step down. As support for him grew, Tony resolved this would not be him. By now it was clear to everyone that he was the frontrunner.

Did Mandelson's 'exoticism' really decide the issue, and the fact that he rated Tony on a higher scale of male physical attraction than Brown? One day the leader before last, Kinnock, had expressed discomfort with Mandelson's style: he was wearing lurid pink socks – or were they blue? – at a crucial interview. Kinnock, perturbed, asked Hattersley, 'I know he's . . . that way, but why does he have to flaunt it?' The hidden, or only partly revealed, agenda of Mandelson's personality would surely have opted for Tony's sexual attractiveness as an image over Gordon's, and as such he was an image-maker too, representative of the shift in the culture towards same-sex partnerships.

Only two days after Smith's death, Mandelson began to 'out' himself in favour of Tony, stating on Channel 4's *A Week in Politics* that contenders for the leadership must register 'who will play best at the box office' (i.e. one or the other had to withdraw). Two days later, on 16 May, he played trimmer and turned the tables on Brown, advising him not to stand while hinting (in order at the same time not to appear disloyal) he would support him. Written before any campaign for leadership had even begun, his letter deserves, as an example of double dealing or facing in two directions to be quoted at length if not in toto:

Monday

Gordon, I think I should give you my best view of the situation from the media standpoint.

You are attracting sympathy from the Lobby for your position. You are seen as the biggest intellectual force and strategic thinker the party has. Most people say there is no one to rival your political 'capacity'. I have thought a lot about your fear that you are being written down (out) by the press, and I have re-read everything very carefully. I don't believe your fears are justified. Nobody is saying that you are not capable/appropriate as leader, merely that the timing is bad for you or that you have vocal enemies or that you have presentational difficulties.

You have a problem in not appearing to be the frontrunner. It's not that people question whether you could catch up . . . [but] it would now be difficult for Tony to withdraw in your favour (how would it be explained in the polls, etc.?) and that by standing you would trigger Cook and possibly others and this would surely not be in the interests of the party.

If Tony felt he had to stand, and you did too, what would be the consequences? . . . Because you would be appearing to come in as second runner, you would be blamed by the media for creating the split. I think the media would attack you and that your standing in the party would suffer.

The only way to overcome this media resistance to you is to mount a massive and sustained briefing which concentrated on your political skills . . . I have not encountered much trouble in selling this so far but to be effective it would have to be greatly escalated, begun immediately and, I am afraid, only done by explicitly weakening Tony's position.

Even then I could not guarantee success. Ultimately, the card the media are playing for Tony is his 'southern appeal'. He doesn't need to point it out or build it up: it is there firmly in their minds and it is linked to their (and our) overriding question, is Labour serious about conquering the South?

My fear is that drift is harming you (cf. BBC lunchtime news). You either have to escalate rapidly (and to be effective I think I would need to become clearly partisan with the press in your favour) or you need to implement strategy to withdraw with enhanced position, strength and respect.

Will you let me know your wishes?

Peter.

Perhaps the letter should be preserved as a masterpiece of political equivocation, or, as Freud might say, an example of the veiled inability to reconcile the love and hate of the father figure which lies behind much betrayal. Mandelson faxed it from Hartlepool, adding a palliative 'if you want to chat now I am in the office'. On receiving it Brown most certainly did not want to chat: the missive angered him, his two brothers and the close circle to which he showed it. He recalled what Smith had once said about Mandelson: that 'he was so devious he would one day disappear up his own something or other'. It is needless to add that this letter, when published, served to put Tony in Mandelson's debt. But although Brown never again spoke to Mandelson, he still had not stepped down. Mandelson subsequently insisted on his intense loyalty to Brown, and that if Gordon were ahead, and signalled his support, 'I would not have thought twice.'

The triumvirate of protean personalities – Tony, Peter, Alastair – was driving hard for Blair even so, with Mandelson at it most, carrying everything before it, and, as with such historic moments as Caesar crossing the Rubicon, or Molotov and Ribbentrop signing the infamous Nazi–Soviet pact of 1939, Tony and Gordon met at Tony's initiative, on 31 May, at the 'Spartan-chic' Granita restaurant in Islington, to create the first but lasting scene of New Labour mythology – 'The Deal', as it became known in the version directed by Stephen Frears. A historian likens it to the alleged Hitler offer to Churchill in May 1940 filtered through the Italian residency, as described in John Lukacs's *Five Days in London*: 'Leave me free in Europe; you have the rest of the world.'

Tony will one day give us his own version of what was said, but at this meagre meal he ate rabbit (if that is what he did eat) and drank white wine, while Gordon, who had come from a drinks party, sipped water. Tony argued that he would make the stronger candidate to win the next election – stronger, not better, he is believed to have emphasised. There is little doubt that he would have pointed out that Brown should have stood against Smith after Kinnock resigned, and by not doing so forfeited his chance of election. Many people would love to know why Tony should have thought he would make the better Prime Minister – as opposed to one who would win the election against the Tories. There is little doubt that at that stage Brown was better equipped to be Prime Minister, while Tony would have made an able deputy, ready to learn from one who was essentially an elder-brother figure. But Tony was always accountable to Cherie as well, and what would she have said? She had been putting it about: 'Could anyone imagine working under Gordon?' And women especially: Labour was set to recruit and swear in a hundred new female candidates.

While the vital ingredient of vanity had never been exactly lacking in Brown, an iron band of vanity held Tony, Peter and Alistair together and bound all three in passionate dependence on one another; and of course alongside Tony there was Cherie, who disliked Brown and often voiced her view that he was 'not our sort of person'. This meant, as like recognises like, he was perceived by her as a rival, a control freak, and that he bordered often on the rude, bit his nails and never looked at her, acknowledging only Tony, who deferred to him. But Gordon was, in fact, very shy of women, a cultural trait once approved of by society, but which for the moment anyway was definitely no longer considered attractive and a vote-winner.

Tony promised as part of 'The Deal' that in return for Brown's withdrawal from the leadership contest, Gordon, as Chancellor, would be granted greater freedom than any Chancellor in recent history, with executive powers over a wide range of policies normally the province of other ministers. In fact, as Peter Oborne wrote in the *Express*, 'he demanded, and got, something approaching a dual premiership'. Yet reality is never quite as sensational as peak-time drama, and apparently the two men had met over the previous days at least ten times and held numerous telephone conversations. They had hammered out some kind of agreement as to what should happen if Tony became Prime Minister: would he ultimately stand down in favour of Brown and name him as his successor? The timing suggested by Brown was halfway through a second term, should Labour be elected again. In Brown's view this was the point at which Margaret Thatcher should have stepped down.

Subsequently both men had very different notions, or versions, as to what actually was said and what was agreed as 'The Deal'. John Mortimer airs a much clearer and more succinct account, told him by Neil Kinnock. In this, both Tony and Gordon went to Kinnock and asked him which of them should be leader. Kinnock said it should be Tony, because of the wife and family, but that Tony should leave after the first parliament. There can be no reasonable doubt about the truth of this. But Tony, maybe guilty at being ahead of his cleverer rival, was full of promises he had no intention of keeping; and it was easy to promise what you hadn't got when you had no idea what might happen. Then, as later, Tony's impulse was to avoid confrontation and conflict. He always wanted anyone he was with to leave the room feeling happy – or at least feeling he or she had got something. And as says he Mortimer found when in his company, he was 'always asking how he's doing'.

Brown kept everyone waiting for the announcement of his withdrawal and stepped down on 1 July. Everything from then on was plain sailing. On 21 July Proteus One (Tony) was crowned with 57 per cent of the Labour Party votes; John Prescott, who became deputy leader, won 24 per cent, and Margaret Beckett, who had been acting leader, 19 per cent. It is a lasting testimony to the levity and despair to which the Labour Party had both risen and sunk in the long wilderness which bedevilled it that it elected the lightweight Blair. But the Labour Party had suffered long from injured self-esteem; hungry and at the core feeling inferior, they leapt to embrace someone whose airy grandiosity compensated their deficiency. An important element, too, was Mandelson's own erotic-idealising transference of feeling from Gordon to Tony. In the dissolution of the old differences between male and female identities, primarily and ultimately engineered by Mandelson, the victory went to the one with more allure, the one with the greater charisma:

> His main weapon (and armour) is charm. His charm conveys not only his magic power but also all his delicate need for love and protection. He yearns to be not only a man, but also a woman at the same time; his inner balance is precarious because of the concurrence of active domineering and submissive seductive strivings. It is an eternal wish of mankind expressed in the mythic idea that once man and woman were one . . . The biological basis of charm

and the modes of mutual attraction, shared by bodily characters in the male and female of the human species, are relevant to the psychological characteristics of the charismatic leader. For he fascinates by a display of both male and female qualities, simultaneously or in more or less rapid alternation, just as in some hypnotic procedures. (D. Wilfred Abse and Lucie Jessner, 'The Psychodynamic Aspects of Leadership')

Amor vincit omnia. The Labour conference anthem, 'The Red Flag', had reached its sell-by date.

Part II

1994–1998

14

The dark shadow in the background

She has the eyes of Caligula, but the *bouche* of Marilyn Monroe.

President Mitterrand on Margaret Thatcher

New Labour approached its general election win of 1997 with a cynical deployment of the Machiavellian principle 'the end justifies the means'. A prudent ruler, wrote Niccolò Machiavelli in *The Prince*, 'ought not to keep faith' if it prove to be against his interest. The justification for this was that men were 'bad', so 'you are not bound to keep faith with them.' But who were the bad men and who decided if they were bad or not?

The simple answer for Cherie and Tony from 1994 to 1997 was that the 'bad guys' were anyone and everyone who resisted or stood in the way of their will to power. Virtuous intentions and noble motives could cover a multitude of sins, so Tony set about establishing a 'holier than thou' philosophy as soon as he took over command of the party. The first intention was to have the British press in the palm of his hand, and especially the *Sun* and other Murdoch-owned newspapers – this in spite of Cherie banning the *Sun* from her house, and in December 1995 informing Anne Robinson, a fellow Liverpudlian and at that time a *Sun* columnist, that she had done just this. She almost upset Labour's apples ripening in the *Sun*'s rays.

Campbell offered 'Blair exclusives' to all the papers, but *Sun* articles were more exclusive than others. Blair became 'the most prolific journalist in Fleet Street', and most weeks would see the publication of half a dozen Blair articles, 'sometimes rising to twenty or more', written mainly by the

Campbell press office. In a similar way virtuous intentions were top of President Bill Clinton's agenda in 1992.

Even before he became elected Clinton promised his wife Hillary equal billing. Equal to him in ambition and political motivation, Hillary would be an integral part of his government, and he pledged to his people 'two for the price of one'. Dual government ('Billary' as some called it) had arrived. Hillary headed the Task Force on National Healthcare Reform, with her own staff and a White House office. But she rapidly over-reached herself and provoked outrage and protest, enabling the Republicans to recapture Congress in 1994.

However, there were differences between Bill Clinton and the new Labour leader in the United Kingdom. For a start, Clinton was grounded in demotic language and fluently articulate, way beyond Tony's capacities. Tony's thought processes and verbal range were modest, so that largely he relied on others for his vocabulary. At the age of fifteen, Clinton showed this feel for words not only in his appreciation of how Shakespeare spoke the truth about human nature, but in an autobiographical school essay in which he said:

> I am a person motivated and influenced by so many diverse forces I sometimes question the sanity of my existence. I am a living paradox – deeply religious, yet not as convinced of my exact beliefs as I ought to be; wanting responsibility yet shirking it; loving the truth yet often giving way to falsity.

Tony and the Labour Party wanted to do more than copy Clinton's electioneering strategies, while Tony and Cherie wanted to become a presidential pair similar to the Clintons. Tony should have noticed the essential difference between the two traditions and the two men – when Clinton came to power aged forty-six he had been governor of Arkansas for twelve years, so had a long experience of wielding power. The President was head of state, both symbolically and with powers way beyond those of the British Prime Minister: for instance he was commander of the armed forces. While both Clinton and Blair were elected, the UK, a constitutional monarchy and not a republic, did not elect its head of state.

But as for now. The love affair with America, centred on the Clinton pair, began just before Tony became leader in a visit he had made to the United States prior to leadership. In Clinton's first year, Tony visited Washington to talk politics with senior Democrats but did not meet the President. Democrats were triumphant over their victory and wanted to tell Tony how to pull off a similar electoral feat to the one they had secured. Tony, 'hesitant and banal', kept looking at the British representative, Christopher Meyer, who had been appointed as John Major's press secretary and who as such accompanied Tony. Meyer, later to became ambassador in Washington, wrote that Tony was 'eyeing me nervously'.

Tony adopted the title 'New Labour' from Clinton's brand name 'New Democrats'. Meantime through his performance in the Commons he acquired the reputation, which became characteristic, for belligerent blandness: Brian Sedgemore, a Labour backbencher, pointed out how Tony was 'quite stoically bland. The sheer blandness of it is difficult to penetrate, if he can hold it and not be embarrassed.' But there was a significant shift from traditional Labour values in Tony's enthusiastic if vapid praise for 'a dynamic economy . . . in which enterprise of the market and the rigour of competition are joined with the forces of partnership and cooperation to produce the wealth the nation needs'.

Blandness typified the interior decorating style at home too, in Richmond Terrace, with its Magnet units in the scruffy kitchen, and the John Lewis pleated curtains (with tiebacks) and sofa in the upstairs living room. Out-takes from a Labour Party documentary film shot for the conference reveal Tony in the kitchen, leaning against the worktops and chatting informally, promising that if elected he would never hang on too long in office. Upstairs in the antiseptic lounge, he holds forth in different style, pompous and full of political rhetoric – the actor showing the two faces of power.

A little while into his presidency Clinton suffered setbacks and became mired in the scandal, dubbed 'Whitewater', surrounding real estate that he and Hillary had bought in Arkansas in the 1970s. Paula Jones, the first of Clinton's paramours or alleged sexual targets, accused Clinton, too, at this time, of sexual harassment. 'I hadn't sexually harassed her,' Clinton wrote later in his *Autobiography*, but the private life of the President of the most powerful nation on earth was of little concern to Tony when he met him for the first time on 29 November 1995, just before Clinton visited Northern

Ireland, the first US President ever to do so. 'Impressive,' Clinton patronisingly called Tony, while in Northern Ireland, he 'warmed' to the people on both sides ('two of the best days of my presidency') and was more enthusiastic about Gerry Adams, the leader of Sinn Fein: 'I told him I was reading *The Street*, his book of short stories about the Falls, and that it gave me a better feel for what the Catholics had been through. It was our first public appearance together, and it signalled the importance of his commitment to the peace process.'

Tony ignored Clinton's back-pedalling on liberal domestic reforms when in 1994 the Democrats lost the control of Congress, and the Republicans dismantled the reforms implemented in the previous years. A cautious pragmatist might have read the signs, while the commonsense application of some psychological observation, plus a little awareness of Bill's amatory inclinations, now splashed over the media, together with the power-hungry, complaisant wife, might have prompted circumspection.

But high-sounding rodomontade appealed to both Tony and Bill, for it served two purposes. First, it enabled them to act out in front of adulatory audiences who at best listened to 17 per cent of what was being said (according to the PR gurus and the confidence-building self-help books) and spent most of their speeches mesmerised by image and vocal impact. The intention of these 'dynamic' youthful leaders, who had a brotherly similarity of style and manner, was to have the men in their audiences envying or wanting to emulate them, and the women ogling their handsome figures, entranced by expansive gestures and cajoling voices. Second, it made them believe they had a theoretical basis, a shared conviction, known soon as the 'Third Way', which Tony and Bill often met to discuss, which came from their immature, idealistic urges: it was hippiedom in impressive language. As Meyer described it:

> As these Third Way meetings reached out to embrace an ever-wider circle of political leaders with vague social-democratic leanings, I could not get out of my head that song by the Bonzo Dog Doo Dah band, in which Vivian Stanshall recites an endless litany of world figures, dead and alive.
>
> Clinton and Blair were too glib. The rhetoric was fine but there simply was not enough political ballast.

As I sat there, fighting off sleep in the front row, it became ever clearer that the Third Way was less a coherent philosophy of government, more a tactic for winning elections.

All kinds of academic notables were wheeled in and out for these occasions, with names soon to be consigned to the dust heap of history. Tony wanted everyone to know his crowd of carpetbaggers and opportunists were serious thinkers, and could win the battle for ideas, and climbed on the New Democrats' shoulders, spouting their mantra of 'opportunity, responsibility and community'. Self-interest was best served, Tony felt, when we act for others, not ourselves. It was all a magnificent melange of hot air and self-deception, while what mattered happened elsewhere.

Even Cherie found the seminars they held on the Third Way boring and would wait till near the end before joining her spouse.

*

Over the last decade and a half, the influence of unacknowledged parentage in world affairs has become a big subject. Bill Clinton's biological father, William Blythe, had five wives and a whole host of illegitimate progeny, but died before Bill arrived, who was then brought up in a violent, dysfunctional home, in his teens defending his mother and breaking down locked doors, and even swearing a deposition to the police to keep his violent step-father within bounds. Here again was someone who sought to appease, to make everyone happy, but who had at the same time serious unresolved problems.

That Tony found a mentor, a political older brother, whose early difficulties even exceeded his own would have profound consequences: here was, if he hadn't enough already, another mirror in which he saw himself. Here was another mimetic double.

All these underlying reasons revealed with hindsight may now appear dark and sinister, but the urge to appear cosy and friendlily familiar in photo opportunities, to smile, to seem benign and harmless, was from the heritage of emotion all the stronger. In contrast to the clear, pristine image of Tony, the Tories in power, in spite of building up the economy from the Black Wednesday of 1991 to an unassailably strong position, were their own worst enemies. Tales of sleaze and sexual misdemeanours fell thick and fast into the hungry maws of the Labour spin machine, driven by Tony's two main power-brokers, Mandelson and Campbell. With the cavorting of Neil and Christine Hamilton ('Mr and Mrs Cash-and-Carry'), the antics of Jeffrey Archer, the perjury of Jonathan Aitken and the toe-sucking of David Mellor, the Conservatives, under a repackaged, grey, morally fervent John Major – later to be shown up by Edwina Currie as by no means practising what he preached – were predictably heading for a fall. They even tried to ape Tony: John Major sent Howell James, his political secretary, a picture of Tony kneeling to lay a wreath where a policeman had been murdered. 'The picture does all the work: Blair's suit, the way he's kneeling, the look, the association with a fallen policeman,' records Gyles Brandreth, at the time a Tory MP. 'It delivers everything.'

But there was a deeper cause for Tory decline, especially in the midst of unrivalled material strength and prosperity. Margaret Thatcher's eleven years of unbroken rule had eaten away the soul of the party and almost irreparably weakened its psychological strength. As Chris Patten said, 'She destroyed the Conservative Party . . . she encouraged the suicidal element and became more radical and fundamentalist.' John Major concurred: 'She had the same gift of shifting the blame for unpopular things onto other shoulders.'

Tony, when later in office, voiced his opinion that he was one of her most avid fans (on his list also were Mick Jagger, the Bee Gees, Bono and Silvio Berlusconi, for Tony was nothing if not catholic in his tastes): 'She had a tremendous clarity of objective, matched by huge determination and vigour . . . she never yielded her ultimate goal.' When they met she told Tony when things got rocky to 'trust his instinct' – with fatal results, it might be said, so it could be claimed she helped destroy Tony too.

Cherie was also enamoured of Thatcher, as revealed in her book *The Goldfish Bowl*: 'By the time Margaret went to university in the 1940s,' she writes in her conclusion, not shared with her co-author, Cate Haste, 'a new breed of career woman was becoming established, but what marked her out was the fact that, unlike most of those women, she did not remain single and childless . . . As someone who sat the Bar exams myself, I know just how determined she must have been to give birth to twins and then within a couple of months take and pass those exams.' She pats Thatcher on the back along with herself.

Earlier in *The Goldfish Bowl* Cherie and Cate quote Thatcher's resentment at what most male MPs felt about combining family responsibilities with being an MP: 'Beneath some of the criticism I detected a feeling that the House of Commons was not really the right place for a woman anyhow.' 'Wake up, women,' Thatcher wrote in a 1953 article at the time of the coronation of Elizabeth II: 'Women can – and MUST – play a leading part in the creation of a glorious Elizabethan era,' but adding the sensible caveat for that leading part, 'should a woman arise who is equal to the task.'

Thatcher was, without doubt, equal to the task, but here illogicality swung into action in New Labour's politically correct coming of age. Because Thatcher was a woman it followed, in crazed logic, that there must be many women who were just like her, and therefore, if women were promoted they would, QED, become as good as her. This principle was to be applied in every walk of life, across the whole of society.

15

One fire, one nail

So our virtues
Lie in th' interpretation of the time . . .
One fire drives out one fire, one nail one nail;
Rights by rights falter, strengths by strengths do fail.

William Shakespeare, *Coriolanus*

Tony and Cherie applauded Margaret Thatcher. Cherie Booth, left wing in principle, a good Thatcherite in practice – and now in April 1995 a QC – could have had little time to devote to her growing family. Her areas of concentration were employment, discrimination and public law, and as a public lawyer she took the opportunities as they came, such as a brief from a Westminster City Council in 1995 to pursue poll tax defaulters, or action for Brent Borough Council against accusations of racial and sexual discrimination from union members. As a public lawyer she rose quickly in reputation, and believed strongly in unlimited legal aid, by which everyone had the means to be defended in court, even if they could not afford to; an American author gave tongue to his doubts: 'This is a wonderful country where pornographers get the best lawyers in the land.'

Tony tried hard to take Euan on the Tube to school in Kensington every morning, but later admitted, 'with my older children, if I was looking after them Friday, Saturday and Sunday because Cherie was away doing something, I'd go back to the House of Commons and be completely whacked out'. According to a friend, Cherie was not a morning person, so 'he didn't have much choice, and it was always up to him to sort out the cereal and end the squabbling'. Perhaps he should not have been so self-pitying because the recuperative comforts of all kinds that the House of Commons can offer its members are legendary.

'A barrister is an old taxi plying for hire' was the motto of Rumpole, John Mortimer's fictional advocate. The cab-rank rule for barristers was also the foundation of both Tony and Cherie in their political ambitions. The same attitude transferred into politics could mean that the only important thing was winning the vote – it didn't matter whose. Rumpole claims that it is an advocate's 'sacred duty to take on anyone in trouble. However repellent I may happen to find them.' The defence against criticism of such a practice is that the adversarial system in the end is fairer than any other. 'The truth is more likely to be revealed, and error and bias avoided, if all the issues are rationally debated by the presentation of divergent points of view.' But judgments of right and wrong were to be made only after this process was completed. Lord Hutchinson of Lullington, for instance, said he was proud that he had spent 'so many hours in defence of alleged child abusers, rapists, traitors and even terrorists . . . To cross-examine children and unhappy women or even corrupt policemen . . . is but painful work.'

Cherie was of a similar inclination to defend the underdog. But she was not per se a criminal barrister, and later, when she joined the new Matrix Chambers in 2000 as a founder member, human rights became her special province.

*

By 1996 Cherie was, in the footsteps of Hillary Clinton, pledging that New Labour would give 'unprecedented legal rights to gays and the disabled', and it would not have been out of place if she had lobbied for Derry Irvine, the 'Blair Cupid', to become Lord Chancellor if (when) Labour came to power. She voiced her political opinions all over the place – something she continually praises the old-fashioned wives of Prime Ministers in *The Goldfish Bowl* for never doing – so much that Tony felt he had to issue a largely untrue disclaimer:

> Cherie is a successful career woman in her own right and wants to get on and do that. She has no desire to do my job. People should just accept the position for what it is. I think it is a shame that people always have to look for this sort

of stereotype – someone is either living in the shadows of their husband or alternatively is trying to run the country through them.

Yet she was, and would seek to influence Tony and run the party and then the country through him. As a leader from the favoured *Sun* later comments, 'She was the power behind the throne.' Tony wasn't quite yet on it, so, coaxed to dispel the harsh legal image, Cherie told readers of the September 1996 issue of *Prima* magazine, which she edited, how much knitting enthralled her and how to 'produce a meal that's interesting and nutritious in thirty minutes'. Help for this came no doubt from Ros Mark, the full-time nanny that Cherie had recruited from a Montessori notice board. The pair soon legally gagged Mark from making rather harmless and admiring disclosures about their domestic and family life. A film director recalls Tony telling Cherie that her make-up for a documentary shot made her look 'like an old slapper', while in pique she sharply replied, 'I wear less make-up than you.' If it was attention they were after, they certainly got it. Help also came naturally, from Carole Caplin, who had filled the Richmond Terrace house fridge with juice drinks, herbal tea, nut cutlets and lentils. As for diet, the disc jockey Zoë Ball told Tony he had bad breath, and he now avoided eating garlic and gave up his favourite pesto.

16

The school of political projectors

The first Project was to shorten Discourse by Cutting Polysyllables into one, and leaving out Verbs and Participles; because in Reality all things imaginable are but Nouns.

Jonathan Swift, 'A Voyage to Laputa', *Gulliver's Travels*

The campaign racing up to the 1997 election projected a Tony more assured than before, but still hesitant with significant lapses. The performance, a life's role rather than, as in the case of professional actors, a taxing role that could be put aside after one intense and concentrated day or evening of work, had been riddled with gaps and lapses: we had not yet moved into the culture of continuous, seamless and unremitting self-presentation.

Tony famously brought about the dropping of Clause IV – the Labour Party's commitment to continuing nationalisation – in 1994. This had met with initial opposition from John Prescott, the deputy leader, but Alastair Campbell went out of his way to humiliate the BBC correspondent who dared to make it clear that for Prescott, conversion to the abolition of Clause IV had been a laborious process. At interviews Campbell was always beside Tony. One journalist said, 'You are interviewing two people. Alastair will sit on the other side of the table, writing notes and handing them across. Blair gets incredibly nervous.' At TV interviews Campbell placed himself in the interviewer's line of vision and made signs such as tapping his watch. Joy Johnson, a media aide, went even further. 'When you heard Bernard Ingham speak, you heard Margaret Thatcher and when you heard Margaret Thatcher speaking you heard Margaret Thatcher. When you heard Tony Blair very often you heard Alastair Campbell.'

Verbless sentences removed for Tony any need or sense of action. Verbs were the 'doing' words. Nouns were concrete, the reality. This is what he said in 1995, at the Labour Party Conference:

> Today I place before you my vision of New Britain. A nation reborn. Prosperous, secure, united.
>
> I know that for some of you, New Labour has been painful. There is no greater pain to be endured in politics than the birth of a new idea.
>
> One Britain. New Labour. New Britain.

Tony ended this hypnotic tirade of turning down alternative visions of the past with 'New Labour. New Britain. The party renewed. The country reborn. New Labour. New Britain.'

*

All things imaginable are but nouns. Another instance of 'reshaping the narrative' happened in early 1996, when it was stated in the *Sunday Express* that Roy Jenkins, the former Home Secretary who had previously defected from Labour, had become personally and politically close to Tony. Alastair Campbell rubbished the story, categorically saying that since Tony had been leader the two men had met only once. The *Express* ran its story, but when the *Sunday Times* tried to follow it up, now Peter Mandelson denied the truth of it. But a month after this, Michael Cockerell showed in a *Panorama* report how accurate the original statement had been.

This seems minor beside the election campaign whoppers, which existed on both sides as they battened down for the 1997 contest. Labour's manifesto simply lied about the strength of the UK economy. It claimed that the economy was weaker than its European counterparts, and had fallen from thirteenth to eighteenth in the league of world national incomes. The political journalist Peter Oborne pointed out that this was false: 'According to the OECD Economic Survey of the United Kingdom for 1996, Britain's national income topped one trillion dollars in 1994, ranking it fifth in the world behind the United States, Japan, Germany and France – up a place since 1979 thanks to the collapse of the Soviet Union.'

New Labour, New Life for Britain also asserted that 'our growth rate has lagged behind our main competitors over the 17 Tory years'. In fact, according to World Bank figures, Britain had achieved an annual growth rate of 2.3 per cent per head since 1979, second only to Japan among G7 countries. The manifesto went on to claim that people were having under the Tories 'to work harder to stand still'. This was another pure fabrication. In the previous ten years, median real wages in Britain had increased by 19 per cent, and even the lowest-paid workers enjoyed a 10 per cent increase. Further, *New Labour, New Life for Britain* claimed that Britain 'had the worst job creation record of any major industrial economy since 1979'. In fact, according to the OECD, Britain provided jobs for a higher proportion of its working-age population in 1995 than Germany, France or Italy. The OECD's 1996 Economic Survey, cited by Oborne, concluded, 'In short, the United Kingdom's policy of maintaining an economic environment conducive to job creation has paid off in a better jobs and unemployment record than in many Continental European countries.'

So how would Labour get round these impressive statistics? Create fear, frighten the voters into obedience? During one week in which Labour support was perceived to wobble, Tony came forward to warn in a campaign speech that the Conservatives planned to abolish the state pension – of the Tories' pension proposal he said, 'There is no doubt, when up and running, the purpose of this is to replace the basic state pension with a private pension.' This untrue claim had an apocalyptic impact. 'The attack on pensions was just one part of a New Labour strategy to distort the facts and mislead the public in order to demonise the Tory Party,' writes Oborne in *The Rise of Political Lying*. Gordon Brown also waded into the controversy, confirming to some extent Cherie's future comment on him. 'It is plain', Brown said, 'it amounts to nothing less than the demolition of Britain's welfare state.' This was electioneering, it can be argued, yet by licensing themselves to lie for short-term advantage, weren't they in the long term threatening trust?

But it was not really solid argument at all which was going to win this election. Instead it was personalities, image and the previous stated reasons, together with a Clintonesque confidence and battle plan and a Cromwellian efficiency based on management gurus and, increasingly, Professor Anthony Giddens, director of Cherie's old college, the London

School of Economics, and a former Thatcherite intellectual. Giddens propounded the political 'Third Way', which was not yet in published form: 'holistic government' and 'flexible networks' would help to achieve it, but the 'Third Way' would go beyond those on the right who say 'government is the enemy' and those on the left who say 'government is the answer'. It was, in a word, the panacea for insecure political leaders who wanted to be all things to all people, 'somewhere between the Second Coming and the fourth dimension', according to Francis Wheen in *How Mumbo-Jumbo Conquered the World*.

Tony loved it, while Cherie was too busy in the 'cab-rank' (rat-race?) to give it more than a summary glance. But was it suited to the UK? Hillary Clinton, who hosted the seminars on the 'Third Way' in the US, had been coquetting with the idea for some time. These seminars were no doubt in her and her husband's minds achieved, by 1998, no less, when Bill Clinton would announce proudly in his State of the Union address, 'My fellow Americans, we have found a Third Way!'

Did no one see the dangers? Well, there were some, but they were voices crying in the wilderness, and they were silenced. Outside England, Pope John Paul II, for instance, despised by the liberal elite of Islington, denounced the way that 'godless anti-evangelisation', supported by the West's great financial resources, was striking at the very foundation of human morality and spreading 'another form of totalitarianism under the appearance of democracy'. Little did he know that the crypto-Catholic Tony and his devout wife would in time become for ten years two of the main leaders of this degenerative trend of Western cultural capitalism.

David Goodhart, editor of *Prospect*, warned twelve days before the election that Labour's new role would be like the Conservatives' following the 1951 general election. 'Then the Conservative Party managed without significant change for thirteen years to manage the reforms of the Attlee government which it bitterly opposed. New Labour has similarly accepted the Thatcher settlement.' They were set to do more than this and profit from it, for Thatcher had prepared the way for government intervention on an unprecedented scale 'by hacking her way through the lower levels of bureaucracy and the institutions of local government' (Norman Davies, *The Isles*). Tony had battled down the real Labour modernists who, clearing the way, had in effect dissolved its previous dogmas and rigidities. Another critic condemned Tony as arrogant, a raging egomaniac, intolerant, given to preachy self-righteousness, and a 'cynical symbol of the politics of opportunism'. Martin Jacques, an eminent Marxist, wrote in his journal, 'Blair is a minor public schoolboy without the self-confidence of an Old Etonian . . . he never kicks against privilege.'

Tony had caught the whiff of real power. Gordon Brown, active behind the scenes, but criticised by Mandelson as too 'dour' and too 'dull', was left well out of the way. Testosterone rich, the Mandelson–Campbell campaign flaunted its virility, but the Millbank staff also minutely mapped every shift of public opinion, every rise and fall of support. In charge of the press office, Campbell bullied and controlled reporters: prior to an election battle bus tour, Jeremy Vine of the BBC asked him for a daily schedule, but then said to him, 'My job will be to report the things that aren't necessarily in it.' Campbell went ballistic. 'You will report exactly what I tell you to report, you'll stick to the fucking schedule and nothing else!' Tony himself became unearthly, orbiting securely in tested messages.

The Millbank staff, sworn to sobriety and dietary virtue, the denial of all setbacks and mistakes, admired Tony, but did not love him as they had loved Neil Kinnock in 1992 and could have loved John Smith at this time. Tony was cast as the invincible media star, coaxed and cultured in hairstyles and wardrobe choice: public school suavity versus Major's 'speaking-clock limitations'. Here was chat show Tony with all the Oxbridge charm of Hugh Grant, his screen double in the film *Love Actually*. True, there were the hiccups: Jeremy Paxman on *Newsnight* made him look distinctly uncomfortable and even shifty when he asked if he found photos of naked women in the *Sun* offensive (the whole, successful Campbell strategy had been to win Murdoch's *Sun* to New Labour's cause). On 7 April David Dimbleby accused Tony of changing his mind on important subjects and made him look insubstantial and rattled.

But Campbell, the media impresario, already wielded power greater than any newspaper proprietor, and the bigger battalions were by now on Tony's side implementing Campbell's rule that 'if Mr Blair looked uneasy it was the interviewer's fault'. The party liked best Adam Boulton of Sky News; the BBC was the exception, its political flagship, *Panorama*, damned as a 'vicious, nasty affair'. This planted the roots of a vendetta which was to grow and grow into a giant triffid.

On balance, in the opinion of political pundits, Blair performed on the hustings less well than John Major. It was the party machine, driven by Campbell, the claqueur master, and Peter Mandelson, the party stylist, with its minute mapping out of every detail and its adherence to their guiding mantra of 'remind, reassure, reward' that drove all before it like an overwhelming tide on the crest of which Tony balanced often rather insecurely. This was Cromwell's new army, admonished by Mandelson to abandon alcohol, eat a lot of fruit, and, a homophobic wag cracked, eschew the thrill of sex with strangers on Hampstead Heath. Tony had established his style, even so, to lead from beneath: image, smile, charm, spin. 'Tony's a great man but a bit of a fruitcake,' said one of his court. 'Fred and Rose,' said another when Tony and Cherie appeared on screen. 'I mean, they're so bloody normal it's weird.' It was, wasn't it, the boy and girl from next door, the face in the crowd who was going to win the people's confidence. This double act could play many different people, put on many faces, as the various opportunities arose.

17

The most dangerous moment comes with victory

It is a General complaint, that the Favourites of Princes are troubled with short and weak memories.

Jonathan Swift, 'A Voyage to Laputa', *Gulliver's Travels*

'Earth has not anything to show more fair,' thought the hard-working party faithful as they contemplated the 'the beauty of the morning' from Westminster Bridge on 2 May 1997. They had won. The hours brought an even bigger and better count of the stunning scale of the Labour victory, a landslide majority of 179 seats. Taxis hooted deliriously, champagne flowed and, as John Mortimer says, everyone thought a new era of hope and change had dawned as they trailed off for a greasy-spoon breakfast.

But not quite everyone. When flying south to join the celebrations with Labour leading lights at the Royal Festival Hall, Robin Cook's first response to Tony's election success was gloom and depression. He feared government might bring out the worst in those he knew.

The victory was a foregone conclusion, but the heights of subsequent euphoria were unseemly. Instead of offering a healing embrace, the petty triumphalism displayed over the other two parties, and over the many millions who had not voted Labour, was more in the nature of winning the FA Cup or the Laurence Olivier Awards, and it set the stage for what became in effect, instead of rule by Parliament, rule by one party, and in time rule by one pair and their court.

The blindness, the self-deception straightaway evident was that Tony and his entourage had been voted in for their positive, new 'modernising' politics, which was not the case. They had merely won the cup. Many had warned that New Labour had no policies, merely hot air and attractive catchphrases pinched from over the water. But the landslide vote confirmed how the public, the voting public, had voted in a highly plausible bunch of untried celebrities, and it too was accountable and must share the responsibility for what followed.

The lustre of stardom comes as a reflection and need of the audience, not from the stars themselves, who answer it by playing up to it. Pop idolism had in its varied forms overtaken real life. Tony and Cherie were by now well-authenticated pop idols, with a surrounding cast and all the promise possible of fresh and fruity storylines ahead. For 'spin-doctor' read 'TV executive producer' and 'newspaper editor': they could see in Tony and Cherie the desires of the public magnified a million times over. Good celebrity, bad celebrity, it's all the same; as the critic A. A. Gill writes, 'The energy of a big pop concert isn't on the stage – that's just amplification. It's in the dark, in the collective generator of the crowd.'

From Tony's first appearances on *Spitting Image* in 1994 as a schoolboy with a high-pitched voice and a bottle-green uniform complete with cap, shouting just after John Smith's death, 'I'm going to be the leader! I'm going to be the leader!' the public had laughed and identified with him in contrast to his 'Tory nemesis', William Hague. They had taken to Cherie too, on the principle that every female brainbox, with a mouth constantly joked about as resembling a letter box, and with as much dress sense as a clothes horse, who commits one visual gaffe after another, touched the heart of the majority of women. She was Ugly Betty and Bridget Jones all in one. 'Look how she juggles everything – but whoops, she's done it again! – those are just unspeakably hideous.'

The appearance, caught by the cameras, at the door of 1 Richmond Terrace on that morning after the election triumph sums it all up for Cherie. A policeman with a florist summoned her from the gloomy depths of the end-of-terrace house and as she opened the front door, in a manner similar to that of Helen of Troy centuries before launching a thousand ships, Cherie's face and figure set a hundred camera motors whirring. To put it mildly, she did not look at her best: 'her hair, still caked in yesterday's styling mousse, had contrived during the night to rearrange itself in the manner of a cartoon character which has found itself the victim of a prolonged and particularly high voltage electric shock,' writes Paul Scott in *Tony & Cherie*. With her eyes rimmed black with smudged mascara, she clutched desperately at her short and flimsy blue-grey nightie from Next, and beat 'a horrified and hasty retreat behind the door'. She would, as we shall see, make sure that never happened again – whatever the cost. But the next day, almost, she was in Hillary mode, proclaiming to a fellow barrister that she wanted 'to set a new climate for the spouses of prominent people'.

*

Tony, no doubt with Cherie's approval and active support, committed two grave blunders in the first four months of his premiership. Both of these, in the froth and heat of his arrival, were overlooked. That they were blunders at all will be considered controversial. The first concerned mainly those who had engineered the victory. The second, over the death of Diana, Princess of Wales, is dealt with in a later chapter.

From the very moment Tony and Cherie entered Downing Street there was no relaxation in either his government or his style, everyone working on at the hectic, fevered pace at which they had won the election. There was chaos everywhere. With equality rampant in all directions, in all places, there was at once no chief and no hierarchy of command. The respect that Tony had acquired was by virtue of his winning the election through his presentational skills, but there had to be something else, which was beyond this bundle of aspirations, to command respect.

'The most dangerous moment', Napoleon said, 'comes with victory.' A leader has to establish himself as a great personage, which Tony's predecessor had notably failed to do, as well as being unbiased and without self-interest. At the very start Tony failed to make the obvious perception that those who had contributed to Labour's victory were not necessarily the right people to run the country and wield the responsibilities of high office. He might have had the wisdom and prescience to have worked this out in his own mind before he came to power. But he lived in the fight, in the flow of the struggle, and not beyond it. To have the power, to keep it: these were the ends, and again like Mark Antony in the Capitol he was acting the part but had no idea where he was going.

Moreover, he was quite unable then, as ten years later, to keep his mouth shut. Secrecy, or at least discretion, is the essence of national affairs, and the whole semblance or dissimulation of openness, beginning with his 'call me Tony' attitude, of bowing to media pressure to know everybody, descended, as it was bound to, from feeling good and comfortable into over-familiarity and contempt, then into conflict and recrimination, then into farce, and finally into a form of psychosis.

Charles I lost his throne and his head by telling his wife of his plans regarding certain members of Parliament; she told a trusted lady-in-waiting, who then named the threatened members, and they fled to the opposition. No one was as taciturn as Bonaparte. 'Nothing', wrote Charles de Gaulle, 'strengthens authority as much as silence.' Denis Thatcher added the Downing Street refrain, saying, 'Better keep your mouth shout and be thought a fool than open it and remove all doubt.' For Tony this would forever be impossible: first, he and Cherie had absolutely no grasp of history, nor had Tony an instinctive sense of authority or leadership. While a good memory is the first and most important requirement for intelligence, or so Aristotle pointed out, history is national memory with literature as its living memory. But Tony was garrulous as well as grandiose: he turned out instant ideas and intuitions with extreme rapidity probably because he had never successfully interiorised a healthy self-esteem.

Blair's first action after the election could have been to part company with those who had devised and executed the plan to bring him to power. He could have planned this before: common sense could have prevailed, for in the words of John Reid, Blair's last Home Secretary, used in 2006 about his own ministry, they were 'not fit for purpose'. But neither Cherie nor Tony seemed to understand that to govern, to lead a country, was a task and involved demands vastly different from winning a general election. Of the five who had seized control of the Labour Party in their breathtaking coup d'état – Blair, Gordon Brown, Peter Mandelson, Philip Gould and Alastair Campbell – three should have gone at once. Gould was anyway a theoretician and instantly dismissible, but Tony should tactfully and skilfully have distanced himself from Mandelson and Campbell, then dispensed altogether with their services. Tony had neither the boldness, the strength of mind, nor the brilliance of perception to part company with them. It took time and cruel events for both of them to be wrested from him, and he clung to both as long as he could. He was codependent on them, as an alcoholic is for his daily tipple: this came from very personal reasons.

Mandelson, a politician of high talent, had grasped that the route to power lay through conquering the media. But the media could in some ways be likened to the *canaille*, the bloodthirsty mob of the French revolution, which once the appetite was awoken would forever be demanding more and more victims. A truly astute political leader would have seen that the brakes needed to be put on the media, and that the enemy within the government were those who believed the media was the be-all and end-all.

Gordon Brown was a different kettle of fish: brooding and complex, his brilliant political mind (he had studied history in depth, albeit with a narrow and limited focus on the Labour movement in Scotland) quite unable to come to terms with everyday human life, he was already a passive figure on the political stage. Yet he made bold decisions at once, ceding interest rate control to the Bank of England, making it an economic not a political decision. He also knew, as he said himself, that 'the key to running a successful government is discipline, and that stems from the Treasury'. 'His personality kept Labour in order' (James Naughtie, *The Rivals*).

Meanwhile Tony quickly began to slide into the time-honoured pattern of mediocre politicians, devising schemes and preaching doctrines, as if desperate not to be seen lacking what the elder President Bush later called 'the vision thing'. In health, in foreign policy, education, in institutional legal terms, his ministers talked endlessly of 'structural reform' and of inventing faultless 'social systems', 'plans for peace' and 'the alleviation of world hunger'. It was all genuinely felt and stuffed with good intention, but a cursory blast of clear thought would have blown away all the theory, and especially the specialists upon whom the mediocre minds of Tony's government came increasingly to rely in order to expand the 'parameters of choice'.

Every 'specialist', in whatever field he or she practises, believes sincerely that his or her patients or subjects all suffer from the same disease or deficiency in which he or she specialises. With such advice ministers started to clog the statute book with a plethora of new laws which were over the ten years to exceed 3,000 in number, many of them unnecessarily interfering as well as unworkable. There were not only 300 new sex offences, for which the equivalent in other European countries had fewer than ten registered, but also such new offences as causing a nuclear explosion, disposing of a zoo animal without permission, docking a dog's tail for cosmetic reasons, or importing Polish potatoes.

Instead of ensuring government policies could be implemented, Tony gave the masters of presentation a free rein, Campbell as chief press secretary and Mandelson as Trade and Industry Secretary. The essential rhythm of good government – patient control, quiet management, the flexing of authority and the gaining of experience – was lost in the tempo of sustaining the same breathless media excitement which led up to Blair's victory.

Tony had his moment of illumination. 'There's a sense of exuberance, but journalists are not friends,' he told the *Times* on 5 May 1997. 'Stories are too easily generated. There's too much chatter. We need to move into a different modus operandi. The constitutional commission was leaked to the *Scotsman*. Cabinet committees must stay confidential, I will come down very hard on leaks.' But the moment passed quickly. Like many assertions this was hollow, for in the same breath almost he handed over a dozen or so muzzles to Campbell, to curb others but not himself. 'All media interviews', Blair decreed, 'should be cleared through his office at No. 10, otherwise newspapers will feed off this kind of thing.' He worried, he also said, about media criticism, first, that they couldn't handle power and 'second, that they were arrogant and drunk with power' (quoted in Oborne and Walters). He couldn't make up his own mind what to do, and cited Clinton confessing to him that he, Clinton, had failed to communicate enough with the press. The moment of illumination had been brief and passed quickly.

No one would dispute that Campbell was a brilliant opportunist, cheeky, a completely dedicated and hard worker, and soon, as became apparent, a control freak. His management of the press, in particular of getting and keeping Rupert Murdoch on the side of New Labour, became total and ensured Tony's superior popularity in the opinion polls well into the second term and even beyond. But he had lit the fuse under himself and sooner or later he would bring about his own destruction. Spin-doctors ought to be invisible, like God in the universe, as Flaubert advised authors should be in their work: 'present everywhere, but nowhere visible'. As soon as we became too aware of Campbell, the game was up. Anyway, it would have been much better for Cherie and Tony at the start if they had not been so popular. For most of Margaret Thatcher's premiership and particularly in her first term until the Falklands War in 1982, she was very unpopular. Her learning curve was achieved by bucking the trend, not riding with the tide. Her effect on the culture of her era and the future of the Conservative Party may have been disastrous or tragic in so far as she presided over the overriding obsession with 'the product', but there could never be any doubt she was an original, her own person, and she made her decisions mainly in isolation and from within herself. She may have emulated other great leaders, but she imitated no one. Unlike Cherie and Tony, she and Denis were the opposite of mirror images of one another. Good government should not be about being popular: moreover the kind of overwhelming popularity that Blair enjoyed actually resulted in another limiting factor – a loss of contact with reality. People who succeed in show business keep their heads by knowing it's only show business.

Blair's brand of socialism jumped on the bandwagon that proclaimed that unfettered capitalism, now euphemistically blurred into the word 'enterprise', was the only way to run the world. But the ever-expanding markets and the rampant consumerism had no check, and the trend was inexorably set for a world of pop princesses in their early teens (to take one example) demanding the earth in response to adult advertisement, and the complete squalor of sexual and moral values. The value of a society is not measured by a U2 or Madonna album selling forty million, or by ecstasy tablets in the UK free market costing less than a pint of beer.

Ten years later, 'Children growing up in the UK suffer greater deprivation, worse relationships with their parents and are exposed to more risks from alcohol, drugs and unsafe sex than in any other wealthy country,' according to a 2007 study from the United Nations.

18

The big move

She often puts her head round the Cabinet room door to enquire, 'Anyone want a cuppa?'

Tony Blair on Cherie's mother, 1998

'Call me Tony' was always, given the opportunity, declaring that he was just an ordinary chap, a family man, with phrases such as 'what does one do?', 'now, look' and most of all 'frankly' and 'honestly, I think'. In the complexity and fundamental ontological insecurity of a character who constantly leaned on others and practised a continual *égoïsme à deux* with his wife, he was anything but this. Cherie moaned to friends about the move from Richmond Terrace to Downing Street, but it was also a big mistake for which she would later pay, her decision not to separate government from the domestic needs and life of a growing family, which were and would always be at odds with the demands of political life. If they had remained in Islington, because of the need for police protection they would have brought inconvenience to their neighbours, as well as a security headache to Special Branch because of the house's position in the terrace and its lack of space at the back. But Downing Street was not built to accommodate government and a large family, so to move a growing family of three, later four, children into the top floor of a cramped terraced house, without there being even a separate entrance, was miscalculation with consequences as grave as any political decision. It not only must have been confusing for the children and household servants to keep bumping into a stream of visiting officials and visitors, it raised puzzled eyebrows among senior advisers who, as one told me, would find heaps of luggage, including a guitar case and packed-up toys, piled in the corridor as the Blairs prepared to depart on holiday to Barbados or Tuscany. Further complication stemmed from their occupation not of the small flat above No. 10 but, at Cherie's abrupt insistence, on taking over the more spacious Chancellor's flat above Nos 11 and 12, which 'greatly offended' Gordon Brown, who was hardly to use the smaller residence.

The move with young children was a bad idea. Cherie justified the sharing of the informality necessary for family life with the cauldron of decision-making government on the grounds that it allowed Tony to be near his family, as all he had to do at the end of the day, at seven o'clock, was to pop upstairs, switch off and concern himself with domestic matters. She said before the election, 'As far as I'm concerned we are a family. Wherever Tony goes we all go. If that means Downing Street so be it.' This was patently naive, but the probability is that it suited Cherie much better, both for her work and for keeping tabs on what was happening downstairs in government; also it looked good in the press. Here was a Prime Minister who, after sitting at the Cabinet table, receiving calls or visitors all day, issuing orders, could bound upstairs, engage with his children and wife, open the baked beans and cut up the onions for supper, or roll up his sleeves to do the washing up.

Cherie wailed constantly to friends how selling the Richmond Terrace house for £615,000 had set them back financially and that they could make no investments, and especially she complained in an undignified way about the newspapers militating against any increase in her husband's earnings. This picture endeared her to the nation of shopkeepers, but she could never get the image right, even when, for instance, on an official trip to China with Tony in October 1998, rivalling Margaret Thatcher in quick changes, she took twenty costly outfits with her. 'I can't win,' she screamed in defiance when picked up on this. 'If I buy nice clothes, I'm accused of profligacy; if I don't, Lynda fucking Lee-Potter will crucify me in the *Daily Mail*.'

She shook off the hair fashion low on the front step of Richmond Terrace in May 1997 by taking a leaf, or rather stylist, out of Clinton's book. Probably it was Bill who told her that he had once kept Air Force One waiting for him at the cost of £50,000 while Cristophe of Beverly Hills gave him a 'runway trim' for which the President paid him £130 out of his own pocket. The next time she met Bill, at the G8 summit in Denver, she was 'tappylappying' or accepting homage in full First Lady fashion with a personal stylist in her entourage: André Suard, from Mayfair, cost her £2,000 for the trip and had the ambition to create a Jackie Onassis image for her. 'Mrs Blair is scrupulous in ensuring that the public purse meets no private costs,' Downing Street said of this extravagance, which would have paid for twenty local hairdressers, but no one quite knew at what point public and private met.

Now, on the China trip of 1998, she insisted on Suard travelling with her to administer twice-daily haircare, this time to the tune of £5,000, while government officials insisted that the taxpayer would not foot the bill. Thus began a whole swelling tide of speculation about the hairdresser's role in Cherie's life: 'Someone who admires and obsesses and thinks, at least for a certain allotted time, only about you . . . It is an intimate relationship involving weakness, yearning and raw need . . . It is the luxury of untrammelled power over a man . . . a complete and utter reversal of the usual gender roles,' wrote the *Guardian*.

On the subject of Cherie's body self-image, Piers Morgan, if not with tongue in cheek then licking his lips, reports that at a lunch with her and Tony he told her that he had a good reason for her to be nice to him. Before the Downing Street move he'd been offered grainy, paparazzi pictures of her sunbathing topless on holiday, which he turned down. Cherie said nothing. Dropping the subject until the pudding was served she leaned over and asked Morgan, 'Did you see those pictures yourself?' Morgan confirmed he had spied Cherie's naked breasts. 'Did I . . . well, did I look awful or was it OK?' 'You looked fantastic,' Morgan said. 'Shame we couldn't have published them, or you'd have definitely increased the male Labour vote.' Cherie giggled. 'Oh don't, Piers, I'd be so embarrassed.'

'You campaign in poetry, you govern in prose,' Cherie told Tony, who repeated this proudly on the *Parkinson* show in March 2006, together with all manner of his own 'I'm tough' assertions (for example, on the exercise of power, 'you've got to harden yourself to it'). These statements and Cherie's might put the reader in mind of the *Noddy* books parents read to their children, whereas it should be pointed out that the kinds of image politicians ought to have in mind when they govern are better found in Wilfred Owen's trench poems of the First World War, or T. S. Eliot's *The Waste Land* –

examples of twentieth-century poetry earthed in reality. Moreover the easy ride Tony had in his first term in office was the reverse of 'tough'. With their voracity for power, and sustaining praise and flattery that went with it (with the Downing Street enforcer behind), Tony and Cherie gathered around them as a chorus a wide circle of sycophantic celebrities. As Jonathan Swift noted, 'climbing is but horizontal crawling'.

Driven by hyper-sensitivity to their own images and this relentless emphasis on the youthful dynamic quality of leadership, which it took years for the public to realise was illusion, the momentum of their domination of political fashion was quite extraordinary. In Parliament the actor, by now the experienced parliamentary tactician with his 179-seat majority, was in charge and set his own terms, as he did at Cabinet meetings, for example consolidating or in effect reducing the format of Prime Minister's Questions in the House of Commons from two fifteen-minute to one thirty-minute session a week. At his first Cabinet meeting he had already copied the US presidential style, the rejection of distance and formality, with 'call me Tony'. The informality he introduced was primarily a comfortable way to cover insecurity, and echoed that of the dissembler Horder in Congreve's *The Double Dealer*, at which Laurence Olivier had been past master:

No mask like open truth to cover lies
As to go naked is the best disguise.

Tom Bower in his 2001 book *The Paymaster* listed the pledge of £1 million from Matthew Harding, a businessman, the same from publisher Paul Hamlyn and lesser amounts from Chris Haskins of Northern Foods and printer Bob Gavron, while 'media aristocrats Waheed Alli, Melvyn Bragg, Gerry Robinson and Clive Hollick all promised thousands of pounds with the hope of a place in the House of Lords'. This shift of emphasis in the constant employment of show business terminology reflected how the new union of magnates, the 'tycoons for Labour' who expected honours, jobs or access to ministers for their money, had supplanted Labour's exclusive relationship with the trade unions.

As for Bragg, thus described as one of the show business bankrollers of New Labour (together with David Sainsbury and David Puttnam the film-maker), he has written of Laurence Olivier in a short book to accompany a *South Bank Show* interview with the actor, 'The appearance or complete illusion of the truth . . . presumes that we believe what he says and take it for granted that he believes it too.' Never a truer word was written about Tony, and from now on massive governmental failures, such as the Millennium Dome, were simply to be written off as 'flops', for this was the new yardstick. 'That's show business for you!' is the common adage.

Two well-known writers, responding to a 'Cool Britannia' Downing Street invitation, were struck by how few (if any) other writers were present. Instead they encountered actors and soap stars, musicians and television celebrities, now joined by newsreaders. Tony spent most of the party at a photo-shoot with Noel Gallagher of the pop group Oasis in another room. When he appeared he came straight over to greet actor Ian McKellen, filming as Gandalf the magician in *Lord of the Rings*. 'May I kiss you, Prime Minister?' McKellen asked – to which Tony enthusiastically acceded. Writers even of a left persuasion such as Harold Pinter or John Mortimer were not invited, as they might seriously probe and ask awkward questions. Premier Zhu's words were definitely not on the invitation here in Downing Street. One recalls almost with nostalgia Anthony Booth's drunken confrontation with Harold Wilson (see Chapter 3).

When asked how he justified having Noel Gallagher, a self-acclaimed drug abuser, at his party, Blair answered, 'Well, we should celebrate great British bands like Oasis,' but tempered this when Alastair Campbell passed him a hurriedly scribbled note from which he then took his cue: 'Though as far as his views on drugs [sic], I can assure you this government will do everything in its power to crack down on drug abuse. Like most parents it is the thing I worry about most with my children.'

More than the pomp and ceremony, and the Blair promises packed into the Queen's speech on 14 May 1997, the real investiture of the new and true cultural supremo of the United Kingdom took place a fortnight later.

19

Policies flow from values

The Bulk of the People consist in a manner wholly of Discoverers, Witnesses, Informers, Accusers, Prosecutors, Evidences, Swearers, together with their several subservient and subaltern Instruments; all under the Colours, the Conduct, and pay of Ministers of State, and their Deputies.

Jonathan Swift, 'A Voyage to Laputa', *Gulliver's Travels*

As Bill Clinton expressed it, alighting from Air Force One on 29 May 1997:

I flew to London for my first official meeting with the new British Prime Minister, Tony Blair. His Labour Party had won a big victory over the Tories in the recent election as a result of Blair's leadership, Labour's more modern and more moderate message, and the natural ebbing of support for the Conservatives after their many years in power. Blair was young, articulate, and forceful, and we shared many of the same political views. I thought he had the potential to be an important leader for the UK and all of Europe, and was excited about the prospect of working with him.

Hillary and I went to dinner with Tony and Cherie Blair at a restaurant in a restored warehouse district on the Thames. We felt like old friends from the start. The British press was fascinated by the similarity in our philosophies and politics, and the questions they asked seemed to have an impact on the American press travelling with me. For the first time, I had the feeling that they were beginning to believe there was something more than rhetoric to my New Democrat approach.

The simplistic 'we felt like old friends from the start' revealed how the older legal pair, and leaders of America's pop psychology generation, were almost at once on the London scene, the world capital of pop, ready to take Tony and Cherie under their wing. Both leaders were nervous smilers, out to disarm any potential hostility, out to please and appease, but Bill had the whip hand, while Hillary was the stronger and more psychologically integrated woman. Hillary at once mesmerised Cherie, up to now an admirer of robust political matrons such as Barbara Castle, who subsequently were sidelined when they began to dissent. Here was someone who was just as Cherie aspired to be, and more, as First Lady, a power-sharer with the most powerful man on earth.

Hillary, a seasoned politician, was also a mistress of the art of political spin, as Christopher Anderson shows in his exposé *American Evita* (2004). Trying to exploit the horror of the 9/11 tragedy, to take a later example, Hillary claimed Chelsea, her 21-year-old daughter, was out in the street jogging perilously close to Ground Zero, when she was in fact safely watching the news on television in a friend's flat thirty blocks away. Hillary claimed she spent countless hours consoling the victims and their families, which proved also to be untrue. At a concert of police officers and firefighters she was booed off the stage as she started to make a speech about the victims, and a firefighter whose brother died in the explosions dismissed her as talking claptrap: 'She says', he told the audience, 'whatever she thinks will fit the moment. I think it comes through, and in serious times people just don't want to stand for it.'

Bill Clinton had always been a flattering, even unctuous, supporter of Pope John Paul II: 'He sure knew how to build a crowd. I just shook my head and said, "I'd hate to have to run against this man." ' The Pope, however, failed to return the admiration, and called him 'a bad listener . . . who never paid much attention to what I said'. He could never make eye contact with Clinton, not surprisingly, because in eye contact John Paul generally struck home, saw right into your heart. Clinton was the only world leader with whom, said the Pope, 'I never managed to have a proper conversation . . . while I was speaking he was always looking somewhere else, admiring the frescoes and paintings.' Probably of the naked Eve, or nymphs in the Sistine Chapel.

Tony and Cherie had no such problem with the presidential couple, with whom they were to begin to all intents and purposes a platonic love affair. All four were infatuated with one another. An insider commented:

> It wasn't just a matter of them being *simpatico* politically; they genuinely warmed to the Clintons from day one. I remember that everyone was very excited because we had been in office less than a month and there was an element that we all were, the Blairs included, a little star-struck by them. But Clinton is a master at putting you at your ease. In person he has a slow effortless charm, which is completely seductive. What was, and is, amazing about that guy is that he was just as adept at being charming to the waiters . . . there was a large element of the showman about him. (Quoted in Paul Scott, *Tony & Cherie*)

Bill loved to talk; a number of points of similarity with Tony need to be made for they were now imitative rivals, although Bill had the bigger clout. He was first of all someone who could outline a policy, then change his mind about it, despite having been in power now for more than four years he still appeared to make his decisions during hour-long telephone conversations. He had opened his first Cabinet meeting at Camp David with a discussion of 'vulnerability', informing his new secretaries of state and education about how he had been a fat kid and how other kids had ribbed him for it. He had already shown the way – and not the Third Way – that Tony in his future years in power was in uncanny similarity, but more slowly, to follow.

The big issue Bill had to face when he first came to the presidency had been whether to use force and become involved in the break-up of the former Yugoslavia. 'We don't want America to get into a quagmire that's essentially a civil war that we can't solve and that may not be worth the lives of Americans.' Instead, maybe they could work within the United Nations 'to restore territorial integrity to the newly independent republics'. This, as well as being an international problem, became Clinton's own personal psychodrama, a means for him to resolve and work out internal conflict, which he adopted all kinds of different ploys to contain. To stop the needless slaughter, the mass extermination of people, he said, 'I specifically would not foreclose the option of the use of force.' It took him several more months, hesitating and tergiversating, to become 'a real American President'. A psychologist commented:

> While it is undoubtedly good for Bill Clinton to talk his way through his problems, it was not so good for Bosnia. Every time he thought aloud about intervention, the Bosnian Muslims kept hoping and kept fighting; every time he went into relapse, the Bosnian Serbs took the fluctuation as a sign of Western weakness. Peace plans fell apart and cease-fires failed to hold while Clinton worked out his feelings; outsiders, and foreigners in particular, don't always understand that the President's statements are not meant to be taken seriously.

The process of self-discovery got a fillip in the psychological breakthrough of 27 June 1993, when Clinton clipped Saddam Hussein's nuclear wings by firing fifteen missiles on Iraq. 'I feel good about the bombing,' he said, integrated at last with the sense of his own power.

You can be sure there was plenty of 'feelgood' chat between the two pairs, much expression of mutual adulation and 'bonding' that went on at lengthy lunches and dinners. The final one, held at Terence Conran's Pont de la Tour restaurant at Tower Bridge, held up for hours the President's departure on Air Force One.

Matched as its members were in comparable insecurities as lawyers (whose ultimate aim is to win briefs and secure clients' fees – in this case, redirected to press and voter or poll approbation), the Clinton–Blair quartet strengthened its resolve to resist enemies (primarily the press) and to further abstract aims, a habit frowned on by more seasoned diplomatic observers.

20

Trapped on Planet Diana

A woeful pageant have we here beheld,
The woe's to come.

William Shakespeare, *Richard II*

At the start of Tony's premiership Princess Diana was another supreme media star. Piers Morgan wrote in May 1997, 'I'm trapped on Planet Diana, a crazy place where she calls all the shots and is famous enough and important enough to newspapers to get away with it.' Morgan had just scooped a story on Diana's former bulimia from another patient at the clinic she had attended ('One day your addiction can come back to haunt you,' she told Morgan on the phone, when approving the story; next day she turned ferociously on the editor in a radio programme). 'You have to hand it to the little minx. Even by her standards it is breathtaking behaviour,' commented Morgan.

Tony's sycophancy and slavering at the presence and universal popularity of Princess Diana soon became a spur to Cherie's determination to rival her, although she was contemptuous of her intelligence, calling her 'an airhead'. In the short summer idyll of 1997 Diana and her sons visited Chequers on Cherie's invitation and there were merry scenes of the Blair boys and the young princes William and Harry gambolling and splashing in the open-air pool. Prince Charles took a dim view of the fraternisation and stopped it. Alastair Campbell had already astutely directed Blair in the conflict between Diana and the rest of the Royal Family: 'On all political issues we back Diana.'

Diana's death, in the early morning of 31 August 1997, led Tony to commit his next serious and personal mistake, one which was much applauded by Cherie in the privacy of the No. 11 flat, and outside earned him near-universal admiration.

A private secretary on duty at No. 10 phoned Blair at Myrobella at 2 a.m. to give him the news of Diana's death. He made his decision at once: his journalistic antennae told him this was the biggest story of all time and he would place himself at the centre. With Campbell to help him he crafted the oration he would deliver outside St Mary Magdalene Church, Trimdon for ITN. He seized that moment, instinctively feeling he had to ride the crest of the surge generated by the media. Not for nothing, once again, had he played Mark Antony at Fettes, capturing the mood and exploiting the popular grief over the death of the beloved Caesar. Examine on film the way he walks to the microphone and you can see the swagger, even detect something of a hidden smile.

'I feel like everyone else in the country today, utterly devastated,' he replied to ITN's Michael Brunson when asked for his response to Diana's death. 'Our thoughts and prayers are with Princess Diana's family, in particular her two sons, her two boys. Our hearts go out to them. We are, today, a nation in shock, in mourning, a grief that is so painful. How many times shall we remember her in how many different ways, with the sick, the dying, with children, with the needy? With just a look or a gesture that spoke so much more than words, she would reveal to all of us the depth of her compassion and her humanity. She was the People's Princess and that is how she will remain in our hearts and our memories forever.'

Campbell had poached and passed on the clichéd phrase 'People's Princess', which had been used before about Diana. (But in 2007, interviewed by Michael Cockerell for BBC2, while looking down rather coyly at his feet, Blair says, 'I came up with the phrase of the "People's Princess".') By now the quirks of self-presentation, which themselves were to become Tony's own clichés, were stock-in-trade political theatricality: thumb and forefinger squeezed together, sweeping open-palm gestures, the haunted look and trembling lip, the pregnant mid-sentence pause, the 'I feel your pain'. The Tory leader, William Hague, then did what Brutus had done after Caesar's death: delivered a public response which was restrained, dignified and proportionate. It moved no one.

By any reckoning, Tony's speech was an act of extraordinary vanity. That the Prime Minister should extol in such maudlin terms the virtues of a paper princess, idolatrised as a celebrity, crossed too many boundaries at once and became in some people's eyes the nadir to which a great country's culture had sunk. Moreover Diana had by now become something of a cheapened image, not only through her interviews and well-publicised affairs, but only weeks before her death in photographs of her near-naked canoodling in a Mediterranean setting with Dodi Fayed, son of Mohamed al-Fayed. Tony subsequently hammed up his reading from Corinthians at Diana's funeral, which ended with Elton John crooning:

> You called out to your country
> And you whispered to those in pain.
> Now you belong to heaven
> And the stars spell out your name.

This lyric had been recycled from an earlier requiem for Marilyn Monroe in gratitude for Diana comforting him at Gianni Versace's funeral some months before.

Blair's eulogy set the pattern of mass recreational grief to come, the main feature of which was that, while it looked and felt genuine, it was a compensatory delusion, satisfying some core, inner hunger of a narcissistic society. The histrionic display signalled a break with traditional restraint, and a move into Middle Eastern mourning patterns. In a country which had lost its religious faith people did not know how to react; they mourned, they laid flowers, but felt inhibited about prayer. They had forgotten what it was all about. Just like the girl who marches into the jeweller's looking for a cross to buy, and after being shown some crosses to choose from, tells the jeweller, 'I'll have the one with the little man on it.'

Following Tony's seizure of the limelight, Queen Elizabeth, badly advised by her courtiers to follow the tactics of Tony and a consensus of Fleet Street editors, abandoned a protocol of not lowering the flag over Buckingham Palace, which had not even been done at the death of her father King George VI, or Sir Winston Churchill, the greatest Englishman of his day. The Queen compromised her reputation as the epitome of the British stiff upper lip, and made a concession to Blair populism by addressing the nation on TV with a largely Downing Street script. This concession may well in the future come to be judged as one of the darkest moments of her reign. It signified that the monarch, if only for a guest appearance, had signed up for one episode of Soap Opera UK, and as such laid herself open to narrative manipulation by Cherie and Tony. On the other hand, there is some force in the view that wittingly or unwittingly Blair did the Queen and the frail monarchy a big service, and that the Queen, by her presence at the Westminster Abbey funeral, brought definition and dignity to a scene of self-indulgent grief.

The 2006 film *The Queen* recreates the drama of how in those days following the death, the Queen and Prince Philip at Balmoral, both disinclined for quite valid personal reasons to play the hypocrite and display feelings they did not feel or believe in, were wooed and cajoled by a monarchist Tony into changing their minds and returning to London to join in the funeral. The film shows Campbell savouring parts of the speech they prevailed upon the Queen to deliver live on TV, and inserting words for her to use such as 'speaking as a grandmother'. The writer Peter Morgan's intention, perhaps in the politically correct and feelgood mood of the moment, he says, was to show the Queen as 'a cold, emotionally detached, haughty, difficult, prickly, private, uncommunicative, out-of-touch bigot'. Unintentionally, in the alchemical transformation brought to the part by Helen Mirren in her Oscar-winning performance, and with the truthful, meticulously rendered filming of the context by Stephen Frears, the director, it turned out to have the opposite effect.

The British public, put up to it by the press, had misunderstood the Queen. Mirren, in playing the part with tenderness and sympathy, and tapping into the Queen's hidden resistance to what she was doing, redressed the balance. It also brought into play the power of time passing. But Tony's pro-monarchy stance was in time to emerge as shallow, for the monarchy was inextricably entangled with hereditary privilege, virtually swept away (but with a token retention) in the House of Lords Bill of 1999: 'All the princes of the royal blood, from the Prince of Wales to the Earl of Essex, were automatic members of the House of Lords. For the British government to abolish the hereditary peerages . . .

without damaging the monarchy was well-nigh impossible' (Norman Davies, *The Isles*).

*

In the short term Tony's response to the death of 'the little minx', as Piers Morgan called Diana, with 'her breathtaking behaviour', may have seemed wonderful, but in the long term it was a grave mistake. A clear-sighted spouse, who could see, as in Blake's great phrase, not just *with* the eye but *through* the eye, should have pointed out that Narcissus loves himself, not others. But the two personalities were now inextricably entwined, and it was never to be quite clear again where the boundaries or limits of one another lay. Cherie gave her unflattering nightshirt from Next to an exhibition at the Museum of London called 'Power Dressing: the Fashion of Politics'. Tony echoed her in sartorial gaffes when he appeared with nudes on the inside of his shirt cuffs, or in purple slacks as a 'plum vision' with his shirt hanging out, to embrace German Chancellor Gerhard Schroeder.

In the new 'me' society, ruthless self-worship and unbridled self-interest were now becoming sanctified in the leadership of Blair and Blair, and society bathed both in praise and approbation. Narcissistic personalities not only require excessive admiration, but also have unreasonable expectations of especially favourable treatment (entitlement), and automatic compliance with this. They take advantage of others to achieve their ends, and show arrogant and haughty behaviour. The approval of something so similar to their core values was irresistible. With Cherie and Tony functioning as mirrors to each other, the armour plating of their narcissism acted as a shield against insight.

*

'Grief is a vital safety valve,' pontificated the pro-Blair *Sun* eight months after Diana's funeral, in contrast to which Euan Ferguson lamented in the *Observer* the orgy of narcissistic emoting as 'part of the Liverpudlianisation of Britain ... [which has] turned us into a country that fills its gutters with tears for girls we've never met and scrawls mawkish thank-yous to the most privileged woman this land has ever known'. But Diana, her defenders said, spoke to every woman's woundedness, and to the battle of women everywhere to be heard and to be loved. When in April 1998 Anthony O'Hear, a professor at Bradford University, wrote that the reaction to Diana's death lacked a sense of proportion, Tony waded into the resulting furore, in which O'Hear was denounced by the *Mirror* as a 'rat-faced little loser'. Tony, visiting the Middle East at the time, saw fit, as the British Prime Minister, to call O'Hear an 'old fashioned snob'. Diana's power, Tony went on, was such that 'is born out of emotion, and there's nothing wrong with that – I'm an emotional person, too'.

Cherie put Tony up to this retaliation because she now identified strongly with Diana. The dead were not rivals. And who was more fit to assume Diana's mantle in this new order of government by raw emotion, in the Liverpudlianisation of Great Britain, than a genuine Liverpudlian lass, ready to embark on turning herself into the most privileged woman this land has ever known?

Cherie's subsequent anti-monarchical antics were constantly applauded by her Islington claque, highlighted as they were during the Blairs' traditional annual visits to Balmoral, when she refused to curtsey to the Queen, hectored the company in legalistic mode, and wore trousers unbefitting the occasion, which upset the Queen Mother. She also fell out with the short-tempered Princess Anne, whom she called a 'bitch' when the Princess disdained to shake hands or engage on Christian-name terms. There was a further incident showing a blatant attempt to hijack royal protocol and usurp the Queen. At the death of the Queen Mother on 30 March 2002, Tony, fiercely supported by Cherie, tried to upstage royal mourners by proposing to walk from Downing Street to greet the Queen or meet the coffin for another Diana moment. This caused a furore of criticism, and he climbed down. For the funeral itself modern 'Teflon' Tony refused to wear morning dress, while Cherie not only yawned during the proceedings but wore a low-cut lacy top showing her décolletage, and a ridiculously wide-brimmed hat.

The tendency to become show people, to engage in self-dramatising behaviour, had become obligatory for modern leaders of a narcissistic bent. Tony and Cherie were to show they could outdo all comers in the power and frequency of media exposure. In stern but lovey-dovey affection they surpassed Chairman and Madame Mao; they even outdid the Filipino love-pair Ferdinand and Imelda Marcos, who fluttered round each other 'like nectar-sated humming birds'. The British people now had two celebrity leaders for the price of one, while 'fame is not fastidious about the lips which spread it'. The addiction to fame began with the death of Diana, as if in some extraordinary transformation or metamorphosis Blair himself wanted to devour the reputation of the dead woman and transexualise her mantle of fame by wearing it himself (an irony to this was, as an echo, that he would later come to be dubbed in some quarters 'Princess Tony').

21

Screw your courage to the sticking place

We want you to get up the arse of the White House and stick there.

Jonathan Powell, Tony Blair's chief of staff, to Christopher Meyer,
UK ambassador to the United States

The 'feelgood' closeness between the Clintons and the Blairs could have beneficial effects. Bill undoubtedly gave Tony the green light to meet Gerry Adams, which he duly did at Stormont in October 1997, so at least some progress was made to bring together the parties to talk peace during the IRA ceasefire which had been restored some months earlier.

A battle of rival compliments was now building up between Tony Blair and Bill Clinton, which climaxed with Bill's remarks at the state dinner in February 1998, when the Blairs visited Washington. Cherie confessed before going that it would be a daunting prospect to look radiant, and that she feared dancing with the President. But Tony had to rule out hopes of having an impromptu jam session with him. Proposing the toast, Bill praised Tony: '[He] has acted with lightning speed to bring renewed vigour to the political institutions of his country,' which was a polite way of covering up the fact that while he looked impressive so far little had been done. Tony had begun his mission of being 'a direction post, which is always telling the way to a place, and never goes there', like Mr Pecksniff in Dickens's *Martin Chuzzlewit*.

The 'entertainment' after the dinner was provided by the Clintons under canvas awnings on the West Terrace of the White House. Elton John, together with toupee and the objets d'art he valued more than people, had been flown over to give the 'Anglo' angle. Show business royalty – Tom Hanks, Steven Spielberg, Barbra Streisand, Harrison Ford – were presented as if they were the Dukes of Burgundy and Aquitaine – while Stevie Wonder crooning 'My Cherie Amour' reminded Cherie, unhappily perhaps in her euphoria, that her name came from a music hall trouper's song. To attend such an occasion, never mind be the centre of it, as were Cherie and Tony, must have been the dream of a lifetime for many, and the world vicariously partook of the feast.

To go backstage for a moment or two behind the banquet niceties we find a different storyline. Tony must have frowned or turned the other way, pretending not to hear when Newt Gingrich, Democratic Speaker of the House, sitting on Hillary's left – with Tony on her right – informed her that the sexual charges against Bill were 'ludicrous' and 'even if they were true, it's meaningless, they were going nowhere'. Tony repeated this formula in 2007 during the police investigations into the 'cash for honours' affair.

Tony and the more ethical and motherly Cherie, who refused to have the *Sun* in the family home on account of Page 3, knew about the Lewinsky scandal, which had blown up just before their arrival, and that Monica Lewinsky had made tapes revealing the 'inappropriate encounters', as Clinton called them, he had had with her since November 1995. Here is how Clinton 'confesses' it in his autobiography *My Life*:

> What I had done with Monica Lewinsky was immoral and foolish and I was deeply ashamed of it and I didn't want it to come out. In the deposition, I was trying to protect my family and myself from my selfish stupidity. I believed that the contorted definition of 'sexual relations' enabled me to do so, though I was worried enough about it to invite the lawyer interrogating me to ask specific questions. I didn't have to wait long to find out why he declined to do so.

Even so, to go back to the time he still believed he could get away with it – with no confession to his wife but a complete cover-up, and certainly no confession to his new best friends Cherie and Tony, for whom he had become an idol – the state investigator Kenneth Starr's inquiry into the affair had intensified, with subpoenas to give evidence issued to potential witnesses. Bill had gone on and on lying to the press, saying, 'I did not have sex with that woman.' Hillary stood by him, telling the NBC *Today* interviewer she did not believe the charges against him, and that 'a vast right-wing conspiracy' had been trying to destroy them since 1992.

The next passage of Clinton's later confession makes further revelation of his double-dealing mentality:

> Hillary's difficult interview and my mixed reaction to it clearly exemplified the bind I had put myself in. As a husband, I had done something wrong that I needed to apologise and atone for; as President, I was in a legal and political struggle with forces who had abused the criminal and civil laws and severely damaged innocent people in their attempt to destroy my presidency and cripple my ability to serve.
>
> Finally, after years of dry holes, I had given them something to work with. I had hurt the presidency and the people by my misconduct. That was no one's fault but my own. I didn't want to compound the error by letting the reactionaries prevail.

What he says, in effect, is not that there are double standards (and this is significant for Tony, for he is to undergo a similar scandal in some ways in 2006–7), but that there are two standards which are different, and have nothing to do with each other. In other words, a set of values that applies in one place or circumstance does not apply in another; there is no consistent morality that can be applied, for everything is relative to the situation. Clinton did something wrong in his personal life, he says, of which he was ashamed. What he was more emphatic about was that his enemies were using this to cripple his ability to do his job – not that he himself had crippled his own ability to serve. He naively or ruthlessly then completely missed the real point, for which later he was indicted: namely that, as President, he lied under oath. The position he adopts here is called in ethics and philosophy 'situationism': everything is relative to and depends on the situation in which a person finds himself.

Into this swamp of charge and counter-charge, Tony and Cherie rode into Washington as saviours, bringing with them their own firm ground or at least firm pedestals. 'Whiter than white' Tony had established himself on his banner as *Private Eye*'s 'Vicar of St Albion', and he alighted among huddled senatorial ranks and acrimonious hacks to rescue his beleaguered friends. At this point Tony and Cherie's pristine image counted for much in the eyes of the American public, and to Bill, who wept with relief. 'They were a sight for sore eyes for both Hillary and me. They made us laugh, and Tony gave me strong support in public.' In the eyes of the American people it made all the difference, and arguably they saved the President.

But what about the trust placed in Bill Clinton not to lie? It was to be some months before the American President, with the grand jury testimony looming, told the truth to Hillary ('after a miserable sleepless night' – note, he had no miserable sleepless nights not telling her for three years). Having told Hillary, who was 'almost as angry at me for lying to her in January as for what I had done' – a wonderful admission which belittles both forms of misconduct – he moved to the couch downstairs to plot air strikes on Al Qaeda (Tony went along with this, giving RAF support without even telling the Cabinet).

As is well known, Slick Willy acted superbly during the impeachment, although, as some commentators noted, his evasive and slippery personality betrayed itself in his defensive body language. But, or so he said himself, people 'needed to hear my admission of wrongdoing and witness my remorse'. No question of honourable resignation?

As for Hillary, in her own autobiography, *Living History*, in a much longer account of the impeachment but one which is carefully coordinated with Bill's (he repeats much of what she says), she sets out once again the dual personality defence. This also protected and secured her future political ambitions because, had Bill resigned, she could have said goodbye to these. She drew on, she writes, 'a reservoir of different emotions – requiring different thinking'. Sure, she went on, Bill had 'violated my trust, I wanted to wring his neck!' But he was not only her husband – wait for it – he was also '*my President*' (emphasis added). As such he did not deserve the 'abusive treatment he had received'. Her crowning judgement is that 'his failing was not a betrayal of his country'.

Here was Hillary's Third Way. But from now on for two years Bill, even with Tony's endorsement, was a lame duck President. At no time did he acknowledge that his 'heartfelt' admission was merely consequent on the discovery of his crime, at least in the Arab world, of adultery (punishable in some countries with death). He was setting a precedent to be followed religiously by Tony when such scandals arose with his ministers.

But at a deeper level there was something much worse in all this.

*

President Thomas Jefferson, one of America's Founding Fathers, once said, 'When a man assumes a public trust, he should consider himself public property.' Even at the start of his career Bill Clinton had been a skilled lothario: Gennifer Flowers, an early paramour, alleged in her book *Gennifer Flowers: Passion and Betrayal* that in their twelve-year affair, begun when he was Attorney General in Arkansas and she had been sent to interview him, he was 'not particularly well-endowed' but great at sex and insatiable (this happened at the Excelsior Hotel in Little Rock). He never used a condom, and he introduced Gennifer to oral sex. Bill called Gennifer's breasts 'the girls' while Bill's testicles were 'the boys', and she would know he was not alone when on the phone he would ask, 'How are the girls?', to which she'd reply, 'How're the boys?'

Now Bill believed adultery was wrong, but produced this weird let-out, as he once told Trooper Patterson in the White House, that he had researched the topic of oral sex in the Bible and decided 'oral sex isn't considered adultery'. Hillary reports that in 1992, during the presidential campaign, 'Like a rampant virus [!], the Flowers story hopped between species of media, from the *Star*, a supermarket tabloid, to *Nightline*, a respected network news show.'

Western civilisation had taken a step backwards with Bill and Hillary, but Cherie Blair, the stern moralist and Catholic, never, as far as I have read or heard, talked of the scandal and never took down the framed photographs of her and Tony with the Clintons which stood on the table and mantelpiece in their flat in 11 Downing Street. The Clintons remained for the power-sharing Blair couple the ideal and a pattern of perfection to be imitated. Tempted to comment later on whether she found Bill 'sexy', Cherie, who panted with laughter at the question, answered, 'Well, I can see what people see in Bill Clinton, but as you may have noticed – um – I enjoy – nice-youngmen [*sic*]' (*Times*, May 2006).

What could Cherie and Tony's children have thought of those shots of the mutually adoring quartet set against the great splashes of Bill Clinton's lies and the impeachment drama on the screens and the media front pages, when Bill's body language only too strongly betrayed guilt? How could Tony and Cherie defend Bill, as did most Americans, by claiming that their friend's behaviour, however objectionable, was irrelevant as it did not affect his job performance? Just as an alcoholic's spouse who covers up his or her drinking is an enabler in the illness, so the US Congress, excusing lies, condoned and enabled Bill's Don Juanism, which only came to light because Monica Lewinsky kept the incriminating dress covered in dried sperm. What did Cherie now think about their joint hero, a man who saw no problem with having sex in the Oval Office while his wife and daughter slept upstairs? What mixed messages must have resulted, what confusion of the personal and the professional must have occurred in a family where Tony, the primal father, always claimed he put his family first?

When Tony appeared on *Parkinson* seven years later with the actor Kevin Spacey they brought up the link between actors and politicians. Spacey called Clinton 'a great actor'; Tony enthusiastically followed suit and emphatically went on that Clinton was 'the best politician as politician I've come across'. And he added, 'He's a really, *really* good guy.' He had added another double to his repertoire.

This might have been a strange learning curve for Tony, this shocking experience of Clinton as the fallen idol. But of course he already knew what Clinton was like. At the height of the Lewinsky scandal in late 1998, before the impeachment trial in the Senate began and the two motions, one on perjury and one on obstruction of justice, narrowly failed, defeated by the Democratic support, Tony was in Washington with Cherie for the annual opening of the UN General Assembly. Christopher Meyer reported here that Clinton's testimony on television was not

> the nail in his coffin that the Republicans had hoped it would be. On the contrary, most Americans took a dimmer view of Republican partisan vengefulness than they did of Clinton's priapism.
>
> By lunch, everybody knew the crisis had passed and that Clinton would survive. At the end of the afternoon, the British and American teams went off for a drink.

The Americans were almost light-headed after surviving another near-death experience. The Blairs and Clintons huddled together in a corner, the two couples intimate and alone.

That evening, I accompanied the Prime Minister to Kennedy Airport in the official limo. To my astonishment, Blair asked, 'What exactly is the charge against Clinton? I mean, what is he supposed to have done?'

'Bloody hell,' I thought to myself, 'have you read nothing of what I've sent you?' (I had been instructed by Downing Street to send as much as possible on Clinton's fate, because of the Prime Minister's intense interest.)

So I began once again to explain the dreary litany of charges against Clinton, his rebuttals, the risk of impeachment, when is sex not sex, and so on.

I tried to keep the sordid tale short and simple. But I could see that the Prime Minister had lost interest well before I had finished.

On their return from Washington, Piers Morgan lunched with Tony and Cherie, asking, ' "So, Cherie, if, hypothetically, Tony had a fling with a Downing Street intern, do you think you could stand by him, like Hillary Clinton has Bill?" She took dreadful offence – scowling at me and saying, "I hardly think that is an appropriate question." '

As well as Meyer's charge against Tony that he failed to exploit the political opportunities Clinton's weakness now provided the UK, the personal impact was extraordinary, and Tony's reaction no less. He was in denial. The learning curve proved to be illusory. Tony either pretended not to know, or actually denied knowledge of what he knew, and went on thinking of his hero as before, as 'a really, really good guy'. Later he would even go so far as to demand and get a payback when his own government and leadership had sunk into disrepute, by seeking Clinton's public endorsement at his very last Labour conference. He introduced Clinton as a 'rock star', one of the two major influences on his politics – the other apparently being Bob Geldof.

'I like these Labour conferences,' Bill drawled before the delegates, then praised Tony's earlier speech as 'proud but humble, hopeful but cautionary, appropriately full of gratitude, devotion and love'. He pushed his groin against the lectern like a cow rubbing its flank on a tree trunk – 'Good burghers of Manchester, lock up your daughters,' quipped Quentin Letts.

'His left eye closed, slowly, with creamy pleasure as he said "lurve".' The old trouper's last performance on an English stage came over as very tired and jaded: maybe Tony could have done without it.

Later, a plan Bill and Cherie had for touring India delivering talks at hot-air seminars (the Fourth Way, the Only Way etc.) in order to command exorbitant fees was quietly dropped when few tickets were sold in advance, to the ignominy of both parties. 'I'm crazy about his wife,' was Bill's parting shot. 'If she ever campaigned for office and wanted me to go ringing doorbells for her, I'd be happy to do it.' Had Cherie, as the human rights lawyer, ever brought up the episode when Bill, as governor of Arkansas, ordered the execution of a mentally handicapped man to prove he wasn't soft on crime? She would have no scruples about raising the death penalty issue with George W. Bush – at the start, although in time she seemed to lapse into wifely compliance.

But for Tony the significant moment had arrived. The damage had been done. For most of English political history, at least in the nineteenth and twentieth centuries, the morality and accountability to truth of British leaders, and their political and leadership performances, were not held to be divisible into separate compartments. There had been signs and portents that this could happen, but given the trumpeting of 'moral purity', 'truth' and 'incorruptibility' by the dyadic pair, they had been given the benefit of the doubt on this score. The two people they worshipped and imitated had given the go-ahead for something else, no matter that these mentors were now tarnished, were now damaged goods.

All through the dramatic disclosures of the Clinton scandal Tony had been on a learning curve different from the one that might have hoped or supposed. From now on he would be two people, and often these two people would need to operate independently of one another.

At the end of 1997 Tony faced the second big scandal of his rule. Even the *Sun*, sweetened and hand fed from Downing Street as it was, cried out from its Dockland winding yard, 'This affair stinks, stinks, stinks!' Still in its first act, the tragedy that was now unfolding began to reveal the flaws in its main characters, from which ultimately they would not escape.

22

Parting is such sweet sorrow 1

The inability to determine where Tony finishes and other people begin was never more clearly shown in the way he appointed the Osrics of his court, the apes and sycophants, whose position there owed most to the way they functioned as significant reflexes of the Cherie and Tony temperaments and states of mind.

Indicating a poor, uncritical understanding of others, evaluated more on the scale of narcissistic and presentational values, in 1997 Blair appointed Geoffrey Robinson Paymaster General, the first or most prominent of these ill-judged choices. Known as 'the richest Labour MP ever', he embodied New Labour's naive belief in wealth, so he was Blair's obvious choice for the post.

According to Tom Bower, Robinson's biographer, before joining the government Robinson had netted a fortune of at least £20 million, as well as various properties left to him by Jaska Bourgeois, a French millionairess twenty-five years older than him. The full content of their attachment to one another, Bower relates, was not entirely sexual, as Bourgeois was 'so old. It's all hanging out,' according to one associate, while Robinson's wife, Marie Elena, an opera singer, added the jocular riposte, 'Well, she wouldn't want to go to bed with Geoffrey. He's so small and no good in bed.' Whatever it was, Robinson wove a powerful spell over Bourgeois.

As well as the money, he had the essential New Labour qualities: charm in buckets, unlimited persuasiveness and coquetry, the kind of temperamental, worn-on-sleeve sincerity and explosive (or sly) self-justification in which Tony and especially Peter Mandelson could see their own image. No noxious self-doubt ever raised a miasmic discharge around Robinson, nor could words of criticism be uttered in his presence.

Did it ever occur to the gullible New Labour apparatchiks to find out anything about Robinson's past? Apparently not. History was anathema to Tony, who made constant reference to 'the bad old days'. What mattered was the present and pious fervour, and how much money there was to back it up. No one actively probed Robinson's business record, believing his wealth's origins lay in industry, nor questioned his probity, his poor grasp of the many aspects of the financial and industrial world. Before his wedding in 2000, Robinson invited Gordon Brown (who accepted) 'to join his holiday party in Cape Cod, generously paying many of Brown's personal bills. Money was the passport to fulfil his, Robinson's, ambition of ministerial office' (Tom Bower, *The Paymaster*).

Events in Robinson's early months in office came to a head with the Ecclestone affair, about which Tony had misled the public by saying he had rejected a second donation from the Formula 1 boss, Bernie Ecclestone, while not admitting the first. (Ecclestone had visited Downing Street when Tony confirmed to him that the long-planned sponsorship ban on tobacco advertising in sport had been amended to exempt Formula 1.) This remained in force for a while although five days before Tony's climb-down, Ecclestone admitted he had donated £1 million to New Labour before the election (with promise of more, which had been obtained through the intercession of Lord Levy).

Tony, 'purer than pure', refusing to admit any wrongdoing, then delivered his master hoodwink act: 'I think that most people who have dealt with me think I'm a pretty straight sort of guy.' (Pause for pout.) 'And I am.'

Peter Mandelson subsequently pointed out the main inference to be drawn from the Ecclestone affair. 'Honesty', he told a conference, 'is the first principle of good communications . . . and the purpose of communications is not to stall or to hide but to put in context and to explain.' But Ecclestone emerged the winner: he got the delay over the ban he wanted, he had his money returned and he strengthened his position.

Robinson's real crime, wrote the pro-Blair Peter Riddell in the *Times*, was 'being a successful businessman and a multi-millionaire who is a member of a Labour government'. There was a lot of unconscious double irony in this statement, especially in the following year as ugly revelation mounted on ugly revelation ('He has nothing to hide,' said Brown's treasury aide and chief publicist, Charlie Whelan). Tony and Cherie felt, that, as a result of this generous provider of funds for their private office now increasingly mired in accusations of sleaze, they would have to sacrifice their third free holiday in Tuscany at Robinson's villa.

Robinson hastily convened a Tuscan neighbour, Prince Girolamo Strozzi, to lend the Blair family his own villa. Tony was by now called in the Italian press '*lo scroccone*', the scrounger, while a priest in a nearby village complained that he, an Anglican, took communion in a nearby church. According to Robinson's biographer, 'Blair accepted without apparently expressing concern about his host's inconvenience.'

On 23 December 1998, Downing Street forced both Robinson and Mandelson to resign over Robinson's loan of £373,000 to Mandelson without interest or plan for repayment. This was the end, after nineteen months in office, of Tony's Osric: 'I have done nothing wrong in any of these areas,' were his last ministerial words, but in the following years more allegations of his concealment were to emerge. In 2000 Robinson's autobiography, *The Unconventional Minister*, which the government tried hard to persuade him not to publish, compounded his decline. Tony vouched for him as a 'high-calibre businessman', a 'brilliant minister . . . who had done everything according to the rules'. Of course, he had been unfairly hounded by the press. A critic wrote of *The Unconventional Minister*, 'Every jilted courtier has a poisoned dart to shoot, and he has now shot his.'

We can all claim to have commitments to different kinds of truth according to what we are up to, thereby explaining our attachment to them. Nietzsche leads us to these astonishing New Labour justifications: 'Our job is to create the truth' (Peter Mandelson); 'I am the Prime Minister and I don't lie' (Tony Blair, November 2001); 'I only know what I believe' (Tony Blair, September 2004). We don't need to be reminded what Nietzsche's fantasy of superman and his fantasy of superman power led to in the twentieth century.

Part III

1999–2002

23

The government of appearances

When Parties in a State are violent, he offered a wonderful
Contrivance to reconcile them. The method is this: You take an
Hundred Leaders of each Party; you dispose them into Couples of
such whose Heads are nearest of a Size; then let two nice Operators
saw off the *Occiput* of each couple at the same Time, in such a Manner
that the Brain may be equally divided. Let the *Occiputs*, thus cut off,
be interchanged, applying each to the Head of his opponent Party-
man.

Jonathan Swift, 'A Voyage to Laputa', *Gulliver's Travels*

In its run of mistakes, the Tory Party, after John Major's defeat by Tony, had
chosen William Hague, the wrong leader for the wrong reasons, or rather it
had chosen him under the misapprehension that he could prove a mimetic
rival, a youthful counter-image to Tony. Again, false advertising standards
prevailed: your rival has a successful product (i.e. Tony); to compete you
have to choose one as near as possible, that is to say, one just as young and
youthful.

The natural leader the party should have chosen was Kenneth Clarke, the
successful Chancellor of Major's last agonised days. But he came with too
much baggage, rather as Churchill had carried in the mid-1930s; pro-
European by instinct, he was rebarbative, spoke his mind, made enemies
and had the huge disadvantage of being reasonably honest. He also, God
forbid, smoked – leaving the aroma of stale cigar smoke behind in the flat of
No. 11, now occupied by Cherie and Tony. He was a political heavyweight,
and heavyweights could never be pop stars.

The electorate in those early years smooched along with Tony, cheek to cheek, eyes closed, in a slow, lazy foxtrot, mesmerised by the verbless sentences, and enjoying applause from the subservient media. The country still reaped the rewards of a buoyant Tory economy and the bonanza of North Sea oil and gas, to the management of which Gordon Brown applied discipline and a hawk-like control of detail. With one or two exceptions that remained effective in their long-term impact – the Good Friday agreement of 1998 in Northern Ireland, Brown's decision not to join in the launch of the euro in 1999 (and, by his allocation of public spending, Gordon had from Tony control of virtually the whole domestic front) – during Tony's first term, the Labour Party and public opinion were in a state of continual reverie.

The pressure on the media to conform was absolute. 'You were told', Peter Oborne says, 'you were being chippy and Tory if you said anything against him . . . Professionally it was impossible to operate if you thought Blair was less than brilliant. If you knocked Blair you were a griping old Tory.' This was the high-water mark of the press and public's complicity with the Blairs' mutual narcissism, within which they were now firmly imprisoned. It seemed they could be forgiven anything that went wrong – the Ecclestone scandal, the fiasco of the Millennium Dome – because the dynamic, youthful image prevailed, with its promise of regenerative policies.

Margaret Thatcher as Prime Minister had battled and succeeded in the face of three years of almost constant opposition, mainly in her own party, because of the residual male fear of a woman being in charge. But in addition, the right, especially the extreme right, tends to a pessimistic view of human nature, seeing it as flawed and limited. It believes, to varying extents, that 'degree', rank, a sense of hierarchy, as preserved in rules, gradations, institutions, are what restrain humankind from anarchy and crime. It suspects change and grand schemes and the alterations of society to fit a theoretical ideal. This is what conservatism is, and means, and the Tory Party should stick to it.

Tony's bromide 'I want this country to be young again' overlooked the biological shortcoming of youth: lack of experience. The archetypical 'youthful' American President, John F. Kennedy, had taken the United States into the Vietnam War; the 'New Democrat' Bill Clinton, who embodied the empty myth, resounding with false power, that if you overcome early obstacles you are somehow inevitably hallowed and able to lead, by his manipulative skill destroyed trust in democratic institutions. The average age of Attlee's 1945–51 government – the best since the Second World War, it could be argued, especially if you were a committed socialist – was sixty-three and a half. Whether you loved or hated its policies the Attlee government was consistently principled and exemplary in conduct and style, while sleaze was at an all-time minimum.

Tony penned his own 'globalised' recommendations on 21 September 1998, a Fabian Society pamphlet entitled *The Third Way: New Politics for the New Century*. But

> if the Holy Grail had indeed been located by the Clintons, why was Blair still searching for it? In the Fabian pamphlet he insisted that 'our work is at an early stage'. This might explain the lack of detail in some of his preliminary findings. 'The arts and the creative industries should be part of our common culture . . . Education is not enough . . . We support the efforts of peacemakers and peacekeepers abroad as an extension of our mission at home.' Who would have guessed it? Blair also revealed that the Third Way was 'vibrant' and 'passionate', rather like Bill Clinton's libido, but also 'flexible' and 'innovative', like Clinton's definition of sexual relations. It rejected 'selfishness' and 'inefficiency', preferring nice things to nasty things. (Francis Wheen, *How Mumbo-Jumbo Conquered the World*)

Much of this language fluttered down from the clouds of two professor mentors, Anthony Giddens of the London School of Economics and John Gray of Jesus College, Cambridge, who were still considered to be among the main intellectual stimulators of New Labour. 'There are claims that it is unprincipled,' Blair admitted. 'But I believe that a critical dimension of the Third Way is that policies flow from values, not vice versa.'

The great British public, happily indifferent by now, still believed it had a principled man in charge, just as it swallowed fast foods by the container-load, enjoyed the Thatcher boom economy, began to watch reality TV and fell for Jordan's tits as it had fallen for Diana Spencer's sly and baleful glances. Later on the day when he published *The Third Way*, according to

Wheen, Tony jetted off to New York on Concorde – the 'only acceptable method of transport for Tertiary Voyagers – to participate in a multi-lateral workfest on this fashionable but enigmatic catchphrase'.

*

One crucial but overlooked aspect of the collapse of the Millennium Dome project was the degree to which it embodied Tony's basic philosophy of life. Tony neatly sidestepped his responsibility for the failure, which had had his personal endorsement (he said he would be tested by his son Euan's response – and not surprisingly, incidentally, we never heard what Euan's response was), by passing the 'poisoned chalice' to his trusty standby, Lord Falconer, as the 'lightning conductor'. A great shrugger-off, Falconer, who belonged to no particular faction, kept buoyancy and good humour flowing through any project to which he was attached. But while Tony could let Falconer take the flak, which he was more than capable of weathering, the core belief, or attachment, remained in Tony.

This was the dedication to what now could be summed up for the first time under the ugly word 'undifferentiationism'. Tony was committing himself to the principle of removing all difference, all distinguishing features, from every possible aspect of social or political life. Odd that it should be so, but this tendency to 'level down' had the same drive of scientific and rationalist justifications as the state religion of the former Soviet bloc. What Tony had embarked on in that first term of government is perfectly summed up by Václav Havel, the playwright and first President of the Czech Republic, in his description of a communist totalitarian government of appearances: 'a mere ritual, a formal language deprived of contact with reality and transformed into a system of ritual signs that replace reality with pseudo-reality'. The idea was that this would recharge the batteries when they went flat. What could be more of a symbol of soulless culture than the Millennium Dome, with its Benthamite promises for the greatest ('the greatest happiness of the greatest number'), or 'the greatest monument to [Falconer's] oldest friend's hubris' (Morgan)? Although Piers Morgan said the Dome had become a 'white elephant' – most likely because at its opening Fleet Street editors were kept waiting too long at Stratford station drinking warm wine – the vacuous space ended as more of a rogue elephant for vain salvage attempts by French managers; it also led to the second demise of Mandelson. In late January 2001, now reinstated as Northern Ireland Secretary, he was in trouble again, for his attempts at pressurising the Home Office to fix a passport for Srichand Hinduja, who with his brother had financed the Dome. Alastair Campbell told Morgan, 'He didn't make any calls himself, he's sure about that, so it's not a problem.' Two days later, when it came out he had made a call, he had to resign, denouncing the media as he did so in a wonderful dash for the moral high ground. 'I want to remove myself from the countless stories of controversy, feuds and divisions and all the rest,' he commented suavely. This will be the end of him, mused Morgan, because 'nobody can come back from two ministerial resignations'. But he reckoned without Macavity Blair, who could defy every human law – especially the law of [political] gravity, and who needed to keep the special 'double' close to the heart of his government.

24

Some fallen idols

Within the hollow crown
That rounds the mortal temples of a king
Keeps Death his court; and there the antic sits,
Scoffing his state and grinning at his pomp;
Allowing him a breath, a little scene.

William Shakespeare, *Richard II*

Mo Mowlam, one of the first 'Blair babes' to be appointed to high office, said, 'I enjoy sex,' and talked about it a lot, told blue jokes, didn't want children and once, when pregnant, had an abortion. Her feistiness endeared her to Americans and, appointed as Northern Ireland Secretary in 1997, she helped move forward the peace process begun by John Major and enthusiastically continued by Tony, in which Jonathan Powell's contribution ranked highly. Her drinking exploits with the Republican leadership in Northern Ireland have been well documented, but, as the figurehead of the progress made, she became the personification of hope for peace among the people themselves.

A lust for power can apply to all politicians, but in Mo's case this led her to become the most popular figure in the first Blair term, for at the party conference in 1999 the delegates gave her a two-minute standing ovation right in the middle of Tony's conference speech when he called her 'our Mo': from then on her fate was sealed. No one upstaged Superman, no one could receive such acclaim and survive for long. No doubt Cherie was whispering in his ear as Tony began to make up his mind that she had to go, and now talked directly to Northern Ireland leaders behind her back.

Crucially, Mo had also become more popular in America than Tony, with Madeleine Albright, Bill Clinton's Secretary of State, declaring 'she was too popular for her own good'. The popularity went to her head. While Mo quoted Barbara Castle ('beloved of the party'), who said about her work in Northern Ireland, 'I'm very pro-Mo. If it hadn't been for Mo, there wouldn't have been a Good Friday agreement,' she would seem often a prisoner of her own lusty rhetoric, so she offended one half of the peace process. But her real sin, in terms of Tony and Cherie, was that she maintained her popularity outside the New Labour court. Cherie, she said, was not her 'kind of soulmate', and although 'Cherie and I chat amicably when our paths cross at social events . . . we are not of the same social circle and have never got to know each other'. She added, significantly, 'I feel I know enough lawyers.'

In the peace process, the dyadic influence of Cherie and Tony was strong, for it also owed a great deal to Cherie's Catholic sympathies and her own early experience of the Liverpool sectarian divide. Later Mo blamed Peter Mandelson for wrecking her career by putting pressure on Tony to give him her Northern Ireland post. 'Well, I'm sorry she feels that way,' the Prince of Darkness responded when taxed to answer by Piers Morgan. 'Mo thinks everyone was out to get her, but the truth is that she had gone as far as she could in Northern Ireland and it needed some fresh impetus.'

Morgan then asked, 'Did you knife her, then?'

'"Oh, Piers, please. I don't knife anybody." And with that he carved expertly into his chicken.'

The much-loved Mo Mowlam died on 19 August 2005.

*

While she bestrode the theatre and film worlds as a commanding and powerful goddess with her two Oscar-winning performances in *Women in Love* and *A Touch of Class*, what impelled Glenda Jackson into politics, as Tony's second female icon, was anger, again an emotion or passion, mainly directed at Margaret Thatcher.

As a celebrity fledgling politician, a protégée of Neil and Glenys Kinnock, who were her neighbours, Jackson had little trouble being selected as the Labour candidate for Hampstead & Highgate in 1992. She had passed the Liverpool test, delighting Cherie by playing Elizabeth I on TV in the 1970s with a Scouse accent. When Tony became leader she stuck so close to the New Labour party line she was accused of sycophancy. However, after four years in Parliament, on the eve of the 1996 Labour Party conference, the last in opposition, she was voted one of the least impressive MPs of their intake by 100 MPs, along with Sebastian Coe. But in spite of Jackson's poor maiden speech and rating as a 'sour-faced Commons performer, ill at ease pressing flesh', Tony, always with an eye to fame and celebrity – Glenda was an icon on two counts – made her shadow spokesperson for transport, and then junior minister.

But the House of Commons, under Tony's regime, couldn't have been a more inopportune place for Glenda, a deeply theoretical and committed socialist. Her growing disillusionment with fame, celebrity and money militated gratingly against Cherie and Tony's governing ethos. Surrounded by glamorous Blair babes, but in contrast to them, she hated wearing make-up and refused to look starry-eyed. She did something else which to Cherie was unforgivable: she smoked forty cigarettes a day and so became known as the 'Queen of Fags', or the 'Fag-Hag' – and was even, along with Nicky Blair and Stephen Fry, championed by Forest, the smokers' rights group. Clearly she was too differentiated from political correctness, although an ardent feminist, to survive.

Tony snubbed Glenda on a visit to London Underground's HQ, then sidelined her into becoming a potential candidate as mayor of London. To his fury, the position was subsequently won by Ken Livingstone, standing as an independent after being expelled from the Labour Party. (Tony changes his tune in 2007, blithely proclaiming on television, 'I always said Ken would make a great mayor.') In her nomination campaign she condemned local nudity in Hampstead, even when her own naked screen frolics had reached mythological proportions. 'She probably still looks much nicer in the nude than the other candidates, but voters must keep their heads and not get carried away,' cracked A. N. Wilson. She failed to win the nomination. 'I have no friends here – in the Commons,' she said in 1999. Her real problem was that she wanted to be taken seriously as a politician, but the days when this had happened were now in the past. Tony and Cherie's friends by 1999 were bound together simply by fame and money.

She survived as an MP all through Tony's ten years on a plateau of angry integrity. What she thought and expressed about Tony was roughly the same as what she had thought and said about Thatcher. Of course, it goes without saying she now found Westminster far bitchier than the Royal Shakespeare Company. Glenda failed lamentably just where Tony succeeded, so triumphantly, by translating theory into skilful, political tactics and being both a good orator and good actor. The intellectual and tactical sides of him were never at odds.

*

The third fallen idol was Estelle Morris, whom Tony made Education Secretary when he moved David Blunkett to the Home Office in August 2001. The daughter and niece of former MPs, her background was political, which dominated her life. Never much good at academic work, she failed her A-levels at Whalley Range High School, a grammar school in Manchester, but was hockey mad. Later she taught history at Sidney Stringer School in Coventry, during which time she informed one of her sixth-form pupils, Jojar Dhinsa, that he would achieve nothing. He went on to become a multi-millionaire.

Morris was elected MP for Birmingham Yardley in 1992. While in opposition she was part of a team which proposed removing the charitable status of public schools – until Tony told her firmly to drop the idea: 'She was sending out the wrong message.' She obeyed – as the first rule of unquestioning loyalty to New Labour orthodoxy.

When Morris was appointed Education Secretary, she told the *Mirror* she had not read a book from cover to cover for three years. Ungrammatical in her use of personal pronouns, she used 'me' instead of 'I' or 'my', and made such resounding war cries such as 'comprehensive isn't about sameness, you can smell its differentness'. In pursuit of this 'differentness', she displayed New Labour's irrational attachment to ideas which would never work, but sounded as if they could. There was much Cherie-and-Tony thinking behind her view that the teaching profession had to be remodelled, while teachers would no longer pass on the core beliefs of history and society: pupils would decide their own values, while every child should have his or her own individualised lesson plan. 'Skills', 'access' and 'equality' would support the traditional education culture, while computers would enable children to 'take ownership of their learning and shape the curriculum round their individual needs'. But as with much else in the Blair world, targets pledged were not met: questioned in October 2001 by the Commons Education Select Committee about an earlier pledge she had made that she would go if they were not met by 2002, Estelle denied that she said it. She claimed she had never made such a pledge.

Her fall came when she over-reacted to and lamentably mismanaged an A-level crisis which was largely of her own making, after she had told the Qualifications and Curriculum Authority to instruct examining boards to 'come up with the results that the government would find acceptable'. The sacking of Sir William Stubbs as scapegoat led to his subsequent win in seeking compensation for his unfair dismissal.

In his account, Stubbs revealed how in shifting the blame onto him for the marking and results crisis, which was hugely exaggerated, Morris capitulated and ceded the initiative to others, but when after avoiding Stubbs, but then, finally, meeting him – in her usual timid style by then 'surrounded by policy advisers, progress chasers, blue-sky thinkers and delivery czars' – she told him, as Stubbs said, 'If I were to resign she would speak generously of my work . . . if I did not, she would dismiss me. It felt very much like a threat.' Subsequently Stubbs said, 'I felt great personal anguish as a result of the humiliating way I had been treated, especially since I had been so clearly vindicated' (*Sunday Times*, 27 October 2002). This was a classic Cherie-and-Tony blame-shifting procedure.

But nothing defined the new confessional style championed by No. 10 so well as Morris's resignation after this crisis, on 24 October 2002. Her supporters said that she had not enjoyed being the 'ruthless axe-woman' and that the storm caused her sleepless nights, emotionally drained her and led to that new chestnut in the political excuse manual, agonised body language, such as twisting her legs beneath the table. She was, she confessed, out of her depth in running a huge department, and as she told Tony in her resignation letter, lacking in effectiveness in dealing both with the job and with the media. 'If being useless', wrote Libby Purves a few days after this, 'was a valid reason for ministers to resign, what on earth is Lord Falconer (who is also unelected) still hanging around for, on the far side of the Millennium debacle? Or, indeed, half a dozen others at various levels of government.'

'I hold you in the highest regard . . . You can be very proud of your work,' Tony answered the letter of resignation. Later, Estelle made her claim to belong to the victim culture (the form taken by negative narcissism), saying that had she stayed on she 'would have sacrificed the very parts that drive her as a politician. I do get hurt by criticism, and I don't want to stop getting hurt by it because the minute it's like water off a duck's back I think you have closed your feelings in a lot of other areas of your life as well.' She excused herself by saying she had backed the 'relentless pressure on politicians to conceal their humanity and seek to eliminate all error and uncertainty' and gave herself the credit for her own humanity and her feminism. 'Maybe at the final judgment it will be seen that I actually furthered the cause of women because I was not prepared to play the game. I could have played it like a man to further my career, but in the end I said, sod it.'

So ultimately, as did Cherie and Tony, she insisted that 'the deference culture is dead' – meaning the deference culture out there. She might have added the one big exception: the deference culture towards Cherie and Tony.

25

The death of the cardinal

> A tyrant must put on the appearance of uncommon devotion to religion . . . Subjects are less apprehensive of illegal treatment from a ruler they consider god-fearing and pious. On the other hand, they do less easily move against him, believing he has the gods on his side.
>
> Aristotle

Most people still disavow the influence of religion in political life, but the ten years of the Blairs in Downing Street saw the issues of belief, especially that of Tony and Cherie, become of central consequence, even to the extent of influencing the most important decisions and affecting the outcome of elections.

One of the first actions of Tony and Cherie after the 1997 election had been to invite Hans Küng, the Roman Catholic dissident, to a Downing Street reception at the Reform Club. While the local priest near Chequers discerned in Tony the seeds of a more traditional Catholic, it was most likely Cherie who saw herself as the liberal reformer and supporter of Küng, although Tony too expressed his admiration.

Küng, author of *On Being a Christian* among other works, had been an attractive intellectual figure for liberal and dissident Catholics since the Second Vatican Council of the early 1960s. A German colleague of Cardinal Joseph Ratzinger, who in 2005 was elected Pope Benedict XVI, Küng, handsome and articulate, became 'the first example of a new phenomenon in Catholic life – the dissenting theologian as an international media star' (George Weigel, *Witness to Hope*). He crossed swords with the Catholic hierarchy primarily over papal infallibility in the making of doctrinal decisions, which he did not hold to be true.

In 1979 the Congregation (then headed by Ratzinger) deprived Küng of his licence to teach Catholic theology because it believed that he undermined that doctrine of papal infallibility pronounced by the First Vatican Council in 1870. This withdrawal of his mandate to teach triggered worldwide outrage in which the Vatican was condemned for restricting academic freedom.

Küng's international media star charisma was naturally attractive to Tony and Cherie, who agreed with his views, but presumably ignored his crucial challenge to the Vatican. Küng had neither been excommunicated nor deprived of his functions as a priest. Even so, he cast doubts on the importance of papal infallibility, central to the Catholic faith. 'When this essential basis of faith is weakened or destroyed, the most elementary truths of our faith begin to collapse,' John Paul II had written in 1980 to the German bishops.

When Ratzinger was elected Pope Küng declared publicly that it 'comes as an enormous disappointment for all those who had hoped for a reformist and pastoral Pope'. He announced that he would be kindly allowing Benedict XVI a period of grace. Here's some of what Küng wrote in an open email to liberal Catholics:

> The name Benedict XVI leaves open the possibility for a more moderate policy. Let us therefore give him a chance . . . At every turn he faces tremendous tasks which have been piling up for a long time and which were not tackled by his predecessor:
>   • the active advancement of ecumenical relations between the Christian churches;
>   • the realisation of the collegiality of the Pope with the bishops and the decentralisation of church leadership, which is desired on all sides, in favour of a greater autonomy of the local churches;
>   • the guarantee of an equal footing for men and women in the church and the implementation of the full participation of women at all levels in the church.

This last generous invitation of Küng appealed especially to feminist Cherie.

149

*

Cherie had always stressed her Catholic roots and how she was drawn as a child into the church's social reading. Her cousin Father Paul, who had officiated at her wedding, was a distinguished priest, and a visit from John Heenan, Archbishop of Liverpool, who called on her grandpa, was to the girl Cherie, or so she says, 'like a god coming'. (Heenan went on to become Archbishop of Westminster and in 1965 was made a cardinal.) Religion had preceded socialism as a passion, and in spite of abandoning mass when she was at the LSE and in spite of being a feminist, she admitted to 'an enduring soft spot for the Virgin Mary. I believe there is no more important role in life than motherhood'. She also defended sending her children to Catholic schools, and wanted them brought up as Catholics. 'Part of it was inevitably wanting them to think like me, but also I didn't want them to be too comfortable,' she says. 'I wanted them to have that little bit of grit in their lives that is there in Catholicism, especially in its social teaching.'

Why 'inevitably'? Many fathers and mothers do not necessarily want their children to think as they do; it was perhaps also rather presumptuous on Cherie's part to think that Catholicism would stop them enjoying 'comfort' – does she imply that it stopped her? She values, as it later appeared in *Why I Am Still a Catholic*, a book of interviews edited by Peter Stanford, the proposition that there is no discrimination against Catholics in this country. But as a priest points out, 'one of the reasons we are free to practise our faith so openly in this country today has at least something to do with the modern spirit of religious indifference'. One might go further and say that anti-Catholicism is one of the main areas into which the redirected aggression of an unhappy society can be freely channelled: 'You know,' writes Tom Clancy, 'Catholicism is the last respectable prejudice. You can't hate black people any more of course, and you can't hate homosexuality any more, but you can hate all the Catholics you want.'

Even before her move to No. 10, which brought her, as she put it in the book, 'my unique perspective on the Catholic faith within the Establishment', Cherie had begun cultivating Cardinal Basil Hume, Archbishop of Westminster from 1976 until his death in 1999, and as such the head of 'her' church. She suggested to Tony that in the run-up to the 1997 election he should praise the English and Welsh bishops' pre-election statement *The Common Good*, which called abortion on demand 'one of the great scandals of our time'. The whole statement itself – the abortion comment notwith-standing – gave more or less blanket approval to New Labour aims, and never directly confronted the abortion issue in the way the Scottish Cardinal Winning did, just before the 1997 election, promising financial assistance to any woman of whatever race or belief who would have her baby instead of aborting it.

Tony, as in so many of his ethical beliefs, tried to have his cake and eat it; he voted for abortion and the woman's 'right to freedom' by lowering the limits alongside his socialist brethren, but privately he let it be known as a religious believer, that he was against abortion. He also later, in December 2004, publicly supported the Mental Incapacity Bill, which was condemned by priests as 'against basic moral order' in prescribing for a dying person denial of food and water. But he then failed to vote on it, excusing himself with, 'Well, I do not vote on some measures.' Similarly when it came to the ethical problems caused by hybrid stem-cell research using human embryos in 2006–7, he caved in to the powerful bioscience lobby (Labour was heavily in the red) but refused to meet religious leaders to hear their views (could it be that he knew that they had no money?). He knew the public mood, in which sliding or relative principles and rules about 'situational ethics', so skilfully and sensitively demolished by Karol Wojtyła in his early philosophical writings, had become the norm.

Hume distanced himself from Tony's widely publicised vote in favour of abortion, but, in what might be deemed an object lesson in pusillanimous leadership (what even Hume's biographer, Anthony Howard, calls 'namby-pamby toffs' talk'), he wrote to Tony a few months after his election:

> My message to Tony Blair would be this. You are an honest man and you see things clearly. I would have thought that you should give leadership within your party and try to convince them that abortion is wrong and that we ought, as a nation, to do something about it.

Leaving aside the naivety and the misjudgement of Tony's character, this was not the kind of talk of someone who could inspire a full-blooded young man to become a Catholic priest.

While the majority of the Catholic bishops were, pro-life issues apart, well to the left of *Guardian* editorials, according to a highly placed Catholic source, and with one exception voted for Tony, Hume himself never much responded on a personal level to Tony and Cherie, and clashed notably with Tony over his taking communion in his local Catholic church. During his cardinalate as many as six approaches were made to Hume to take a seat in the House of Lords but he turned them all down, stating 'it was a boring place' and 'I can say much more outside'. One of his Westminster clergy claimed that he would accept – but only on his own condition, namely that he be made a hereditary duke, for as he was of 'the royal blood of Christ' he should be placed in seniority before the Archbishop of Canterbury, whom he would thereby outrank.

Perhaps this came from his wicked sense of humour, and perhaps he turned down the offers not wishing to confuse in his own mind Christ with Caesar (canon law expressly forbids priests to take part in making secular legislation, although this seems a feeble excuse – a Catholic bishop could voice his opinions and abstain from voting). Declining to sit in the House of Lords could be taken as another sign of weak leadership and of remaining an outsider in a country whose statute book still contained proscriptive anti-Catholic laws. This position has been reversed by Hume's successor, Cardinal Cormac Murphy-O'Connor, who says Hume changed his mind at the end of his life, while Murphy-O'Connor states he would like to be the first British Catholic prelate to take up political office since the reign of Elizabeth I.

One such anti-Catholic law, the Act of Settlement, stipulated that no member of the Royal Family who married a Catholic could become sovereign, for fear the heir to the throne might be raised a Catholic, and no sovereign already crowned could marry a Catholic. When Cardinal Thomas Winning, the primate of Scotland, attacked Tony over a letter he wrote saying there was no need to review this, Tony responded that 'the one thing that made him see red was f— prelates getting involved in politics and pretending it was nothing to do with politics' (Lance Price, *The Spin Doctor's Diary*). Blair, said Price, was under the impression that the Act simply stopped Catholics ascending to the throne – not a problem in Blair's view, because all the Royal Family were Protestants.

But also, according to the *Times* (October 2004), 'The Catholic Relief Act of 1829, Section 17, asserts that no Catholic can offer counsel to the monarch on an ecclesiastical matter . . . there is no such prohibition in law for some of the more obscure religious or bizarre cults on offer.' The *Times* calls this discrimination: 'Prince William could marry a Scientologist, a devotee of the Moonies, or a dogmatic Satanist . . . [But] were he to fall in love with a Catholic . . . either she would have to renounce her faith or he abandon his claim to the throne.' When he came to being challenged in early 2007 Tony told the Commons Liaison Committee, 'When we come to talk about the ten-year legacy [his own] we can pitch that out as a major omission'; in the same sarcastic tone he went on, 'I was just thinking that it might be something for my successor really. It is a useful one to leave around.' The irony here is that Tony's government has passed a law against discrimination on the basis of religion, while it still has a law in place which discriminates on that very basis. It was also still forbidden to carry the Catholic Eucharist in a procession in a public place – as it was similarly in 1976 in Poland under Communist rule.

In his biography it suited Anthony Howard to exalt the timid, liberal Hume, with his appeal to the Catholic elite but not to the masses at large, at the expense of the 'stern Roman traditionalist' Cardinal Ratzinger, who was in charge of doctrinal matters. Elsewhere in his book Howard condemns Ratzinger's 'insensitivity'. That might be a matter of opinion, but he made a serious mistake when he states, 'During the last quarter of the last century the decline in the number of practising Roman Catholics in Britain was remarkable and remorseless.'

This was simply not true. According to Gordon Heald in 'The Soul of Britain', his survey for the *Tablet* and Nottingham University of June 2000, which formed the basis of nine BBC1 programmes, and which Howard uses as his authority and source for reliable figures elsewhere in his book, the Church of England saw the biggest decline in membership from 1957, from 55 per cent to 25 per cent, while practising 'Catholics have remained fairly constant since 1957 at 9 per cent'. Heald continues that churchgoing of all denominations had kept constant over the previous twenty years, with 23 per cent attending a service. The decline in the membership of political parties is much more striking: the Conservatives had 2.8 million paid-up members in the early 1950s but now have only 250,000, while Labour's figures were, and are, commensurate.

Liberal 'sensitivists' in the English Catholic Church to some extent enjoyed a field day under Hume and they were increasingly forming a conspiracy to fend off early 21st-century attempts to revert to more conservative and lasting Catholic traditions. They found natural allies in Cherie and Tony. Now, Hume had said firmly about the Catholic faith that you can't 'take it à la carte'. Cherie and Tony did just this. They were the perfect embodiment of 'pick 'n' mix', liberal Catholic sensitivists. Their Catholic faith, their cultivation of the highly popular Hume, and then especially of Pope John Paul II, is curiously revealing of their inner hearts, states of mind and souls in a way that has hardly ever been explored, although 'the God factor' has provoked extreme reactions and comment. Senior Conservative politicians accused Hume of siding with the Labour Party and like most liberal Catholics he approved of its social policies. Cherie always insisted she and Tony had a good relationship with the cardinal, but was this really the case?

Most likely it was Cherie who initiated the call from 10 Downing Street to request a visit some two or three days before he died from cancer at the Hospital of St John and St Elizabeth in north London. Somewhat reluctantly ('It's not a question of what I *want* to do, it's a question of what I *ought* to do,' Howard quotes Hume as responding) the cardinal assented. Cherie told a friend that she, Tony and the cardinal held a long conversation (twenty minutes) around his bedside on the meaning of the Lord's Prayer.

By then Hume could not wait for the relief of death. When Timothy Wright, the Abbot of Ampleforth, had heard Hume was dying he told him, 'That's brilliant news, I wish I was coming with you.' The cardinal was hugely relieved. 'Thank you, Timothy,' he told his old friend. 'Everyone else just bursts into tears.'

According to a MORI poll after the 2005 general election conducted by the *Tablet*, Labour won the popular vote by just three percentage points, with a 36 per cent share, while the Conservatives had 33 per cent and the Liberal Democrats 23 per cent. But 'had no Catholics voted,' ran the summary, 'the

Tories would have secured a knife-edge 35 per cent to 34 per cent lead in the popular vote, depriving Tony Blair of a popular mandate.' The Catholic vote was higher than at the 1997 election: 'Catholic loyalty to Tony Blair is in distinct contrast to the attitudes of the rest of the public.'

26

Love is like a cigarette

And when it slips,
From your fingertips,
There is nothing for you to forget,
Oh, love is like a cigarette.

Popular song of the 1920s

Cherie conceived her and Tony's fourth child on their Tuscan holiday in 1999, and in spite of the protestations of this very private pair, who claimed they were so sensitive to any child's exposure in the media, Max Clifford soon heard of it and sold 'the secret' for £50,000 to the *Daily Mirror*. Alastair Campbell, rung by Piers Morgan for confirmation, said they were relaxed about the exclusive, but several hours later contacted Morgan to say Rebekah Wade also had the story. Campbell denied Downing Street had told the *Sun*, saying to Morgan, 'Rebekah got word that Cherie was seriously ill and phoned her at the No. 10 flat and put it to her. Cherie didn't think she could lie, so felt compelled to tell her the truth. I'm really sorry, but we can't lie to papers about stuff like this.'

Later Tony himself phoned Morgan, trying rather unsuccessfully to placate him and to back up Campbell. 'I'm only doing this', he told Morgan, 'because I don't want you to think we have been playing politics with our baby, because we would never do that or allow anyone to do that.' But that is just what Tony and Cherie did. Privacy is as privacy does (although the view of the press has always been, largely, as one editor famously said, 'if the public is interested, then it's in the public interest'). But should a Prime Minister ever embroil himself in this way? Later Fiona Millar gave the lie to both Campbell and Tony, telling Morgan that 'Cherie just felt she had no choice [about giving the story to Wade]. She didn't want her pregnancy used as some commercial tool.' About this time, the Tory MP John Bercow said she was like Lady Macbeth and certainly we see something of this in her control of the weaker Tony, insisting to aides, for example over a mooted trip to the Sedgefield constituency to visit hospitals and schools, that he 'shouldn't go into A&E because he's a bit squeamish', and that he 'doesn't like staying in hotels'.

Whether or not caused by the new pregnancy, a resounding insert of truth enters the narrative at this time. As now (it never changes) the UK's rate of teenage pregnancy was the highest in western Europe. Tony, shocked by the cases of two pregnant twelve-year-olds in South Yorkshire, called for the re-creation of a 'national moral purpose'. The Home Secretary, Jack Straw, demanded that councils make more use of curfews for unruly youngsters and implement the laws against bad social behaviour. David Blunkett, Education Secretary, ordered a complete recasting of the national curriculum guide-lines for health, personal and social lessons in school which the year before had given teachers the wrong idea, spreading the message that single parenthood and gay relationships had the same status as marriage. He directed that all 11–14-year-olds 'should be taught about the importance of marriage for family life and bringing up children'. He told the media that the government had to hold to a sense of moral purpose or it would be working in a 'vacuum'. Cherie's pregnancy had a strong impact.

Early on Cherie had said she was planning a Caesarean, which was how Kathryn had been born. When the evolution and IVF guru Lord Winston unwittingly revealed this admission, and that the hospital would be the Chelsea and Westminster, he lost his membership of the inner circle. In fact Cherie in the end bravely decided on the opposite, a natural birth.

But there was little that was Lady Macbeth-ish about her in January 2000, her first day as a recorder, when she was in the papers after having to pay a £10 on-the-spot-fine at Blackfriars station for travelling on the train without a valid ticket. Her excuse was that, having just returned from Portugal, she only had escudos in her pocket. Downing Street said, 'Mrs Blair could not buy a ticket because the Blackfriars ticket office was closed and she did not have enough cash to use a machine, which did not take credit cards.' The statement added, 'She is an upstanding citizen. These things happen.' She clearly thought she never should have been fined. Time and again, in such small matters, she was to suspend the morality which underpinned the law, and which put in question whether she would ever be allowed to become a full-time judge.

Three days before she gave birth to Leo, Cherie was in cab-rank action on behalf of the TUC, putting the case against Tony's government plans for parental leave, insisting on speaking on her feet for three hours. Whether or not this can be considered an example of pregnancy as a commercial tool, the judgment went in her favour.

Nor was she much like Lady Macbeth later, when in the protracted throes of natural childbirth with Tony present, she suffered terrible pain. He was tormented, terrified that something was going wrong. Later Cherie was to insist he took two weeks' paternity leave.

'I don't want it to be spin,' the PM told Lance Price, one of No. 10's press aides. On 21 May 2000 at 12.25 a.m., after nearly twelve hours of labour, baby Leo was finally born, weighing 6 pounds 11 ounces. 'It was a nightmare,' Tony told an insider. 'I never want to go through that again.' The *Mail on Sunday* devoted seven pages to the event. The ensuing polls boost halted the government's decline in popularity as a consequence of crime and NHS issues: this was burying bad news in birth, and here the press took the initiative. The Blairs happily posed for the photographer Mary McCartney, daughter of Paul, helping once again to cement the pop music hierarchy of Soap Opera UK and Beatle UK: his aide gushed, 'TB very casual and hunky-dad-like on Saturday and was so Tony-ish . . . It could have been Rory Bremner.'

However, at the christening, as the press photographed Leo at St John Fisher Roman Catholic church in Sedgefield, they suddenly hoicked up the drawbridge, and Cherie complained to the Press Complaints Commission of intrusion. The PCC exonerated the press. The event was public, and Tony and Cherie's complaint could have carried weight only if the christening had been held in private.

The early months of Leo's life brought Tony close to the fatigue and reality of fatherhood and married existence, which was just what the country needed at this critical moment in his first term. The parallel reality of struggle and fatigue was completely lacking in the government of the United Kingdom, but at least it could be said that Cherie imposed some reality, the birth of their fourth child, on Tony's airy nothings. Here we can see dramatically the split into two people: domestic politics, by contrast, was the non-confrontational, almost abstract endeavour compared to rising in the night and changing nappies, and in his own natural tendency to avoid conflict and dissention, Tony made his control as smooth as possible, relying more and more on his 'sofa Cabinet', centralising power so that he would spend less time neutralising dissent (he left that to Campbell), and above all devolving responsibility to ministers on the difficult domestic fronts (health and education in particular). He would concentrate on the plum of foreign policy and particularly, whenever possible, in being out of the country to act a role on the international stage. The Kosovan war in the spring of 1999 had released in him that long-buried aggression that had lain dormant for so long, and had whetted his appetite for war if it had a moral justification, as this one had: the removal of Slobodan Milošević from power. But now that this was over, on the whole he was back to just collecting and delivering the sound-bites and delivering the rousing speeches, at which he got better and better: he didn't do the detail.

*

Cherie left Downing Street for a well-deserved rest with Leo in Tuscany, and took Tony with her. Euan and the rest of the family were left behind. 'Mrs Blair may have considerable intelligence,' Leo Abse wrote at the time, 'but simpler mothers-to-be, not wrapped in themselves, not preening themselves on their own creativity, know how much attention during pregnancy and following the birth of their new baby must be focused on an existing child, lest he otherwise feel displaced and betrayed.' A few weeks later, in June Tony, too, found pressures mounting on him to such a degree that he delivered a ferocious attack at Tübingen University to the Global Ethics Foundation on the anti-social behaviour of young people.

Before he came to power he made a touching promise to Kathryn (see Chapter 38): 'I dream of a nation where as a parent I am less worried about you going out on your own, where crime does not breed insecurity and fear.' A short while before the Global Ethics speech the *Sun* and the *Times* published a leaked memo written by Blair, in which he said he believed the government was 'out of touch' with gut British instincts. Now back in his natural habitat on a platform he was staging his response, tuning in. To rapturous applause, and echoing his earlier promise of a crackdown on crime, he proposed to give the police powers to arrest young drunks and disturbers of the peace on the spot, march them off to cash machines and force them to withdraw £100. He was certainly playing to the gallery now, and the audience cheered, and as usual he won wide publicity back home, although it was not that popular with one young man who lived in Downing Street.

Almost straight after this speech, Euan Blair, aged sixteen, impelled by a predictable feeling of maternal neglect, possibly made worse by post-examination fatigue, left home, strolled the half-mile into the West End, and a few hours later was discovered drunk in Leicester Square by two women, lying close to a wall, and covered in vomit. Although Downing Street had an agreement with the press about covering private incidents involving the children, it now sanctioned the reports, which went into full detail. At first the media was in a quandary as to what angle they should take: as Adam Boulton of Sky News put it,

> You think to yourself, is this politically significant? What are the questions that are asked? How hard or self-righteous, or whatever, should you be? And you just have to take a judgement at that point because that's the nature of twenty-four hour news. I was one of the first people telling the story and I said, 'In the end, we've all been teenagers.'

Cherie watched the news on Sky in the British ambassador's home in Lisbon, and rang Tony, berating him for his neglect of Euan while she was away. The next night, on BBC1's *Question Time*, Tony had decided to face hostile questions. The first one asked, by a barrister called Christian Mole, was, 'Who should be dragged to the cash machine to pay the £100 fine, the father or the son?' Shocked and mumbling, almost in tears, Tony muttered, 'I guess that most of us at the age of sixteen have done things they regret. Not everyone has to see it the next day in the papers,' lapsing into incoherence next: 'I don't know what behaviour he did . . .'

Undoubtedly sincere, yet working the misery or poignancy angle, Tony won sympathy, as did Euan, who was deemed universally to be behaving in a normal way for his age. But this overlooked the important issue that Euan's drunkenness had first of all been a public act of rebellion against the family circumstances, the pressure caused by the birth of his brother, and his mother's handling of him during it. Second, Tony, unloading too the private aggression and feeling incurred from the family situation in his Tübingen speech, lacked insight to what he was doing, and as a result sacrificed his right to claim privacy in family matters. What happened in the domain of his family had a profound impact on his public policy and decisions, and on what he said. The two were inevitably intertwined and were to remain so.

In September 2000, before Cherie became fixated on her idea that the press, and especially the Rothermere stable of the *Daily Mail*, the *Mail on Sunday* and the *Evening Standard*, was on a 'mission to destroy us', she and Tony gave a private dinner party to court these papers. They invited Jonathan Rothermere, the proprietor, his wife and Paul Dacre, editor of the *Daily Mail*. In the course of the dinner, which was amicable and progressing smoothly, Cherie suddenly got up and left the table, only to return moments later carrying Leo. She sat down, proceeded to unbutton her dress and started to breast-feed Leo. The guests were shocked, while later a friend of the editor joked, 'Paul is still in recovery.' The episode found its way only too quickly into a daily newspaper. But if the episode is not extraordinary enough, it's surprising Tony took no action, perhaps saying to Cherie, 'I don't think this is appropriate,' even nudging her to take Leo out of the room to feed him. He could then perhaps have defused the situation with the throwaway line he was so good at, such as, 'Wonderful, isn't it, what women get up to these days.' We might imagine Michael Sheen or Hugh Grant playing the scene perfectly.

But who knows, by fracturing any potential rapprochement between herself and the Rothermere press, this little act of Booth defiance might significantly have changed the course of history. And where was Hazel during all this? We'd love to know what Tony's voice of 'absolute common sense' thought.

To cap this particular narrative motif, for Christmas 2000 Tony put himself, Cherie and Leo on his official card – prompting the loyal press aide to comment that it 'makes a bit of a monkey of our efforts up to now to stop people using pictures of the baby'. The *Times* floated this spiky observation: 'The last time the babe appeared on a Downing Street Christmas card, it was Jesus. This year it is Leo Blair.' On whose promotional insistence, we wonder, did Leo appear on the card?

In spite of the opportunity the new birth gave to the couple to spend more time at Chequers, Cherie, in contrast to Tony, hated the countryside, preferring, as she said, the smell and comfort of concrete. How anything natural to her was anathema should by now be clear. Or rather, it was truer to say that anything natural had to be wrapped up in magic and esoteric ritual to appeal. Not a trace of this distaste appears in *The Goldfish Bowl*, in which Denis Thatcher, the exemplary Downing Street spouse, is quoted as saying, 'I loved Chequers. I think it's a magnificent house and an ideal house to entertain in. And it's a lovely part of the world – Buckinghamshire was a new stamping area for me [did they mean "stomping ground"?].'

Canon Timothy Russ, the local priest, was a frequent invitee to the Tony and Cherie Chequers weekends. Here he met Tony Booth – 'a delightful man, right over the top' – whom he also called 'the kind of man who would give instinctively if asked, and one of the nicest men you've ever met'. On one family occasion at Christmas Tony Booth led a Bible reading and a silence for a dead friend: 'It was a moving, instinctive gesture,' says Timothy: for him Tony Booth was the kind of man who would say, 'I love God but I can't keep his commandments.' Both men enjoyed smoking, as had Charles de Gaulle, who, proud Frenchman though he was, smoked ninety Players Navy Cut a day, and Winston Churchill, two of the greatest world leaders of the twentieth century. Not far away, in Wootton Underwood, John Gielgud, now well over ninety, savoured his untipped Gauloises *noires*.

Cherie banned smoking in Chequers, so the priests and actors would have to go outside for a smoke. She was draconian in the way she imposed her ban: 'If she had her way, she would ban all smoking everywhere,' says the priest. When I asked if she ruled the roost, the reply was frank: 'There is no roost. When she comes to Chequers she is the mother who spends most of her morning doing her law work, and ignoring the children . . . "I must prove", she says to herself, "that I'm a lady who can follow her own career." ' Timothy found that Tony would be alone there over the weekends, often while Cherie was away working. He would give the priest a call and ask him over. But where were the children? 'They voted with their feet – never turned up.' He had the impression Tony was lonely.

Uninhibited in bravely expressing his opinions to the point of reproof by his superiors, Timothy would tell Tony that he was wrong in doing this and doing that. He once suggested, with Cherie present, that they ought to go to Blackpool instead of Tuscany for their holidays, but Cherie 'would not have any of that'. He asked Tony to go fishing with him in Scotland. He felt that Tony and Cherie were far too interested in wealth and believed that success first and foremost meant making money. Tony was unduly impressed by people who made a lot of money, for he would say to back up statements, 'I've met a lot of successful people.' One day he turned to Timothy, furious in the argument they were having. 'How much do you make?'

'Five hundred pounds a year.'

'Five hundred what?' stuttered Tony, aghast.

All the same, in these discussions, and their frequent exchanges of handwritten letters, the priest believes the Prime Minister is a genuinely modest person who aspires to be good and decent. If Timothy took him too severely to task, he wouldn't reply, but did on occasion – for example in the early days when someone wanted to paint his portrait – say, 'I'm worried about hubris.' Timothy told him he had made a moral surrender back when he had moved away from his belief in unilateral disarmament and changed his view on possessing a nuclear arsenal. Tony, he says, was genuinely proud of the continuing effort he made to obtain peace in Northern Ireland, and felt this should be considered his main achievement.

The intimacy and closeness of their contact is shown in the letters, Tony's scrawled in a regular, large, open hand – clearly the autograph of a confident and outgoing person. There is a frankness about them which is appealing too; they also demonstrate that the pair share a dislike for emails, text messages and mobile phones. 'I'm not into any of that,' Tony laughingly told the priest, showing his ink-stained fingers.

At the time there was a furore in the press criticising Tony's appointment of Ruth Kelly as Education Secretary, as she was known to be a member of Opus Dei. Tony asked Timothy, 'What is Opus Dei?'

'A rather strict organisation of the church,' the priest told him, and then added, 'General Franco had eleven members of Opus Dei in his government.'

'I've only got one – what's wrong with me?'

Timothy argued with Tony on the issue of stem-cell research, and the increase of the threshold for performing abortions from twenty to twenty-four weeks. This made Tony furious, but when later the priest, with the Blairs in church, delivered a sermon against the permissiveness of society, quoting the philosopher Giambattista Vico – 'as you get more secure you become unresponsive' – he could see that while Cherie dismissed it as arcane, ancient theory, 'Tony was looking very uncomfortable'.

When in October 2003 Tony went into Aylesbury Hospital, near Chequers, with a heart murmur, the priest was on the scene after the treatment. Tony told him that the nurse, when he entered the operating theatre, asked, 'Do you want the black box?' Timothy asked, 'Do you mean the black box which blows up the world?' Tony said yes. 'How utterly ridiculous!' said Timothy – and then: 'They both laughed at this.'

In 2004 the Vatican sent out a directive to its priests worldwide to tighten up respect for the liturgy, ruling that at the moment where the priest celebrating mass gives the sign of peace he shouldn't, as had become the fashion, race up and down the nave glad-handing his flock, but only give the sign of peace in the immediate vicinity of the sanctuary: this rightly, thought Timothy, brought the focus to bear on the blessed sacrament and the most solemn moment in the mass which was to follow. One Sunday at mass, Cherie, noticing the change in the priest's behaviour according to the tightening of the rules, came up afterwards: 'This is ecclesiastical fascism!' she berated him furiously. 'This is ecclesiastical fascism!'

Tony expressed his strong desire when he stepped down to become a deacon – and a Roman Catholic deacon at that, confirming the often speculated belief that he would convert to Roman Catholicism sometime in the future. 'Would this be possible?' he questioned Timothy, who told him, 'It usually takes two or three years.'

'The fact that I'm PM,' replied Tony, 'could this make a difference?'

But Tony's fast-tracking to deaconhood – was he thinking of following in John Paul II's footsteps? – wouldn't happen quite yet. 'If he was free from politics, do you think he would accept the authority of the Roman Catholic

Church?' I asked. Timothy is convinced he would. He is the male, he says; hierarchy and procedures fascinate him: 'He has a lot of potentiality for good,' he adds. 'He is still looking for the meaning in his life.' But for the time being he was, the priest emphasised, 'two different people'.

Although no longer seeing the Blairs, Timothy writes to Tony weekly, still sends him his sermons, which he says have coded messages to the Prime Minister. In a recent one he comments, 'The politically correct flow of information leads to a sort of alienated obedience . . . Repressed is *joie de vivre.*' When tightened security around Tony's person after the Iraq invasion made it impossible for the family to attend the local church, he would celebrate mass in the drawing room at Chequers. But for statements about Iraq, such as one in the *Times* – 'Tony Blair is a lazy thinker when it comes to ethical questions . . . He is quite heroic but I fear he might be doing the wrong thing' – he is in the end excluded from the Blair circle in favour of Father John, a ruddy-cheeked and jovial RAF chaplain who comes from Marham in Norfolk, and is a Liverpudlian to boot. The new priest adamantly refuses to engage in any discussion about the PM and his wife's religion. 'I am bound by the Official Secrets Act,' he says. 'I work on a military base and the rules are very strict.' These touching and revealing asides with the befriended priest apart, the political animal in Tony came first.

*

Canon Russ believes the smoking did him no favours. No such inhibition affected Penny Mortimer, the wife of the writer John Mortimer, a staunch Labour supporter who visited Chequers for a celebratory dinner early in the Blairs' reign. Sipping champagne on the terrace outside, Penny, a chain-smoker, dying for a cigarette, found herself standing beside Cherie. 'Oh, Cherie,' she said, 'you don't mind if I smoke here, do you?'

Cherie answered her in a sneering tone, 'Well, I'll allow you just one if you have to, but it's a filthy habit.'

Penny, leader of the Labour Party lobby group Leave Country Sports Alone, which also included David Puttnam and the actor Jeremy Irons, felt indignant at Cherie's proprietary air. 'It wasn't her house, it's *our* house. Churchill smoked here, Macmillan smoked here, foreign visitors smoked here,' she said. 'Anyway it's surrounded by 1,200 acres.'

At the Chequers dinner she found herself questioned by Philip Gould, who taxed her with brainwashing her husband into supporting publicly her pro-hunting campaign. (John Mortimer wrote articles against the law to ban hunting, telling me in 2007, 'You can't make something criminal that a large number of law-abiding people think is OK.') 'He's getting very old,' said Gould of Mortimer, 'isn't he?' And then, 'Why do you stay with him, is it love or duty?' Penny was outraged. The Mortimers were not invited again and she commented, 'There won't be many people to invite soon.'

The Mortimers met the Blairs at other parties or dinners in the Chilterns area, notably one night at Melvyn Bragg's. This was ten days after the first vote against hunting was passed. Tony came over to Penny and put his arm round her. 'Don't worry, Penny,' he said, 'it's going to be alright, but don't tell anybody.' But was it? In a Downing Street briefing before the 2004 Labour Party conference, Tony placed a high priority on the abolition of hunting, so that Labour, as he put it, 'can reconnect with its members'. It is now generally known Cherie was behind the ban: he was indifferent or emollient, but she turned to him: 'Well, you do know what you have to do, don't you!' To this day Penny Mortimer is livid at the breach of this private pledge he made to her.

At that same dinner, when they were leaving, Tony stood outside admiring the writer Robert Harris's new £30,000 car. He asked Harris if he might sit in the driving seat. Harris gave him the keys and he duly opened the door, climbed in and had a fiddle with the controls. He then asked if he could take the car for a little spin – just up and down the road. Harris assented, but the detective standing nearby stepped in and told Tony this was not possible. John Mortimer comments, 'But why didn't he? He could have taken no notice of his detective. Robert drove off, leaving a dejected Tony in the street, looking very sad for himself.'

27

The plough and the stars

Botvinnik: We are enemies! *(A beat. Then softer.)* Because Americans, who never had to confront themselves as conquerors, are still under the illusion that they are idealists.

Lee Blessing, *A Walk in the Woods*

Towards the end of New Labour's first term in office, Roy Jenkins wrote Tony up as 'A good Prime Minister, and possibly a great one.' He went on, 'But you don't tip the waiter until the meal's over.' This peculiar analogy failed to take notice that meals are cooked by chefs and only then served by the waiters. Who were the chefs? Disillusioned Labour voters were swelling in numbers, while party membership began its steep decline, from 360,000 in 2000 to 198,000 in early 2007. But in 2000 the donors were still there, giving or lending generously, perhaps in the expectation of honours. And here the change developed, the gap widened, between the 'two different people' in both Tony and Cherie, as a direct effect of their being in Downing Street.

Lauren Booth reported Tony as telling her, 'I'm not a different human being, say, from ten years ago, but I am different politician' (*Daily Mail*, April 2007). With some justice Booth claims this was only 50 per cent accurate and she confirms with other observations the split in him which she saw as having occurred: after the move to Downing Street, 'there was a nagging feeling that behind Tony's good nature was a more sinister animal, one that demanded compliance from backbenchers and fed on spin'.

As for Cherie, the change had became even more evident, for one day, at a function, while Tony did his shy-boy act, blushing at Charles Dance the actor bathing him in praise, raising his hand in an 'aw, shucks' kind of way, Cherie marched her half-sister over to Fiona Millar. The latter then dressed her down for her support for a cause, animal welfare, disapproved of by Cherie. 'Sorry,' Lauren blurted in front of the two angry women. 'I just thought . . . What about freedom of speech?'

'What about it?' came Cherie's stern response.

Yet Tony and Cherie gave the directly opposite impression to many others, one of unaffected kindness and courtesy. Nicholas Hytner remembers:

> In the summer of 1997 I happened to be at a party in New York thrown by Tina Brown and Harold Evans for the Blairs on their first US visit after the election. It was dauntingly full of the political and media elite. I had never, at that time, met either of them. They must have seen my name on the guest list, because they both, separately, took the trouble to seek me out and ask after Ben [Benet Hytner]. In Tony's case he let Kissinger and Barbara Walters wait while he talked to me. Shortly after *Stuff Happens* I was at a Downing Street reception, and again Tony took trouble to ask after my father, acknowledging that the National was giving him a rough time.

In this middle period, before the defining Iraqi invasion of 2003, Cherie had rather fluctuated in her role both as Prime Minister's wife and independent career lawyer. As the first she came in for some stick from Germaine Greer, who said, 'I find it irritating that Cherie appears like [Tony's] concubine.' Greer was not too keen either on the 'Blair Babes', those 101 women MPs with whom Tony had been photographed triumphantly after the 1997 election. Dressed in fuchsia suits, or subtle beiges and bright red blousons, they had beamed in unison and on message with the mantra 'women have really arrived', and were expected to represent the hopes for change of thousands of women voters. Tony proclaimed that they would 'transform the culture of politics'.

But 'they had done no such thing', Greer said in an interview with the internet company LineOne. Rather the reverse. A complete failure. 'It's true, they've been useless,' she went on. 'They have been bewildered about what they are doing.

'I actually paid a researcher to go through Hansard and found out what they had done. How can they be there and not make any difference at all? A lot of them came in by default.' She added, 'They were a backing group singing "woo woo", while he, Tony Blair, was the teen idol – it's crapulous.'

As predicted, the number of Blair Babes fell sharply in the 2001 election.

But with regard to Cherie, Greer had not strictly been true, because Cherie had, first, been defending the new human rights law and, second, been criticised for becoming a second Hillary Clinton by her highly publicised opinions on parental leave, homosexual rights and the need to change the way judges were chosen, to ensure fairness to ethnic minorities. The Tories accused her of harbouring the ambition to become Lord Chancellor. She wrote in the *Telegraph*:

> The Human Rights Act forms an integral part of the government's pro-gramme of constitutional reform, which has the aim of modernising Britain to make it a strong and confident democracy in the 21st century. We all know the old saying that everyone is free to go to the Ritz Hotel, but in reality, only those who can afford it will get in. Likewise, too often human rights have been regarded as something to be used by the rich and have been denied to those who could not afford them.

Cherie went on that a new culture of human rights would be created through education and good citizenship as much as through the courts. Courts would 'be sensible and discourage the opening of the floodgates' to human rights litigation, she said. 'Liberty, equality and community are indivisible. Unless rights are enjoyed by everyone on an equal basis, they become mere privileges, not rights at all. Unless there are strong com-munities to protect the weak, rights are trampled on by the powerful.'

These very high-sounding intentions, couched as they were in woolly and vague terms, over the next few years, were incorporated into the Human Rights Act (which enshrined the European Convention on Human Rights). According to the Act's critics, they were to throw the legal system into turmoil, inflate the compensation culture to an unimaginable extent, help terrorists evade capture and criminals escape punishment, and cost the country and the taxpayer millions in legal aid. They were also to lead to severe demoralisation among British forces, acting as an occupying army, in Afghanistan and Iraq, when civilians alleging maltreatment, unlawful killing or injury attempted to bring actions against serving personnel. Battlefield conditions were way beyond the experience of any Blair minister, and to introduce a suburban, anti-army correctness or judgementalism into what happened in such extreme circumstances was once again showing an underlying ignorance of, and arrogance towards, history and a disdain for any incumbent system or value.

British law, unlike the Continental system, is not based on a fixed code, and to introduce it here would be to overthrow the common-law system which has grown out of the reality of cases, and which has changed and adjusted with the times. As John Mortimer points out, 'The English system is not logical, but it works.' The government also attempted with more sense to restrict some jury trials, as in complicated fraud cases, and put them in the hands of professional panels.

But there was a personal interest too in this commitment to Tony's new Act. Matrix, the new chambers that Cherie had joined in 2000, specialised in the European Convention on Human Rights, which the Human Rights Act now opened up for British lawyers. Here was a whole new killing field, in which Matrix soon moved into a leading role, with many of its clients having its top fees paid by legal aid. Again, it played its faddish and fashionable card (weren't all lawyers by definition concerned with human rights?) and its close government connections. Many in the legal profession questioned whether there was not a conflict of interest in Cherie, close as she was to government, being appointed a recorder, or junior judge. In five years Matrix became one of the most profitable legal practices in London, with a turnover of £11.5 million. In time it represented terror suspects held without trial but under arrest in Belmarsh prison (a 'ludicrously unjust disgrace, with no respect for Magna Carta', says Mortimer) overturning, in landmark judgments, the tightening up by Tony of restrictions designed to increase security. Notably, Cherie represented Shabina Begum in 2004, the Luton schoolgirl who lost her claim that her human rights were violated when the headmistress of her school banned her from wearing a head-to-toe jilbab. Another member of Matrix, Kenneth Macdonald QC, was in 2003 appointed Director of Public Prosecutions and as such will help to determine what action is to be taken in the cash-for-honours police investigation in 2006–7 which, beginning with the fund-raising activities of Lord Levy, a close friend and tennis partner of Tony's, has led to the questioning of scores of Labour donors and government figures, including the Prime Minister.

Here again, and in the second Blair government, it became a habit of Tony and his ministers to blur boundaries. 'Undifferentiationism', the merging of all distinction or difference of one thing from another, or, as Tony more usually called it, 'modernisation' or even 'cultural diversity' (forgetting difference and individual quality as defined by history and tradition), and 'globalisation' (which often seems to mean having too much information, making decisions too quickly and change for the sake of change to meet lower standards) marched hand in hand with the mindless and universal application of computer technology. New Labour was playing fast and loose with law, history, tradition and ethics. By the end of ten years the situation became reversed, and Tony himself was forced to attack the Tories for putting civil liberties and human rights before national security.

And where did Cherie stand in all this? In some murky, ill-defined no man's land, protected by the cab-rank barrister culture? After all, in situational ethics, another term for moral relativism, all action and morality depend on the situation in which you find yourself. There are no moral absolutes and everything is subject to the scale of optimum remuneration.

*

Admissions (of guilt, of failure) now actually began to count for very little, as the connection to change of anyone making such an admission had grown so tenuous. 'Never apologise,' Churchill had once said in a very different context of political responsibility, and given the number of confessions of wrong-doing and failure that were to fill the second and third Blair terms, it could have been sensible advice. Action, in another word resignations, should have taken the place of apologies. Tony had already apologised over the mishandling of the decision to exempt Bernie Ecclestone's Formula One from the proposed ban on tobacco advertising in November 1997, but denied any wrong-doing. Now at the Labour conference in 2000, the last before the election of 2001, Tony beat his breast in *mea culpa* fashion over pensions and the Millennium Dome, while a few months later Peter

Mandelson, reinstated in the Cabinet as Northern Ireland Secretary, had to resign a second time over the Hinduja corruption affair.

Mandelson had just, in November 2000, added to the mournful threnody by expressing the government's collective contrition and asking for pardon for its over-enthusiasm which, 'by over-selling the enhancements to ordinary life which its policies could bring, had led to disappointments'. The public had become cynical about believing anything the government said, especially over the outbreak of foot-and-mouth disease early in 2001.

But even when opposition to the true face of New Labour began to be more than manifest – Blair heckled by Sharon Stevens, the disgruntled partner of a Nottingham cancer patient, and John Prescott, the deputy Prime Minister, punching a heckler who threw an egg at him ('John is John,' Tony told the press conference after this), the electorate failed to stir from its quiescent mood. In an account of personalities there is little place to record a list of the non-achievements and the gap between expectations and delivery of a government during its first term with a leader who, as one disillusioned Blairite says, if he had not been at No. 10 'would probably be making videos to sell timeshare on holiday homes'. As inexperienced ministers struggled to find authority and master their briefs, the civil service departments continued to function in spite of ignorance and incompetence, and the experienced spin machine prolonged its reign of terror under Alastair Campbell. They were now destroying things they didn't under-stand, and in the process devaluing public opinion about politics. But the voters, given little more than a lukewarm alternative in the Conservatives, still re-elected Tony at the 2001 election.

More than 40 per cent of the electorate did not vote, the worst turnout at a British general election since all adults got the vote in 1928. 'As soon as people have power, they go crooked and sometimes dotty as well,' wrote E. M. Forster in 1939, 'because the possession of power lifts them into a region where normal honesty never pays.' Political life and power were more highly organised than at any time before in human history, but it seemed the more highly power was organised, the lower it sank in the estimation of the electorate. The democratic base of a great democratic society felt distinctly uneasy with Tony at the apex of its pyramid, and gave him only 21.4 per cent of the total vote. But the closer the ship of state came to foundering on the rocks or wild seas of falsehood, the more Tony and Cherie expressed their belief in Belief. Almost incredibly, towards the end of November 2001 Tony told Piers Morgan, 'I am the Prime Minister and I don't lie.' The self-apotheosis went on building and building until it reached its crowning statement at the Labour Party conference of 2004: 'I only know what I believe.'

In the reshuffle of June 2001 Tony replaced Robin Cook at the Foreign Office with Jack Straw, while David Blunkett succeeded Straw as Home Secretary. By now it was lamentably clear that one of Tony's great deficiencies was an inability to appoint the right people in the right jobs, and he now began a habit of reshuffling which was to quicken. A year and nine months after Blunkett's appointment, John Mortimer publicly pronounced, 'We never thought there could be a worse Home Secretary than Michael Howard, but there is. David Blunkett doesn't have a civil liberties bone in his body. It is sad to learn, as a lifelong Labour voter, that our Home Secretaries are worse than Conservative ones.' Of the long-cherished plans, furthered by each successive Home Secretary, to introduce identity cards Mortimer says, 'My father said you've got a horrible government if you're asked to carry papers.'

Unforeseen circumstances were to follow the appointment of Blunkett, just as unforeseen consequences resulted from the ban on hunting with dogs, which took up so many hundreds of hours of parliamentary time and provoked intense hostility to Tony and Cherie in the countryside. By the end of 2006 it was questionable whether the unenforceable law was being obeyed, except in lip-service, while it gave a significant boost to the popularity and appeal of the sport, which now flourishes more than it ever did. Tony and Cherie were both to claim personally not to care about the issue, but the fox-hunting 'unspeakables' as Oscar Wilde called them, or in socialist mythology the demonised 'toffs', came from a wide social background. They now pursued not the 'uneatable' fox, but the anthropomorphised Mr Reynard. The picture was rather different.

28

Parting is such sweet sorrow 2

From the time they met, Tony and Cherie maintained an intensely narcissistic bonding with each other. In this bonding, as in other dependencies he has fallen into, Tony allowed Cherie to be the dominant and driving personality – more than allowed, was happily complaisant while for many years she lifted from him much of the burden of the paranoid party politician who is such a common feature of Westminster. Tony's apparent openness, his commendable failure to bear lasting grudges against those who have wounded him, his ability to relax and listen, owed much to Cherie's knee-jerk, instant reactions, her touchiness and dismissiveness – for she carried for a long time much of the negative baggage of their codependency.

Numerous examples of this are seen in Piers Morgan's account of the interplay between himself and the couple – with Cherie inevitably more forward, abrasive, dismissive, and completely uninhibited, as when she tries to have Morgan sacked as editor of the *Daily Mirror*, while Tony is more unsure, laid back, reflective and, it would seem, non-judgemental. He may not like it, and may do all he can to avoid it and the conflict of having to face it, but he did not harbour resentment against those who inflicted criticism on him; nor did he attack the press in the intemperate way Cherie did – issuing writs as well as lists of their alleged false claims and lies – and of course falling into the trap by so doing of having all the 'lies and false claims' repeated over and over again in the media.

There were no instances which showed Tony to be jealous of the relationships that Cherie formed, either with members of their family, or with her personal or professional entourage. He seemed to have endorsed wholeheartedly her wilder flights of self-serving or self-regard, at least until the fall-out threatened serious repercussions or a slump in popularity, when he left it to others to check Cherie, to pull her in, so to speak.

Far from being threatened, as a rather self-conscious example of the feelgood, new male leader he joined in what she was doing. He did the same exercises, consulted the same health gurus, followed the same rituals of Cherie's Catholic faith – even, if the alleged details are true, phoned Carole Caplin at midnight. Indeed, on one occasion when he was spotted attending Catholic mass alone, and the press speculated and drew the conclusion that he was striking out on his own – even suggesting he might soon convert – he pointed out that he was there by himself because his wife and children had been held up in traffic. Not so the other way round: Cherie's interventions, her personal whims, or expressions of anger or jealousy were all too patently evident throughout the busy schedule of their lives, and here again Tony generally appeared to bear the rows, the outbursts, with calm and equanimity.

One woman, however, in the hothouse of that passionate world which, mirroring the medieval court, politics became, was a threat to Cherie – at least, Cherie perceived her as such. Anji Hunter was in many crucial ways Cherie's complete opposite, but in other important ways a duplication of the loyal, subservient wife that Cherie also functioned as, or tried to, when not fulfilling her own agenda. Both women, with the myriad resources that were theirs to control as Tony rose in power, were magnificent multi-taskers.

Organiser, networker and personal manager, Anji became for ten and a half years Tony's prime fixer and 'mover and shaker' who underpinned the more volatile emotions of his spouse with unerring good taste and advice on how to dress, the pitfalls to be avoided and the people to be cultivated.

Although married to Nick Cornwall, a landscape designer living in Hampshire, during the crucial 1997 election campaign she stayed in Geoffrey Robinson's penthouse flat overlooking Park Lane. She had first met Tony at a Scottish house party when he was seventeen and she was fifteen; he was at Fettes and she was the daughter of a former SOE hero turned rubber-planter who had retired prosperously to Scotland. She attended a girls' public boarding school in Fife but at sixteen was expelled for her anti-establishment views, then went on to St Clare's, Oxford, a popular sixth-form college, for A-level studies. Like Tony's father, her father, who died when she was twenty-four, was a staunch Conservative supporter of Margaret Thatcher. They could offer each other mutual understanding from the early death of Anji's mother in a car accident and Tony's loss of Hazel, his mother, who had died in July 1975. As a lifelong friend, then, when Tony became Prime Minister, she brought him security and continuity, and while they never fell in love, they became very close, which Tony made no effort to disguise. Often as they spent more time together than Tony did with Cherie, the latter soon began to fear and believe that Anji was more important to him than she was herself. Cherie also believed, from Anji's very different and more confident social background, her dependable charm and rock-like obedience which embraced problems with commendable equanimity, that Tony was ignoring her own advice in favour of Anji's.

In some ways Anji stood in the way of the mimetic role Cherie had set herself of becoming a Hillary Clinton, in other words an independent force and power in a shared partnership. But Tony, much as it was believed he would like to be President, and she First Lady, was Prime Minister, and she was merely a Prime Minister's wife. Here again both were making that fundamental mistake about the limits of their function and, especially in Cherie's case, the limits of their power. And alas, Cherie had none of the repose and poise, to be polite, of Hillary; she and her husband shared their identity confusions to such a degree that they found solace and peace only in the constant reassuring sight of their own images.

Anji Hunter would never be a Narcissus like the Blairs; the jaw is firm, the eyes stare out with a warm and bold engagement with the outer world and people. Narcissism reveals what it insists on, exactly what it lacks. When Cherie berates the press for invading her own privacy and that of her children, she is, as she constantly shows, incapable of being a private person. Both she and Tony, in their display of self-love, keep giving out worrying signs that they cannot find adequate means of loving themselves. They hold hands, they gaze lovingly into one another's eyes, then present themselves as a constant photo-opportunity because the love they have, while true and deep to them, is created so that it will reflect back on themselves.

The attachment of Tony to Anji may have been more like a same-sex relationship between old friends, but Cherie still felt rivalry over her exclusion. Suspicion nagged away in her underlying paranoid state of mind. Any romantic link was laughed off: 'Anji said they may have been at the same all-night parties, but they never slept together,' report Peter Oborne and Simon Walters in their biography of Alastair Campbell. But Cherie still clung morbidly on to her jealousy, believing Anji was a terrible flirt, 'petrified of the power she had over Blair'. Once a friend reported to Cherie a compliment Anji made about her. 'Don't ever ask that woman what I think. Do you understand? Don't ever talk to her about me. She knows nothing about me.'

Even further back, at an early Labour conference, Cherie's resentment at Anji's role of emotional confidante had boiled over. Dressed only in her *robe de nuit*, Cherie emerged in rage from their bedroom in the hotel suite to kick Anji out, at that moment huddled in a *tête-à-tête* with Tony. 'Piss off,' she said. Another time she harshly denounced Anji as 'a bloody bitch', when she herself couldn't find some document or other. On another occasion, in a corridor at No. 10 Cherie shoved her out of the way. Anji and Tony grew complicit in keeping her out of Cherie's sight, and if they were in a very close relationship in all but deed, Tony, in his passive way, failed to take a stand for Anji's continuing presence in his life. She was good for Tony Blair the Prime Minister, so what did this say about Cherie? Tony, behind Cherie and Fiona Millar's back, tried to negotiate a new job for her after the 2001 election, but Millar, who had broadened her duties after the election, had been fed the line by Cherie that Anji had designs on Campbell and opposed it, while Anji herself soon wearied of the infighting and backbiting.

Tony at first refused Anji her wish to resign. He clung on to her, going again behind Cherie's back to persuade her to stay on after the election of 2001. It would only be for a few months, he told her, in order to help him reshuffle ministers and reorganise government. Having just returned from the formal meeting with the Queen at Buckingham Palace, Tony was worn out. Then, while he and Cherie were alone in his office but in the midst of needing to make many calls and administrative adjustments, he told her Hunter was going to stay on until September – and not only that but with a new title and status. 'Cherie was furious. A bitter row ensued. She swept out of the room, with a face like thunder and stomped off to the flat' (Oborne and Walters).

How much Anji had, even if unconsciously or secretly, any desire to supplant Cherie in Blair's eyes and affections has hardly been floated as a notion, but it is quite bizarre that, after the refocusing of her life following her Blair era, she should have so rapidly fallen in love with Adam Boulton of Sky News, a feverishly active man, leaving her husband, father of their two children – who, curiously enough, has been described as a Blair lookalike.

Boulton also left his wife and their two children, and in the bitter divorce battle engulfing the two couples and the sharing of their assets, Nick Cornwall, who had by general repute been badly treated by Hunter, retaliated by claiming she had neglected him during the long days and years she devoted to the Prime Minister, thus making him a co-respondent by proxy.

In the fall-out from this broken attachment, which began when Tony joined the Labour shadow Cabinet, yet again showing the bizarrely dramatic or dysfunctional behaviour in the Blair corridors of power, and above all the raging mimetic envy of the main players, Cherie, who showed, contrary to her Catholic or Christian professions of faith, the paranoiac's inability to forgive, wrote Cornwall's lawyers a character reference in which she praised his qualities as a husband and father.

Surely Caesar's wife should not only be above suspicion, but also should not engage herself in the marital disputes of Caesar's servants.

29

Hug 'em close

Botvinnik: How best to be America? Make individual freedom your god. This allows you to attack on many fronts – all along borders in fact – and maintain the illusion that you are not attacking at all. You don't even have to call your wars wars. You call them 'settling the West'.

Lee Blessing, *A Walk in the Woods*

'Hug 'em close,' Bill Clinton told Tony of the new American administration of George W. Bush, elected at the end of 2000. The schoolboy still in the short trousers of power was patted on the back by Bill when he stepped down, or so it seemed. He need hardly have bothered because Tony's *bain de foule* appetite had already been so heavily gratified by his early appearances with Clinton as rock-star soulmates: as Peter Mandelson had said, 'When you see them together they are like brothers. Blair's evangelical style was to the manner born.' Tony was well on the way to becoming an honorary American when he and Cherie first met Bush on 22 February 2001. It was Cherie now who needed Bill's advice more, for from the start she found inside her a deep resistance to both Laura and George Bush. The failure of Al Gore and the Democrats to win devastated her and she believed, as did many others, that some electoral skulduggery had resulted in the close Bush victory: 'I don't expect they are looking forward to this [meeting] any more than we are,' she said as their helicopter descended to Camp David.

'May I call you Tony?' were among Bush's first words of welcome, whereupon the instant mimetic Tony countered, 'Thanks, George – may I call you George? It's great to be here.' Round one clearly to Bush: he knew at once the deferential British public schoolboy would be a pushover. He would make the running and Tony would defer.

For this first meeting, Tony wore close-fitting, dark blue corduroys for the macho look, an open-necked shirt and a jumper. He looked tight and uncomfortable around the crotch and stuck his knuckles self-consciously into his trouser pockets. The impression of him deferring to the older man, in poses of reaction rather than action, is caught perfectly in the photographs of the pair together, walking in the woods, sharing what the White House called 'face time'.

But George also listened to Tony explaining his ideas on Russia and Europe, and, being astute while also needing to conceal his ignorance, the President, as well as having got him talking, peppered him with questions. When Christopher Meyer chaired meetings of the two government teams, he observed Bush's self-confidence and aplomb. There was no sign of the verbal stumbles that plagued his public speaking, and while Bush's entourage, in contrast to Blair's freewheeling interaction with his, showed him deference (and never swore or used obscenities, or abused opponents), he was perfectly at ease to let others do the talking.

There was no defensiveness or awkwardness as yet between the pair, and perhaps they shared, in that relaxed encounter before 9/11 struck with the need for revenge it engendered, a warm, almost complicit sense that here were two similar souls who had deep problems with their fathers, and as a result problems in dealing with their own aggression. For the moment these demons were hidden in smiles. Both were, if you could probe beneath the well-cosmeticised exteriors, not only masters of the honest-man routine, but also massively self-deceived. This is why they clicked so well from the start, but for both the same kind of retribution might well be in store. 'A candidate', says the journalist David Corn, 'who rises to power by denouncing lies warrants more attention when he engages in dishonest behaviour. [Yet] you always know where you are with him.' Says Tony of George, 'a very charming personality, easy to deal with'. Tony had his sights on another double.

*

Let us pause for a moment at the milestone of character Bush: a supremely important one for Cherie and Tony, and not for the reasons usually advanced. Cherie's hackles had risen straightaway at some aspects of her host, as when she tackled him over the death penalty and his record of showing little or no clemency when governor of Texas, a charge he quietly deflected. But he and Cherie met in one significant area, and recognised it in each other. Both felt and showed in their behaviour that they were types who believed normal laws did not apply to them and therefore became what Freud termed the Exceptions: they felt entitled to live outside the limitations applied to normal, ordinary people by dint of their injuries early in life. Tony himself did not feel that far injured, but he hankered after being an Exception too: he was, after all, the Prime Minister. The difference from Cherie in George's case was that he inherited a sense of political dynasty from his father, and from his family wealth and his own wealth – and as a result of curing his addiction to alcohol – he had acquired a sense of almost divine right. As Lieutenant-General William Boykin, his deputy Under-secretary of Defence, said, 'He's in the White House because God put him there.'

This wouldn't be so bad, perhaps, if George hadn't believed it too. The 'Exception' he became had to protect himself from intrusion, from adverse comment and enemies, so he became a tough guy. When asked later to explain the international contempt he earned ('what goes around comes around') he said in broken Bushese, 'Heck, I don't know. I think that people – when you do hard things, when you ask hard things of people, it can create tensions . . . I'll tell you, though, I'm not going to change, see? . . . I won't change my philosophy or my point of view' (Tim Russert: *Meet the Press*, February 2004).

George and Cherie mirrored one another from opposite ends of the social scale: 'Four generations of building towards dynasty have influenced the Bush family's hunger for power and practices of crony capitalism with a moral arrogance and backstage disregard of the democratic and republican traditions of the US government' (Kevin Phillips, *American Dynasty*).

While Tony and Cherie felt both attracted by, and yet on their guard with, George, who first seemed something of an enigma, his certainty, his over-compensated fear and his extreme arrogance were not probed or understood at any deep or significant level. Here was a man who could say unashamedly, 'The interesting thing about being the president is that I don't feel like I owe anybody an explanation' (Bob Woodward, *Bush at War*). Nor was his inner uncertainty and tendency to panic in danger – revealed so graphically on the world's screens in the immediate aftermath of 9/11 when he ran for the bunker and then appeared on TV, looking like a rabbit frozen in car headlights – evident to the pair in their lost realms of innocence. Tony and he showed how unreal the world of politicians had become, in which nothing was as it seemed. When he purported later in the time of the Iraq war to land a jet plane on an aircraft-carrier, he was no more than a passenger in pilot's costume, but he did nothing to dispel the illusion. 'The action-figure toys made of Bush in his flight suit are inadvertently accurate interpretations of his behaviour, the concrete personification of a childish fantasy,' reports Justin A. Frank in *Bush on the Couch*. George gave the Blairs a present of coasters with his photographic image on them, which Tony and Cherie, proud of the gift, placed on the John Lewis coffee table in the No. 11 sitting room.

Such a power-hungry, sharp operator, who hid the fear that drove him but at the same time had an overriding desire for love and approval (as did the United States itself), embodied, it would seem, the country he ruled. But why, one has to ask, weren't the Blairs on their guard? Quite simply, they could not work these things out, they were beyond comprehension. And while Tony had the sense that he was being tough and challenging towards George over the next months, he was far from this; at every turn he was manipulated and outmanoeuvred, while the concessions made to save his face he took and applauded as victories. The United States used a highly classified database for intelligence and combat operations called the Secret Internet Protocol Router Network, but denied Britain access to it, even when involved in Iraq alongside its forces. The Americans hoaxed the British into the belief that they were being kept informed. Yet the more developed, mimetic side of Tony was active in storing up George's ploys and tricks for future use, with the recognised political know-how to implement them, so that he might in time become, as George also believed himself to be, a winner of the next political contest outside the laws of history and responsibility.

George's mother may have been at the beginning the cause of her son's inability to integrate his conflicting sides: over-protective, the beautiful but cold Barbara Bush helped him to become a man desperate for protection, so much so that he had actually remained outside those laws of history and responsibility. According to Justin A. Frank this came about in

> an unconscious mockery of his mother's hatred of the search for truth – whether about her husband who was so often away from home, or about her dead child [the illness and death of George's sister Robin from leukaemia, which Barbara coldly covered up], or even about her own mother [killed in a car accident – Barbara did not attend her funeral].

Shakespeare had a name for the likes of George W. Bush. He called him Coriolanus. It seems the mother who protected and hid from her son his father's decline, and was the 'concrete' in Tony's life, also played a part in Tony's liking for George. Cover-up was the name of the game.

*

But what about our innocents in the fairyland of Bush and his entourage's developing delusion? Flattered, bathing in their own reflected glory, perceiving themselves as empowered not only by the President but by the powerful chorus of voices that surrounded him and that swept the gullible American audience into ecstatic adulation, like a rip-roaring successful musical on tour, the Blairs fell easily, and were only more than ready, when the twin towers melted to the ground in September 2001, to follow Bush. But here again, in reaction to death and tragedy, Tony was at his very best. 'One of the first calls I got', said George, 'was from the Prime Minister.' It 'symbolised and articulated the response of the world,' says a Downing Street aide. But what world? In the aftermath of the terrorist outrage a rock radio station played John Lennon's 'Imagine' every half-hour, as if salvation came in a shocked world from the hippie vision of a world without distinctions in religion, culture and appearance, unified in a rational sameness revered by Western academics as the recipe for peace and global harmony. What could be more 'Cherie and Tony'?

But now the American President, in the enablement given to revenge 9/11, could justifiably in the eyes of the world complete the 'unfinished business' of his father's first Gulf War of 1991. At the same time George W., as the rebel ex-alcoholic son of the impeccable, measured father, had the means at hand to prove, at least symbolically, he was the bigger and better endowed. For example, in what would become a prophetic foretaste of the United States' inability to execute a withdrawal strategy in Iraq, there was in 1967 an extraordinary off-the-record showdown between President Lyndon B. Johnson and sceptical reporters. Forced into a corner by demands to explain why the United States still fought in Vietnam, even increased its commitment of troops, as did Bush in 2007 – and at his wits' end because his political justifications were failing to convince – the President unzipped his trousers, hauled out his penis and said, 'This is why!' As commentators have pointed out, American politics in the final reckoning does seem to come down to men showing who has the bigger penis. We have been subject to repeated assertions by Blair and Bush that we have to 'stick it out'. In Afghanistan the Taliban have equally grim practices. The ancient Egyptians cut off the penises of their dead enemies as a means of showing how many they had killed. Kipling wrote:

> When you're wounded and left on Afghanistan's plains
> And the women come out to cut up what remains
> Jest roll to your rifle and blow out your brains
> An' go to your Gawd like a soldier.

It is madness to repeat the same mistake over and over again. The reader will need no reminding of Bill Clinton's priapic preoccupations, but at least they remained confined to the domestic scene – until, when found out, to distract the process of impeachment, he took to bombing Bosnia.

*

Only eighteen months separated 9/11 from the March 2003 invasion of Iraq, but since 1998, when Clinton had endorsed it, 'regime change', i.e. the overthrow of Saddam, had been US official policy. 9/11 supplied impetus to this policy, which had lain dormant for more than three years, giving theorists such as Richard Perle and Paul Wolfowitz arguments to propound their whole new Middle East power alignment in favour of the West. Autocrats and tyrants were to be driven out by a tidal wave of people power. Although supporters of this speculation, the neo-conservatives or 'neocons', while they called themselves realists, demonstrated that they were in fact in the grip of an imaginative idea to which the eager and idealist Tony was only too eager to sign up. It is, as the great dictator who was also a brilliant political philosopher once remarked, imagination which 'governs the human race' – while he himself failed and fell for that very reason when he invaded Russia.

True realism is by its very nature unpopular and wins little support (no one any more will vote for blood, toil, tears and sweat, while even Churchill could only be truly 'realist' and make such a speech in the context of total all-out war in 1940). If it was imagination which carried the American neocons along with their fierce, barnstorming intellectual justifications, with Tony it was also something more complex and disturbing, which we will attempt to unravel from the inside.

The power of the United States in 2001–3 was awe-inspiring. What made America so seductive, so compelling for Tony and Cherie (as mirror images of one another), was that it was so dramatic compared to the dull old UK. It answered their exaggerated sense of entitlement. The shifting insecurities of the Blairs' backgrounds particularly orientated them to America because America, unlike old Europe with its long and time-honoured traditions, had been *discovered* by Europeans, a new-found land with a destiny, always full of promise, but always and ever – and still today – on the brink of self-destruction. Its founding revolution, unlike anything on the European mainland, from those of France and Russia to the less explosive English counterpart, was not a civil war but a struggle for independence from the Old World, out of which it came into being with its logo and rallying cry of 'freedom'. The United States has never, and will never, take its own survival for granted, for as it was, as a nation, *born*. So it feels mortal, if unbeatable, and above all it hungers after love to prove to itself that it is honoured and it exists.

In other words it is Tony and Cherie to the very core. They (and America) want to do good, to show their virtue, their connectedness; above all their inclusiveness, because seceding in the first instance from empire (or in Cherie and Tony's case traditional values), they have a terror of being isolated, and strive to show their idealism, their well-meaningness and virtue, for which they crave appreciation. Deeply and profoundly the United States is a rootless, narcissistic society, and Tony and Cherie had already demonstrated with the Clintons their *folie à quatre* as the most bonded, twin-ruling pairs the two countries have had in either of their histories. Was this now due to continue with the new President's administration, and if so, would this lead to the defining decision of Cherie and Tony's years in Downing Street?

30

The big decision 1

Tony's decision to go to war alongside George W. Bush should never be seen as a separate issue from life with Cherie and their dyadic leadership, the first time the United Kingdom in its parliamentary history has been mainly governed by a man and woman, one of them unelected. As a *Sun* reader commented online, 'She [Cherie] had been running the country since 1997.'

After five years in power, the dual leaders, living largely with the Mick Jagger ethos that lay at the heart of this government – 'the trick is to keep on the move' (Jagger in a 1995 interview) – had maintained its hold over the 'me-me-me' society of unbridled individualism, where a significant majority of the voting public responded in an almost trance-like state to airbrushed images and the propaganda gushing from the hugest, most dynamically controlled falsehood factory of modern times.

The electorate, it is true, was inevitably beginning to feel unloved. The gap was opening up between the promises made in all areas of public and social life – transport, food manufacture, health, education, pensions – and the practical results, but Tony and Alastair Campbell combined had managed to keep a lid on all that. But Narcissus loves himself, not others; and Tony, wrapped up in himself, lacked the ability to extend love. The public began to feel abandoned by Tony and Cherie and as a result by all politicians. 'Thus politics . . . [became] a dirty word and all politicians [were] condemned as self-seeking.'

But not quite yet.

During 2002 it was noticeable how Cherie grew more outspoken. With Anji Hunter out of the way the previous autumn, she could cut loose without an inner insecurity about holding on to Tony. Relentlessly she attacked Piers Morgan: according to him, 'Cherie told my boss last night [20 June] that I was an immoral little crook trying to get you turfed out of Downing Street and that I should be sacked.'

Morgan demanded satisfaction from Campbell, who responded by sighing for five seconds. 'Christ, that's all I need.'

'Does Tony know what she's done?'

'Of course he fucking doesn't,' replied a clearly angry Campbell. 'He'll be furious about this.'

Campbell did nothing and Morgan went on to fax Tony and email Peter Mandelson.

Other targets of her incontinent tongue were Bush; civil servants such as the Cabinet Secretaries Lord Turnbull and Lord Wilson, whom she reproached over the state of the carpets and refurbishments to No. 10; and Gordon Brown, denounced at one lunch as 'the rot at the heart of government'. However heartfelt it might be to say that young Palestinians 'feel they have got no hope but to blow themselves up', it was hardly constructive for the wife of the British Prime Minister to say this, especially as they killed innocent people. Yet to some admirers, she had done the 'great therapy thingy': found her own voice, become her own person.

No one knew that Cherie was pregnant again in 2002. At the end of July, on a joint constituency visit to a maternity unit in Durham, she cradled a newborn child in the gathering. Tony took fright, and joked publicly that she should give the baby back to its mother, 'Oh dear,' he said to the mother, 'she will be getting broody again. I'm getting worried about this.' Cherie had not yet told him. So Tony didn't know.

Cherie was anxious. This was holiday time and the children and Carole Caplin and Gale Booth left for their holiday in Vernet-les-Bains, France, when the flaunting of tiny G-strings by Carole and her mother next to the pool became an issue with the Blair children. Cherie was forty-eight. Tony, it was evident to her, was self-absorbed on Planet Iraqi War, which she knew would happen in the spring of 2003, exactly the time when their new baby would be born.

In *The Denial of Death*, the psychologist Ernest Becker writes that one of the key concepts 'for understanding man's urge to heroism is the idea of narcissism'; this echoes the contention of Freud that each human being repeats the tragedy of Narcissus – 'We are hopelessly absorbed with ourselves.' Tony's narcissism, enhanced by the trappings of power and his renewed recruitment of those who could expand it for him, had come to know no bounds. It was fast building up to its heroic outlet, or its Götterdämmerung. It may be indelicate to describe what happened next to Cherie as a subliminal or unconscious protest at what was now clearly transforming Tony from the inside and putting him beyond her reach. Whatever that protest was, and knowing who she was, and how much, given that she had become pregnant, she would have wanted a fifth child, this was not to be.

One night in August, with Tony by now informed, an ambulance took her to the Chelsea and Westminster Hospital, where Leo had been born two years earlier, and here, under general anaesthetic, she lost her baby. Events subsequent to the miscarriage suggest Tony did little to counter the grief Cherie felt at losing the child. He was preoccupied and had little time. As a boy he had been dispatched to boarding school during his mother's illness and kept in darkness about it. Visibly tired and in a decided trough in her self-esteem, particularly in respect of the poor image she had of her body, Cherie sank to an all-time low. One may speculate that self-destructively, masochistically, but as a way of keeping Tony within her force field, she now sought reassurance by letting Caplin weave her spell over Tony. She delegated, and therefore derogated, Tony's desire for her to a Cherie substitute in order to control, and then feel, that desire in herself through Caplin. Here was mimetic desire in its most manifest form: a wife encouraging an attractive friend to pamper her husband.

Caplin needed no prompting, while Cherie felt she was holding on to Tony, channelling his sexual needs into a harmless outlet, over which she felt she had complete control. Here her instinct was apparently correct.

What comes next could be a storyline in *Footballers' Wives*, a TV soap opera maintained by Cherie to be her favourite programme.

31

The big decision 2

Thousands, hundreds of thousands of words have been expended on the dodginess of Cherie's health and fitness gurus, so much so that they have become a mimetic double of the dodgy and sexed-up dossiers surrounding the Iraq war: symptoms, both, of the make-believe spun out of Tony and Cherie's attachment to each other.

Tony from the start had proclaimed himself a highly moral person for whom ethics, and a strongly ethical purpose in life, were of paramount importance. So far he had managed for nearly ten years, together with those of a similar conviction, such as Peter Mandelson and Alastair Campbell, to plant this at the very centre of Labour Party belief, so it still remained the core of New Labour philosophy. 'Tony Blair, and many of his colleagues, consistently seem to feel that they are lucky enough to have been granted a privileged access to the *moral* truth' (Peter Oborne, *The Rise of Political Lying*). John Prescott confirmed this in a 2007 BBC television interview: 'Oh yes!' he said. 'He's a man on a mission – with a religious overtone.'

There is a considerable difference between on the one hand a deep understanding of both complication and complexity, in resolving what to do and then presenting it to the electorate and media in the clearest and simplest possible terms to gain support and understanding, and on the other hand actually deciding what to do on the basis of the shallowest and simplest reading of any situation. Here Tony, with his repeated 'it's very simple, it's pretty obvious' mantras or assertions, not only gives himself away, but actually believes what he says. He was not deceiving us, but sadly, tragically, was deceiving himself.

Yet the paradox of this is that both George Bush and Tony, and Cherie as well, believe in God and a spiritual direction to human life. They should be better equipped than most to understand Islam. Furthermore, Tony claims he has read the Koran three times; it was first given to him by Chelsea Clinton. This being so, why should they ever have believed that they could impose a system of democracy and remove the mainly secular tyrant in a country where power – and particular respect for the authority of spiritual power – and not politics held sway in spite of the corruption and secular tyranny?

The answer, simply, is that both men in their different ways were ignorant and deluded. Both shared, crucially and over the same period, two similar deficiencies: first profound ignorance of, and lack of interest in, history or any external opinion; second, an inability to process complex thoughts and ideas. Neither was able to make the distinction between their own perceived notion of what they controlled and what they could achieve, and the nature and challenges of the real world. To put it brutally, neither could any longer distinguish fact from fiction. Or history from personal ambition.

Cherie, too, with the superior Catholic attitudes of the Crosby religious orders that taught her, believed in her own impeccable probity. Paddy Ashdown excused Tony on one occasion of deliberately taking him for a ride over a possible Liberal Democrat–Labour merger: 'He always meant it when he said it.' The same was true of Cherie. They remind one at this juncture again of Pecksniff. Pecksniff seems to say to everyone, 'There is no deception, ladies and gentlemen, all is peace, a holy calm pervades me.'

Tony's promise to the brilliant young woman of immense earning potential was of cement-like fidelity; he would give her the attention her father, the other Tony, never did, and would continually put her centre stage. Moreover, as she was cleverer than him, much cleverer if not actually intelligent, she would influence him, and she could shine in his eyes as someone who could both inform and originate, as well as being the mother of their incredibly bright and high-achieving children.

We have read and heard exhaustively how much Cherie and Tony love one another. This is the example they would like the public to hold onto, the through-thick-and-thin, Darby-and-Joan saga. As far as it goes it is a good example, and it is true in its way that this is an unusual love story which, unlike many celebrity love stories, has not ended in betrayal, divorce or other disaster. They have a blind faith in each other, which bonds the marriage and also sustains it. But the moment has perhaps come to puncture, or at least dent, the pervasive myth about its beneficial virtues in the sphere of political decision-making. There was a personal crisis and it came to a head in the autumn of 2002. It had begun before Tony's election in the spring of 1997.

Hardly anyone today realises in the fast, compulsive flow of political narrative that Carole Caplin goes way back, and first came publicly on the Blair scene on 21 July 1994. Tony won the party leadership, and from her desire to get herself into shape Cherie had met Caplin at her local Islington gym. Caplin, then in her forties, had run a health and fitness company called Holistix, which advocated new age cults – the benefits of goat's milk and unlimited sex – and which had gone bust in 1992.

But not enough for Cherie was just one guru, and Caplin's mother, whom Cherie consulted over channelling energy using crystals and communicating with the spirit world – but in gestures reminiscent of the ungrounded Princess Diana – became more than just back-up. Cherie embraced the theories of other self-styled gurus, licensing her rampant subjectivity to expand to absurd proportions as she fought to contain and limit, and project, a new body image.

Tony never objected when in the march of the Cherie gurus, Caplin, according to a Blair court insider, had blitzed the Islington kitchens (see Chapter 15). Caplin also attempted a Trinny and Susannah-style makeover on Tony's wardrobe, supplied the constant reassurance he asked for and generally 'feminised' him into a faddish lifestyle. She even boasted to friends, 'Tony's body is fantastic and it's all down to me.'

At the time Cherie couldn't have been more pleased. 'Her man' was 'the new man', moulded out of feminist and post-feminist philosophy, the feelgood equal who responded above all to feeling. But, in her lability and irrationality she would not stop at the Caplins. There might have been on Cherie's part some reining in of her guru libidinousness or incontinence. Self-love may urge, but reason should be there to restrain. She was beginning to upstage Tony in the way Vivien Leigh upstaged Laurence Olivier, or Diana Prince Charles: 'Have you seen Cherie Blair this week?' wrote Jean Moir in the *Guardian* at the 1997 Labour Party conference, the first of Tony's premiership.

Tony Blair's wife has transformed herself from an uncomfortable appendage, wearing awkward clothes in the Norma Major tradition, to a svelte political wife like Hillary Clinton. This month's Cherie is wearing tailored miniskirts and sexy leather boots. She looks fabulous, her hair shines like glass . . . we all knew that Cherie was going to have to shape up. None of us expected an executive superbabe and none of us expected quite so much of the Cherie amour routine.

This sycophantic rubbish needs to be printed for one important reason, namely that Tony and Cherie took it seriously: it flattered them, it made them feel gratified in the way both deeply needed.

'The Cherie amour routine' was a prophetic phrase, what with Cherie now linking her fingers round Tony's chest, staring up at him like a calf-eyed newly-wed. But next door to the Blairs' suite in the Imperial Hotel, Cherie had installed Caplin, a move which led to the latter's unmasking in a *Sun* article called 'Secrets of Blairs' Girl Friday', together with a picture of her posing naked, as a former *Men Only* and *Daily Star* nude model. Carole, the article had continued, had told Cherie to rub Tony's body with scented oils and drink infusions of celery leaves. Her lurid and colourful past was also splashed in no uncertain terms. The publication of these nude pictures by a tabloid during the 1994 Labour conference in Blackpool should have put an end to the liaison. But Cherie thought Carole was good for her.

There was, according to a friend, a phenomenal showdown between Tony and Cherie, while Campbell 'went ballistic' over the story, and together with Tony bawled out Caplin, decreeing that she should be known as 'Cherie Booth's personal assistant'. But he didn't get his way with his spontaneous instinct of banishing her for ever, and in spite of further subsequent revelations of Caplin's routine in ritual humiliation cults, during one of which, it was alleged, she subjected participants to act like dogs while shouting at them, 'You're useless. You're a bloody failure. You're not trying,' Tony stood by Cherie's feelgood thirst.

She was then able to add other gurus to the cabal: Jack Temple, an octogenarian 'healer-dowser' who grew herbs and plants in a 'neolithic healing circle'; a shaman in her fifties who used crystals and meditation, and encouraged people to picture animals in their minds – bats, bears or deer –

to protect them against problems; finally, the most bizarre of all, Bharti Vyas, described as 'a cross between a Bollywood matron and Lady Thatcher, an awesome force of nature and a glorified leg-waxer'. A description of her methods contains 'details of colonic irrigation, cranio-sacral courses, depth counselling, phobia management and manual lymph drainage'.

Here was a pattern for authorised and legal self-indulgence on a scale to match that of Cherie's absent father with his alcoholic and womanising excesses. It was a clever and subtle ruse to outdo Tony Booth, for no one could claim she was in the wrong. She had been deprived when young of a father's love and, by God, she was going to make up for it. But at the same time she had a needy, nagging fear, and a limpet-like proprietorship over Tony, forcing compliance on him to validate her selfish appetites, from which he also stood to benefit. Vyas encouraged Cherie to devote time and money to increasing her sexual allure:

> I tell ladies that if their men turn to a younger woman it is their own fault. If they do not look good and have enough energy for sex, then their men will look to other women. A woman should tire her man so much that he does not have the energy to turn to another woman.

But if that man was Prime Minister? Surely there was *some* difference here. In the transactions of mutual narcissism between Tony and Cherie, Tony could not put his foot down and become as his dark alter ego, Campbell, would have liked. Allegations surfaced that Cherie became pregnant with their fourth child while adopting New Age sexual techniques, while Tony kept a grey velvet pouch in his breast pocket containing a red ribbon and a rolled-up scrap of paper without which he could not take a decision. Also, it was said that Cherie practised white witchcraft before important meetings: casting a circle in which a glass of water was placed on a sheet of paper decorated with symbols of earth, fire, and water. Francis Wheen sums this up in his aptly titled *How Mumbo-Jumbo Conquered the World*:

> The emotional populism of modern politicians – as manifested in Al Gore's lachrymose convention speeches, Bill Clinton's televised prayer breakfasts and

Tony Blair's promotion of the Diana cult – may seem to be a form of collective experience. In truth, however, by asserting the primacy of feeling over reason, of the personal over the political, it stands revealed as nothing more than a disguised version of self-love.

The disabling ghosts had been awoken. The Taliban within was on the march. The irreversible decision had been made: the floodgates of innocence were drowned and the anarchy within unleashed of an insecure pop idol worshipper, in curious alliance with a man who deeply feared his own aggression. Jung issued the warning long ago: 'Every psychological extreme secretly contains its own opposite in some sort of intimate and essential relationship . . . the more extreme a position is, the more easily may we expect . . . a conversion of something to its opposite' (*Symbols of Transformation*).

If the groundwork had been done, the foundations laid, the crunch or unexpected denouement in this saga of mutual narcissism came in the autumn of 2002. Cherie was consumed with hidden grief over her lost child, but bolstered and cosseted by the transforming hands and spirit of Caplin, and the energy-charging Vyas. 'The lady of the home is the pillar of the house. If she has a lot of energy, she will radiate that energy.' We must remember this was all being played out in the press and media during the crucial months in which Tony was forming the irrevocable decision to go to war.

Cherie then set out to improve the family's fortunes by acquiring some property in Bristol, where Euan was also about to study, so it would be somewhere for him to live. *Spooks*, the BBC1 spy thriller, is full of agents and criminals who, to dupe their victims, or drop them under electronic surveillance, say to them, 'I know just the person who'll help you with that.' It must be the oldest trick in the book, but apparently one that Tony and Cherie fell for over and over again: 'I know just the chap who'll be perfect for running Work and Pensions.' This was, as David Blunkett called it, a 'sofa government', a perfect phrase, for what do people do on a sofa? They sink into comfortable reverie. They feel good. The multiple roles and actions can be imagined.

Well, Carole Caplin knew just the man to 'help' Cherie with her property ambitions. An ex-lover (or current, it was never quite clear to Cherie), an Australian, Peter Foster. Upon his arrival in Britain in July 2002, and belonging to an ever-increasing network of slimmers and pedlars of holistic cures and therapeutic knick-knacks, he met Caplin at a coffee shop in the King's Road and explained his mission, a slimming project called – with outback economy – Trimmit. With equally abbreviated courting he and Caplin were lovers, and he moved in at once with her in Holloway.

Was there a two-way confidentiality between Cherie and Carole, or was it a one-way mirror fixed for Caplin to know all the secrets of the Blair bedchamber (she put it about that Cherie had told her all the intimate details of their sex life, just as the Chinese had hoped to stitch Cherie up on her visit to Beijing)? While Foster and Caplin were nestling down in Holloway (Caplin became pregnant but later lost the baby, to whom Cherie was to become godmother), Cherie and the children enjoyed a holiday in Bermuda, where she lectured on 'Women in Public Life' and enjoyed free hospitality and air fare. But as every author and lecturer knows, these free trips (she paid a nominal £50 towards the holiday) come at another cost – the loss of time and attention you can give to those close to you.

On returning to Downing Street, Cherie asked Carole to view two flats in a block named Panoramic in Clifton, Bristol, priced at £297,000 each, with a view to buying them with trust money for Euan. Foster, with his own agenda to use a contact with the Blairs to promote his schemes, accompanied Caplin to Bristol, self-styled by now as the Blair's financial advisers. Special Branch warned Tony about his wife's contact with Carole, but he ignored this – after all, what could ever go wrong with Caplin? – while Cherie apparently failed to tell him that she had instructed Foster to negotiate the purchase of the two flats at a reduced price of £265,000 each. It seems hard to believe he did not know. And here again, a second time, Cherie's incompetence over property showed. Why two flats? Just for the deal? Selling as opposed to letting out Richmond Terrace had been ill advised because they lost the freehold value.

Cherie emailed Foster, 'I cannot thank you enough, Peter, for taking over these negotiations for me.' Later, in furthering the transaction, Cherie wrote, 'You are a star. I have sent them off [the forms].'

According to a well-placed informant the *Sun* editor, Rebekah Wade, knew first about this sensational piece of news and the emails while she intended to publish a piece sympathetic to Cherie and Tony – an 'improved fortune' tale, redeeming the bad luck they had with property. The *Mail on Sunday*, meantime, had been trying to check out with Downing Street the rumours about Foster, known to have had criminal convictions, being involved with Cherie. Campbell phoned Blair in Newcastle, who then spoke to Cherie, who was at Chequers, who told her husband that she had never used Foster for advice or help with the flats' purchase.

On 1 December 2002 Tony and Cherie were at Chequers when the *Mail on Sunday* broke the story of Foster and Cherie. It was effectively denied and rebutted by other papers and by Campbell until Wednesday 4 December when, late at night, after an evening at the theatre (a David Hare play), they heard what had happened next. The *Daily Mail* published the emails, which were genuine. Next morning, Campbell and Sally Morgan, who had replaced Anji Hunter, scrolled through them with Cherie to confirm they were correct, which they were. The first offence of deception, and straight mendacity, caused by Cherie not coming clean with Campbell and Fiona Millar, about which they were furious and never forgave her, was about to be followed up by a cunning second thrust of half-truth, devious distancing and media manipulation in which Cherie became the star turn.

Both main participants went straight into denial, acting as one person. After midnight, Cherie called Carole, telling her she would remain her lifelong friend, while the other half of the duo, Tony, called Carole to tell her she would 'stay part of the inner circle'. He followed this with a call to Sylvia, Carole's mother, to inform her that she and Carole had his 'total support'. (This mantra of Tony's 'total support' offered to numerous colleagues and inner circle members would become like the black cross put on doors in mediaeval times to signify the plague had struck – other victims being Geoffrey Robinson, Peter Mandelson, David Blunkett, Tessa Jowell, Lord Levy and many, many more.)

In the days following the publication of the emails the journalists misled by No. 10 turned on Campbell and the press aides. Adam Boulton of Sky News, now Anji Hunter's partner, complained to Tom Kelly, who had been sent into bat, 'If you people just come here and tell us lies the whole system has broken down.' Cherie, trumpeting loudly that it was a private matter and that the press were out to stitch her up, insisted the prices of the flats were dropped before Foster came on the scene and that she had only known him for 'a couple of weeks'.

Rebekah Wade offered Cherie the opportunity to tell her side of the story in a sympathetic interview, but when Cherie refused, the *News of the World* went for her with no holds barred. 'Sex, crystals and witchcraft' headlined an account in which Caplin 'washed off naked Cherie's toxins in the shower' and instructed her in 'bizarre sexual exercises'. It claimed through an unnamed source that Cherie knew Foster 'had a dodgy past'. (In June 2000, showing the bizarre lengths Cherie would go in refuting press claims, when the health pages of a daily paper said she wore a nuclear receptor pendant to reverse DNA change caused by electromagnetic force and radiation by releasing 'harmonic frequencies', she replied, in one of her many attempts to correct the 'record', that it was in fact a 'Bio-Electrical Shield'.)

The emails showed Cherie had been in touch with Foster for more than six weeks. Campbell waxed angrier and angrier at being caught in a deception not – for once – of his own making, and while both subtly and brutally enforcing the fact that he and No. 10 knew nothing of the shenanigans with Caplin and her lover, elicited the public statement from Cherie that 'she and she alone is responsible for any misunderstanding between the No. 10 press office and the media'.

Tony turned on Campbell, resentful of the way he was treating Cherie, and called up Mandelson in the United States to tell him to come back at once and sort out the mess. Meantime, Cherie fell out with Millar, who had anyway been vituperatively labelled by Caplin 'the bitch from hell'. At one moment during all the rows Cherie appealed to Millar, 'Why aren't you giving me more help?'

Millar answered, 'Because you never listen to me and you don't tell me the truth.'

Cherie, as ever, stridently maintained she had done nothing wrong. Strangely, bizarrely, she appeared cold about the whole affair, which could have formed the central scene in a savage satire on truth and political alchemy by Ben Jonson. As a result of her own actions, for which she and no one else was entirely responsible, she went through a humiliating sequel. Hilary Coffman, a senior aide, with Tony's sanction quizzed her on every aspect of her life, including her acceptance of gifts and holidays, while Cherie insisted on having a solicitor present. Henceforth, her private email was monitored by Downing Street: the protection amounted to censorship and near house arrest.

An overlooked incident in this affair, but perhaps the most significant of all, was how Cherie, using her position as a prominent QC, and presumably prompted by Caplin, attempted to influence the judicial hearing on Foster's subsequent deportation to Australia. She knew the rules, yet she asked for and received from the presiding judge the defence case against the deportation, a move first denied then partly admitted (*Scotsman*, 12 December 2002). Here once again was a case of Cherie suspending her own professional ethics.

Caplin complained vehemently in print about how the 'mysterious people were acting to protect whatever they thought they needed to protect' while Foster, on his arrival in Sydney, accused Caplin of being in love with the Prime Minister, and even of choosing his underpants.

> They went for long walks in the woods around Chequers and they phoned each other at night . . . People think that Cherie is the ugly duckling who Carole advised with clothes and make-up and styling. The truth is that Tony relied on Carole too. Carole coached him on how to handle people, how to handle situations and how to present himself.

Later he was to allege, without any foundation in fact, that the baby Carole had been carrying but then miscarried was not his but Tony's.

Tony, completely preoccupied with Iraq, found the whole affair incomprehensible, but stuck blindly by his wife. To bring to an end the messy drip-feed of new stories, the ever-widening ripples of scandal as some further charge was detonated, Mandelson, now back in London, together with Lord Falconer, Fiona Millar and Piers Morgan, penned a confession for Cherie to read out (through autocue) on television. Let us not go on about how, in spite of her dramatic delivery, it was spontaneous and heartfelt. She delivered this sanctimonious piece of drivel, which ended with Millar's unsurpassable line 'I am not superwoman', one pre-Christmas evening when, ironically enough, she was later due to hand out childcare awards.

She never viewed the flats herself. She never told her husband about them. In nine minutes of persuasive pleading, enforced by what the papers called her goggle-eyed innocent look, she voiced the words put into her mouth in a captivating display which showed no remorse or genuine regret, but the consummate family skills of a 'piss-off' apology which was not really an apology. Someone likened her skill to overpower argument with emotion to that of Princess Diana, who was another mother, another martyr. Tony then went straight on to the high moral ground, saying at a EU summit in Copenhagen that 'it was time to move on', as everyone had had their pound of flesh, which was a rather unfortunate reference to the pound of flesh in *The Merchant of Venice* which Shylock proposed to take from the spot nearest Antonio's heart. In fact, like Shylock, and thanks to the rescue operation, the press and public failed lamentably to obtain their pound of flesh. In the falling out between the Campbell-Millars and Cherie, paradoxically it was Cherie's failure to tell the truth and force Campbell to lose face which estranged the Blair media minders from their heroes. Cherie had betrayed her loyal friend and ally. Millar resolved to quit.

But no one caught up in 'Cheriegate' saw the personal crisis at the heart of it, which was that Cherie had not told Tony the truth, for she felt perhaps she was above having to tell him the truth. If she had told him the truth, then he was complicit in her lying over Foster to Campbell and the press, and if he was complicit in her lying – if only temporarily – surely he would have the common sense to see that a continued closeness to Caplin could only lead to worse things happening.

Cherie then became involved in Foster's extradition case. According to the *Scotsman*:

> The Prime Minister's wife reviewed both the court papers prepared by Foster's lawyers and the official Treasury Solicitor papers demanding extradition, according to legal sources. She then advised both Foster and Ms Caplin on the case, including giving an opinion on the likely attitude of the judge who would eventually hear his appeal. (12 December 2002)

Cherie defended herself against the charge that she had acted improperly:

> I emphatically did not try to influence this one way or the other. I was simply trying to help my friend Carole find out the facts . . . It is even being suggested that because I publicly checked the available court list for the name of the judge in some way I acted improperly. I didn't.

But Tony by now was putting things in boxes and while criticised for being distant from her during the paroxysms of charge and counter-charge, he seemed easy after anger, presumably at the disruption it caused, to acquiesce in her version, and to shift the whole blame of the affair onto the press, which was out to 'smear' both of them. Obvious though it is to say this, it was just what a Prime Minister needed.

Peter Stothard, the *Times* editor, wrote, 'The sight of his wife being pilloried for weeks in the press caused miserable stress to Tony Blair.' Of course it did, for she, if now seriously tarnished and murkily brown at the edges, was still his mirror image, in which he saw his own reflection. The shallow but frantic engagement of their minds organising the whole process of lies, half-truths, deception and extrication meant little beyond the exercise of skill; it was part of the lawyer's brief to win the case, and Tony appeared able to brush it off. Any aggression or anger he felt quickly redirected itself towards their scapegoat, the press. He remained trusting of Cherie's attachment to Caplin, which most people would feel was the real intrusion into privacy. This still extended to her being given a free run of the No. 11 flat and Cherie leaving her blank cheques to fill in.

Could *EastEnders* scriptwriters have thought of a better 'plant' to provide drama in a future episode? Yes, perhaps they could: Tony bringing David Blunkett back twice into office. Cherie even blamed herself when Carole miscarried the Foster baby and their joint defiant attachment surmounted Carole selling the whole story to *Hello!* magazine and her and Foster's cooperation with the BBC feature *The Conman, His Lover and the Prime Minister's Wife*. What could, or did, the Blair children make of all this?

Both Cherie and Tony, at a deep and crucial level, refused to take responsibility over the debacle. Cherie was a mother with four growing children, Tony the Prime Minister of the fifth richest country on the planet on the brink of a war which would alter fundamentally the world as we knew it. It revealed a profound truth about their shortcomings, the shallowness of their marriage, but also the no longer hidden but almost palpable dangers that their personalities held in dealing with matters which affected millions of people. As Peter Oborne later wrote, 'Almost every crisis faced by the Prime Minister – examples include the death of David Kelly, the Mittal affair, "Cheriegate", the Hinduja affair, Black Rod, and the foot-and-mouth crisis – has either been accompanied or brought about by government deception and falsehood.'

But we must move on: the story has to keep going, the narrative will soon give way to a new twist, a new development. What viewers love to see in soap operas is the characters – and they love the bad guys as much as the good guys – making the same mistakes over and over again.

32

The big decision 3

The causes that led to the invasion of Iraq in early March 2003 can never be too often investigated because there is no doubt that it is, like 9/11, a defining moment in this new century. Aside from other important causes which lie outside the scope of this book, the mixture of confusions and certainties in Tony and Cherie, before and during this disastrous under-taking, demand close scrutiny. Both by now showed they had little capacity to disengage from one another and lead a separate existence, even though they seemed no longer to be acting in perfect harmony and their paths were somewhat diverging.

The *Daily Mirror* editor had noted on Saturday 9 March 2002, just a year before Bush and Blair unleashed the dogs of war – with red-top prescience, 'We ran a front page yesterday on Blair's trip to Texas to rubber-stamp an Iraq war, with them both mocked up in Stetsons and the headline, HOWDY POODLE.' And yet it went deeper with Tony: the Iraq war became the answer to a long-standing need and supplied the outlet to an inner crisis with Cherie, of which he was unaware.

The crisis was that mimetic doubles do not, and cannot, go on existing in harmony effortlessly and indefinitely without an explosion. Something, somewhere, has to give. What draws a pair intensely to one another in the first place – a recognition of the likeness, a mirror image – may, when the parties wake up and see it is just this, lead to a whole host of things: affairs, separation, illness, intense obsessive hobbies, a complete realignment of ideas. Some displacement activity is inescapable. Given the huge pressures on them in Downing Street, in Tony and Cherie's case this was war. Tony had to prove himself, had to show the world he was a man, able to take risks, that he was not, as a general put it, 'casualty averse'. At Christmas 1997, just before he had gone on television to announce that RAF planes had started bombing Iraq, he watched a video of Harrison Ford's *Air Force One.*

Tony took his first action over Iraq just after the home loan scandal which had caused Peter Mandelson to resign. Over Mandelson he was nearly in tears, and not in a much better state over Iraq, where he had just ordered RAF planes into action in support of Bill Clinton bombing Saddam Hussein's bases:

> You know, people ask what the most difficult thing about being Prime Minister is, and until now I haven't really known the answer [at the end of 1998]. But I can say in all honesty, that taking the decision to send the RAF into battle has been the worst moment for me. I couldn't sleep the night it happened. I was worried sick. (Piers Morgan, *The Insider*)

Anyone could see, except apparently Tony, that Clinton was using him to divert attention from the Monica Lewinsky scandal.

But it had been Clinton first who had enabled Tony to, as Clare Short says, 'enjoy the drama and glory that goes with military action' and get 'a taste for war', but also to 'fail to learn lessons' which could have helped him to manage the Iraq crisis 'with more wisdom and international support'. Clinton had ordered the seventy-hour missile blitz in December 1998 (Operation Desert Fox) ostensibly to cripple Saddam's largely fictionalised capacity to produce weapons of mass destruction, but mainly to distract attention from the Lewinsky affair.

The second milking of Tony as a war leader came between March and June 1999 in Kosovo. Here, PR fixers chose a refugee family and tent and made Tony roll up his sleeves in the search for an image that would lead to many Kosovans calling their babies Tony. Next, in an Albanian refugee tent using the same humanitarian deception, he wore a red top and black trousers, the colours of the Albanian flag. He declaimed heroically of Slobodan Milošević, the Serbian leader, 'There are no half measures to his brutality.' He looked so impressive while doing this. David Blunkett was at No. 10 when the news broke that Milošević had capitulated. He told Nicky Blair, 'Hug your dad; he's contributed to saving tens of thousands of people.'

The Afghan invasion was the legitimate response to the terror of 9/11, and should have, in the occupation by Nato forces in the following years, been backed up to a successful conclusion instead of being downscaled. But it was rated as only a sideshow by the US right-wing consensus which came to power with George W. Bush in 2001 and which had long advocated military control of the Gulf region. If dozens of people share psychotic or delusional beliefs they can be thought of as prophets or truth-speakers rather than lunatics. This is roughly what happened in the higher echelons of the US administration after 9/11.

It emerged in a book published in 2006 (Bob Woodward, *State of Denial*) that George Tenet and Cofer Black, top CIA executives, had warned Condoleezza Rice, Bush's National Security Adviser, two months before 9/11 (10 July 2001) that Al Qaeda were poised to launch such an attack, but Rice took no notice. This 'state of denial' from the American heads of state (and from Blair's government) on the one hand, and over-sensitivity to the extreme reaction of the Islamist media and world on the other, were symptoms of the huge breakdown of understanding, trust and intelligence between the UK and its European neighbours. In time it gave rise to the French, whose intelligence warnings from the best-equipped secret service vis-à-vis the Arab and Muslim world were neglected, calling London 'Londonistan'. Tony, whose occasional strong insights alternated with a trusting naivety bordering on simple-mindedness, was content to abandon his friend Bill's belief in containment, in favour of the Bush 'shock and awe' obliteration of the Taliban and the mujahideen that Margaret Thatcher had so lavishly praised as heroic freedom fighters.

In November 2001, weeks after US, British and coalition forces attacked Afghanistan in their so-called 'legitimised revenge attack' against Osama bin Laden for 9/11, Cherie told a conference she organised in Downing Street, once again breaking the constitutional mould, that women in that country needed freedom from sexist tyranny – needed 'to lift the veil' and show what was happening in Afghanistan under the Taliban. Yet she had nothing to say, nor had Tony, when shocking photos, posted on the official Pentagon website, showed terror 'suspects' picked off the streets of Kabul, hooded and shrouded, in obvious breach of the Geneva convention on human rights. The *Daily Mirror*'s headline, above the grim pictures, ran, 'What the hell are you doing over there, Mr Blair?'

Alastair Campbell at once rang the editor, telling him he should not be sticking the boot in.

This set the Iraq precedent.

*

At the Labour Party conference in September 2002, Campbell emphasised how the government needed to restrain Bush from attacking Iraq. His warning was not heeded, because it was in the sequel to that first Blair–Bush meeting that Tony would seem to have fallen irretrievably under the spell of George. Heart and head were at odds in Tony, for head must have told him to be cautious, not to be swept along by a man uninterested in self-knowledge and incapable of introspection. A 'dry drunk', a former drinker who now abstains but who has not dealt with the fundamental anxieties or inherited aspects of his or her condition, shows a similar pattern of traits which Tony found so appealing in Alastair Campbell: 'grandiose judgementalism, intolerance, detachment, denial of responsibility, a tendency to over-reaction and an aversion to introspection' (Justin A. Frank). So here were reasons of personality why Tony was attracted to George and succumbed to his spell as he had to Campbell's.

For Tony 'head' was Europe, dull, old-fashioned, traditional, the enemy of 'modernisation'. 'Heart' was the United States and his passionate desire to become an honorary American (he was to all intents and purposes now acting President of the UK, with Cherie as First Lady – and was to remain so, at least for a while). Insensitivity, lack of searching curiosity, an emotional conviction overrode all evidence, but what is extraordinary is how Blair and Bush, and Condoleezza Rice ('Probably the worst National Security Adviser in modern times since the office was created,' according to David Kay, the US official later ordered by Bush to hunt and find WMD in Iraq), swallowed Saddam's lies.

It was quite clear that a deep factor in Bush's response was the personality challenge: speaking of radical Islam, Bush said, 'They want to humiliate us . . . we need to humiliate them.' The Iraq war had to be, in typical Bushese, 'in order to make a point that we're not going to live in this world that we want for us [*sic*]'.

Bush did not want to be like his father; he wanted to show the world he could beat him at his own game; he wanted to imitate Ronald Reagan. It was perhaps for Tony to reflect that, making his own independent decision to follow Bush to war, far from 'simply doing what was right' and being 'ready to meet my Maker and answer for those who have died as a result of my decisions', he would never have gone to war had Clinton been President – Clinton would have decided on containment instead of aggression. Wouldn't going to war then have been far from 'simply doing what was right'?

Tony had always been a rebel, so how do we explain this extraordinary volte-face?

In August 2002 during a customary annual break, Tony went for a day's hike in the Pyrenees, after which he stayed the night with his fellow walker in a chalet hotel. At breakfast the next morning, his friend reported that Tony showed irritability of temper, did not drink his coffee and 'said he had to leave at once for London. I asked if he was OK and he apologised for being a bit grumpy. He said he'd been up all night . . . couldn't get to sleep. And then he said, "I've made some big decisions."'

A few months on, in the early winter of 2002, seventy national security experts and Middle East scholars met at the National Defense University in Washington to discuss Iraq. They concluded that occupying Iraq 'will be the most daunting and complex task the US and the international community will have undertaken since the end of World War II'.

The group emphasised that the primary post-invasion task of the US military 'must be on establishing and maintaining a secure environment'. It also strongly cautioned against a swift, uncoordinated dissolution of the Iraqi military. 'There should be a phased downsizing to avoid dumping 1.4 million men into a shattered economy.' What is remarkable is that, again and again, such expert warnings were not heeded or even deemed worthy of a response. Deputy Defence Secretary Paul Wolfowitz – the most gung-ho of the pro-war ideologues – stated flatly in December 2002, 'I think people are overly pessimistic about the aftermath.'

Tony ignored similar warnings and advice from the Foreign Office and elsewhere. He had made up his mind, either 'seduced' by the special relationship, or convinced, Bush and the neocons apart, that he was, as he says, 'doing the right thing'. Determined now not to wait for the threat of Saddam to become reality, he had steeled himself 'to pay the blood price at

207

the moment of crisis'. He would stand side by side with Bush, just as, as he had said after 9/11, 'America stood side by side with the British people in the Blitz'. He got that wrong too, because the United States had done no such thing, not engaging in hostilities until after Pearl Harbor had precipitated it into war with Japan, more than six months later, and even then it was Germany, on 11 December 1941, that declared war on the United States. But that didn't matter to him. The need for war, for action, was deep within the man.

Part IV

2003

33

The God factor

> The seasons alter: hoary-headed frosts
> Fall in the fresh lap of the crimson rose . . .
> The spring, the summer,
> The childing autumn, angry winter, change
> Their wonted liveries, and the mazed world,
> By their increase, now knows not which is which.

William Shakespeare, A Midsummer Night's Dream

Tony's 2002 decision to go to war, fully endorsed in public by Cherie, brought the question of their Catholic faith once again into the public arena. In early 2003, with three members of their family, they travelled to Rome. Stressed by Cherie to be a 'private visit', it was far from this. With the repeated condemnation by Pope John Paul II of any military action in the Gulf, and the insistence of the French President, Jacques Chirac, that the 'region does not need another war', the Blair family visit to Rome from 26 to 28 February gave Tony the opportunity to put his case for a war and seek the pontiff's counsel, even his endorsement. This was very important to him, for, as he was to say on the Michael Parkinson show in March 2006, specifically with regard to his decision to invade Iraq, 'if you have faith you realise that judgement is made by God'.

The eve-of-war visits of other heads of state, including the Iraqi foreign minister, gave the impression there was almost a stampede, or at least a queue, to consult the Pope. Cherie insisted that early in Tony's premiership the Vatican had indicated that the Pope would like to meet him, but planning the trip had taken 'a long time'. There had been 'resistance inside

No. 10' to their meeting, and they had already tried once to arrange it during a holiday in Tuscany. This had not been possible. Finally it had been arranged for February 2003. Disingenuously Cherie claimed it was a 'total coincidence' that the crisis over the invasion of Iraq was at its height: as we now know, invasion had been decided on in 2002. The terms 'insisted on by No. 10', in Cherie's words, were that it was entirely a personal visit, with the Blairs paying for their own flights and accommodation. It is highly possible that Cherie, generally believed at the time to be privately against the war, hoped the Pope might dissuade Tony. Later some of her colleagues at Matrix were to declare the war 'unlawful'.

*

Concerns over, or at least attention on, Tony's potential conversion to Catholicism had reached a peak in 1998. His election in 1997 had added a new twist to the tale of British suspicion, even hostility, towards the Roman Catholic faith. For it was widely known even then, before he became premier, that he took Catholic communion in St Joan of Arc Church in Islington. 'I look back on our time in north London as among the happiest in our family life and I look forward to getting back to that one day in the future,' Cherie said later. 'People didn't know that he wasn't a Catholic,' says Father Michael Seed of Westminster Cathedral.

Cherie gave the impression in 2003 that Tony's attendance at mass had been denounced by the Orange Order as consorting with 'the bride of the devil', and conversion, reinforced by the 'Establishment sensitivity' over Northern Ireland question, she claimed, would have proved 'an electoral disaster'. Whether he will convert, finally, Tony has always dismissed as 'a tedious question'. He had attended mass and taken communion for twenty-five years or more, anyway, so was 'a de facto Catholic', according to Father Seed (which, by the way, would make his advice to the Queen on such matters as the appointment of bishops illegal). But if he were to become a Catholic, 'he doesn't have to make it public. Of course he'd have to confess.'

The Pope in a Vatican directive of 1996 had tightened the practice of refusing communion to non-Catholics, and accordingly Cardinal Hume had written to Tony asking him not to take communion any more. It was alright to do so, he said, if the family was on holiday in Tuscany, where no Anglican church could be reached, but not allowable in London where there were plenty. But even in Tuscany, one year, a local priest strongly complained. Tony accepted the ruling but did not agree with it, answering Hume that he would refrain if it would cause problems, but adding, 'I wonder what Jesus would have made of it.'

Tony called Pontius Pilate in a *Sunday Telegraph* article 'the archetypal politician . . . so nearly a good man . . . caught on the horns of an age-old political dilemma'. Jesus, Tony wrote, 'restlessly searched after truth, he challenged, he changed, he asked why'. When he went on to let slip that 'Jesus was a moderniser', Dominic Lawson, then editor of the paper, objected: 'Mr Blair does not deserve our faith.' Lawson said that it was wrong that 'Blair should have identified himself, however unwittingly, with the Messiah.'

While the 2001 election was brewing Tony had been unusual in admitting that he believed in sin, perhaps the first British Prime Minister since the nineteenth century wholly to admit to so doing. He qualified the admission by saying that 'sin' was a word that 'seems old-fashioned today' and went on:

> Yet the concept [of the belief in sin] is simple and important. In theological terms, it is alienation from God. In everyday terms, it is the acknowledgement of right and wrong. It is the rejection of a purely libertarian ethos. This is an area that will become of increasing importance in politics.

To counteract or soften the impression made by using that taboo word he added, 'I don't mean "sin" in the sense of personal morality, but there is a desire in the modern world to retrieve and re-establish a sense of values, of common norms of good behaviour.' Tony spread his meaning to a wider but more ambiguous sense of social inclusion – the 'undifferentiationism', one thing being just like another, again took away any personal commitment to 'uniqueness', to responsibility.

One Sunday offered the spectacle, in Basil Hume's Westminster Cathedral, of Ann Widdecombe, a member of the congregation, reading out the Ten Commandments with Cherie and Tony sitting in the front rows. The story broke that Blair might soon convert, like the Duchess of Kent a few years earlier, which had been a 'shocking' betrayal of her royal position, as reported in some quarters. If so, in the next election a Catholic Blair might be expected to stand against two Catholics: both opposition leaders at the time, Charles Kennedy and Iain Duncan Smith, were practising Catholics. But the conversion was not to be – not immediately, anyway – while most people in the country now thought of religion as a form of therapy, or something worse. A new high priest of genetic and environmental determinism, Richard Dawkins, was on the scene, calling (in 2006) the Christian God 'misogynistic, homophobic, racist, infanticidal, genocidal, sado-masochistic and a capaciously malevolent bully'. Secular malevolence in the media was spreading: Philip Roth, for example, said, 'I find religious people hideous.' But Dennis Sewell, a writer who surveyed the Catholic faith in Britain, commented on Tony taking communion, 'Few could imagine that a modern man like Tony Blair might simply want to participate in the celebration of the Eucharist.' By taking Catholic Holy Communion Tony felt a personal contact with the God in whom he believed.

For a time – until President Bush came on the scene in 2000 – Blair had refused to answer questions about his faith. Alastair Campbell operated the guillotine: 'We don't do God.' The national confirmation of disbelief was much more important. Agitation in the secular press and the anti-Catholic bias of the BBC, as shown in such programmes as *Kenyon Confronts*, the commissioning of *Popetown*, and *Panorama*'s 'Sex and the Holy City', continued their rise, while even C. S. Lewis, the author of the much-loved Narnia novels and an Anglo-Catholic, became a particular butt. Of the film made from *The Lion, the Witch, and the Wardrobe*, which Tony declared to be among his favourite reads, Polly Toynbee wrote, 'Narnia is the perfect Republican, muscular Christianity for America – that warped, distorted neo-fascist strain.' The hugely successful children's author Philip Pullman described the Narnia series as 'one of the most ugly poisonous things I have ever read'.

*

Before they left for Rome in February 2003 Cherie rang and asked Cormac Murphy-O'Connor how they should conduct themselves in the presence of the Pope. For the audience Cherie wore a black suit and the black lace mantilla of a devout Catholic woman (in contrast to an audience in 2006 with Benedict XVI, when she wore white). It delighted her that they had come with a largely Catholic entourage, including three Catholic detectives, from their pool of fifteen, and a Catholic nanny, who carried Leo. Now aged two, Leo had drawn a picture to give as a present along with official gifts, but as Cherie kneeled to kiss the Pope's ring, he squirmed out of the nanny's arms. Vatican staff let him sit on one of the Pope's thrones. Yet there in the Vatican Tony and Cherie must have known and wilfully disregarded how tenaciously John Paul had ranged himself in opposition to the Gulf War, which had begun in August 1990 with Saddam's invasion of Kuwait – and in spite of the United Nations' favourable vote.

The Pope wrote to the first President Bush to stress the devastating and tragic consequences that war would bring if the coalition of thirty-nine countries resorted to military action. He went to extraordinary lengths, with over fifty initiatives of every kind, to avoid hostilities, then end them, then repair the damage. In spite of the Pope's public and private opposition to the war – and to war as a general principle in the resolution of any conflict – many eminent Catholics were to express complete and strongly argued support for Bush and Blair in the Iraq War, for instance Lord Alton in England and George Weigel in the United States. But as to why Tony had gone to Rome the pundits were mistaken, at least according to Cherie.

How Blair could have thought he might convince John Paul his own case for war just beggars credibility. But he argued hard to convince the Pope. In the twenty-minute audience the Pontiff pointed out the terrible consequences if he took that step, the cost in civilian casualties, and the old warrior of peace, who knew the ravages of war and its aftermath from bitter experience in Poland, would have been forthright – as he had been when he tried to stop the Falklands conflict in 1982, when he denounced it to Margaret Thatcher's very face. 'Today the scale and horror of modern warfare – whether nuclear or not – makes it totally unacceptable as a means of settling differences between nations,' he had said; while at Hiroshima, on a visit to Japan in the shadow of the skeletal Peace Memorial, he had declaimed passionately, 'War is an act of man. War destroys human lives. War is death.' In particular the Pope, according to his press secretary, pleaded with Blair that 'special consideration be given to the humanitarian situation of the Iraqi people already so severely tired by long years of embargo'.

It is impossible to imagine the religious standpoint from which Blair could have formed the notion that God could tell him to go to war, and it stretches his and Cherie's belief in Catholicism to breaking point. The Holy Father was not convinced by Tony's arguments and never would be. Presumably – this is speculation – Tony played the card, as he was to go on doing, that he had not taken his final decision, and still had doubts. But there was a difference between feeling reservations about a decision already reached, and being ready to change it. The Pope, who had received every kind of world leader at the Vatican, would never deny Blair's right to determine what he chose to do. He was of course always saying 'man has to choose' and had in his time held conversations with many tyrants and notorious malefactors, including the man who attempted to kill him.

Cherie then spoke to the Pope on her own for another ten minutes, giving him gifts of a vase depicting the entrance to 10 Downing Street, and a small bronze statue of St Margaret of Scotland. The Pope rose and left his study and presented them with rosaries, medals and a fine icon.

Next morning the Blair family attended mass in the new brown marble-floored papal chapel at eight o'clock (the time, as a concession to the Pope's age, had been moved from seven). Here, as one of the acolytes observed, the Pope sat on a chair ten minutes before the mass, facing the altar, absorbed in prayer. This image he gave was, for Cherie, she says, both 'a symbol of suffering and the defeat of suffering'. When he began to say mass he sprang to life: he said all the mass, the first part in English, but when he came to the Eucharistic prayer, switching to Latin.

Tony, in off-the-peg suit and muted tie (taller and younger looking than he appeared in his photos) read the first lesson from Isaiah, 'I it is who must blot out everything.' Euan read the responsorial prayer, 'Heal my soul for I have sinned against you', and Kathryn the second reading, from Corinthians, 'Jesus was never yes and no: with him it was always yes.' The Irish bishop, host at the Irish College, where the family was staying, read the Gospel from Mark, Chapter Two: 'The Son of Man has authority on earth to forgive sins.' There was no homily, while the Pope stood for the whole Eucharistic prayer. The Pope then gave the family communion, including

Tony, while the other celebrants gave communion to the rest of the congregation. Only two weeks later, the Pope through a Curial directive emphasised the rule that communion should not be dispensed to non-Catholics. But here was an example of Karol Wojtyła as parish priest of Rome making the human gesture, and demonstrating that priests were there to serve the family. It was ungracious of papal critics who pointed out gleefully that the Pope broke his own rules. This was a decision for Tony, not for the Pope.

At the end of the mass John Paul sat in his chair looking at Cherie and Tony. With those big blue eyes, says one of the acolytes, he 'doesn't miss a thing . . . He has that much power. He's saying, "I'm looking at all of you [i.e. the whole person]." ' He saw well into the ugly future too, and from the depth of his experience he probably had the vision that Tony was about to miss the opportunity for a great humanitarian gesture in the cause of truth and peace, and the opportunity to establish himself as a great world leader.

*

The Pope's diction had been distinct and clear – he'd been on new drugs to combat Parkinson's disease since last summer. After the silence at the end of the mass he stood up – head leaning to one side – and spoke in English. 'God bless you all.' He shook everyone's hand, gave out rosaries, held little Leo by the hand while the cameras flashed.

The Blairs had considered it important that Tony put his case for a just war to the Pope, to square his conscience with the man Mikhail Gorbachev had described to his wife, Raisa, as 'the highest moral authority on earth'. But why should he try, when he had already made his decision? The papal visit fitted perfectly this image of wanting to be seen to do the right thing. But how Tony could have formed the notion that God could tell him to go to war is of a singular strangeness. He did so in effect on the *Parkinson* show mentioned earlier, when he claimed, 'God will be my judge.' He told Michael Parkinson that while he struggled with his conscience over the decision, he received guidance from divine authority: to put it bluntly, God had told him it was all right to go to war. The actual words, expressed hesitantly, were that there 'is another judgment . . . made by other people and by God' – the meaning plain to anyone who watched, that what he did, in his words, 'depended on other judgments than your own'. He might have included the Pope in that thought. We are now led to understand, thanks to that appearance, that the question of his religious belief was crucial to the most important political decision Tony ever made. Catholics would be surprised if John Paul would ever go or had ever in his whole life gone so far as to voice publicly that God told him to do something so specific, and in such categoric and presumptuous terms – let alone invade a sovereign country and expose it to the horrors of modern destruction. Had he prayed with Bush before the invasion, Parkinson asked, repeating the question Jeremy Paxman had put to him in 2003. 'No, I don't want to go into that,' answered the Prime Minister.

The critical issue was what the Pope had said to Tony in their private conversation. When I asked her, Cherie said that John Paul had told him, 'Ultimately, it is up to you to decide what to do.' This was, according to Cherie, the exact response. In England on his return, Tony told a friend something different. What John Paul said to him, not once but three times, he revealed, was, 'I am very glad this is not my decision.'

There is a distinct difference in emphasis between the two versions, which can be interpreted in several ways. Cherie may have been conveying that the Pope had less sympathy towards him than Tony seems to be showing in his own words (or perhaps it was Cherie herself who had the less sympathy). But the words Tony relay carry a sense of the pique he must have felt. In either case – and importantly – the Pope made the church's stand clear to Tony; and he might well have added, 'Whatever you do, don't use God to back up your decisions.' Which version exactly corresponds to what the Pope said is a mystery.

After the audience Blair held talks with Cardinal Sodano, the Secretary of State, and Archbishop Tauron, the papal foreign minister. Both reiterated the Pope's message of working through the United Nations, and expressed the Vatican view that war was 'still believed to be avoidable'. The English archbishop Michael Fitzgerald reputedly told Blair, 'If only you could offer to give up something as well' – in other words, make a gesture to Saddam – but this was most unlikely to curry favour.

Downing Street later issued a Tony statement, which might have come out of *Animal Farm*: 'We acknowledge the Pope's concerns and we share the desire to avoid war, but ultimately the decision will be a decision for Saddam.' This was rather like saying Germany's decision in 1939 to invade Poland was a decision for Poland to make. Later Cherie told me the papal visit was 'the highlight of my time' at No. 10.

The bid to have the Pope on his side, the need for 'authentication' of Tony's action by the Catholic Church, failed, but this establishes that 'private visit' to Rome in a very different light.

34

Let slip the dogs of war

And Caesar's spirit, ranging for revenge,
With Ate by his side, come hot from hell,
Shall in these confines with a monarch's voice
Cry 'Havoc!' and let slip the dogs of war,
That this foul deed shall smell above the earth
With carrion men, groaning for burial.

William Shakespeare, *Julius Caesar*

During the final run-up to war Tony discounted all intelligence that did not
suit his decision, and ignored all warnings from European heads of state,
including Jacques Chirac's statement, ten days before war began, that
France would veto the second UN Resolution. This shocked Blair, who
exploded that this was 'a foolish thing to do at this moment in world history'.

The Russian President, Vladimir Putin, had already told him the previous
autumn that Russia had no 'trustworthy data which would support the
existence of nuclear weapons or any weapons of mass destruction in Iraq',
yet in spite of this and the negative French intelligence reports, and flimsy
evidence (if any) from Hans Blix and the UN weapons inspectors, Blair told
the Commons on 25 February, 'Not a single member of the international
community believes Saddam Hussein's denials that he has no WMDs.' On
the very eve of the invasion, on 19 March, Tony informed the Commons of
what was to prove a wholly false prediction, namely that Saddam Hussein
'will be responsible for many more deaths even in one year than we will be
in any conflict'. (By the autumn of 2006 it was estimated by the *Lancet*
magazine that more than 655,000 civilians, or 2.5 per cent of the total

population, had died since 20 March 2003, the day of the invasion. Although these figures were inflated, a nearer estimate being perhaps 30,000 a year, the US military refusing to keep the number of civilian casualties, by then revenge-taking was out of control.)

Tony failed to secure the second resolution of the UN Security Council, so the United States and the UK had to go it alone. Both governments claimed this as a lonely and brave decision by their leaders, but Cherie was strongly behind Tony, resolute that they should stay by America's side. Why did Tony pursue this path, which Clare Short described as 'reckless . . . reckless . . . reckless', and led later to Robin Cook's resignation?

One reason above all. Not the pact between Bush and Blair; Blair could have broken that, for Bush gave him the chance to drop out of military coalition, although the equally short-sighted Jack Straw claimed rather stupidly, 'We will reap a whirlwind if we push the Americans into a unilateral position', but the much more powerful bond of Cherie and Tony. Tony believed he had to stick close to George. But both of them were equally convinced that this was the right decision on the basis that Saddam was an evil dictator and had to be 'taken out', failing to see that Saddam swaggered in the realm of make-believe about his deadly arsenal of weapons, gambling that the menace would deter Bush.

Cherie's philosophy was that you remain inside; you influence and ultimately control by being part of something, such as the Labour Party, and now the Bush administration, not from outside. This meant Cherie increasingly played a highly political role, and although unelected used her prestige as a woman and a human rights lawyer to support what was now called 'the second phase of the war on terror', which in that endlessly repeated phrase was to bring to an end Iraq's 'capability and intention to use weapons of mass destruction'.

*

Now Tony claimed, as we have shown, that the route to war could have been legitimised in the Security Council resolution, had the French not threatened a veto categorically against the use of force. This was also not true. In the Commons debate on Iraq on 4 June 2003 Clare Short delivered an authoritative account of how Tony lied and deceived Parliament and people in his desire to authorise war. She pointed out: 'The Christian teaching on just war . . . and I understand that the Muslim teaching is very similar, unsurprisingly – says that the cause must be just, the remedy proportionate, the war winnable, and that there must be no other way of putting right the wrong.' The possibility, she said, of resolving the problem in another way was not exhausted. 'It was therefore not a just war.' She went on:

> The Prime Minister told us that we could not get a second resolution because the French had said that they would veto any second resolution. A member of the public sent me the transcript of the Chirac interview, and it is plain that he said clearly on 10 March that the Blix process needed to be completed and we had to see whether that could succeed in achieving disarmament, but if not, we would have to go back to the Security Council and the Security Council would have to authorise military action. We were misled about the French position, and the French have been vilified disgracefully, when it was not their position to rule out all military action. We will never know—

Here, on behalf of Tony, Denis McShane, the Minister for Europe, jumped to his feet:

> Will my Right hon. Friend give way on that point? . . . I have the French transcript of the exact words that President Chirac said. Nowhere did he say that he was ready to contemplate the use of force. What he said – I do not refer to the veto reference – was that if there was a majority of nine on the Security Council authorising war, France would vote no. [MPs: '*Ce soir.*'] Not '*ce soir*'. That is in a different part of the interview. He said that France would vote no, and that killed the chances of a UN path to peace.

Short answered McShane's misleading interruption:

> [Chirac] said [on 10 March] that if the weapons inspectors came back to the Security Council, stated that they could not achieve disarmament, and said, '"We are sorry but Iraq isn't cooperating, the progress isn't sufficient, we aren't in a position to achieve our goal, we won't be able to guarantee Iraq's

disarmament," in that case it will be for the Security Council and it alone to decide the right thing to do. But in that case, of course, regrettably, the war would become inevitable. It isn't today.' ['*ce soir*']

That is not only what Chirac said on 10 March but he had also told Tony at a meeting of European leaders the previous autumn, directly to his face, no doubt incurring Cherie's wrath, 'Leo will not thank you in the future if you lead Britain into war.' Tony commented dismissively, as if it was a stupid first-night review of a play of his, 'The dear old drag, he just doesn't get it.'

*

On the eve of war well over 70 per cent of the American public, at least in a poll, favoured upending Saddam's regime (they were hardly well informed: 'God invented war', commented the humorist Arthur Smith, 'to teach America geography'), but in the UK a public demonstration of more than a million registered opposition.

'How do we address the nation?' Tony asked Alastair Campbell.

'My fellow Americans,' answered Campbell, but Tony did not find this amusing.

'This is not the time to falter,' Tony began his speech in a high-pitched, uneven delivery.

And so Tony's third war, Afghanistan, was only too rapidly followed by the fourth and final one. Gradually over that period from 9/11 to the decision to go to war Blair had recognised and built into himself, largely unconsciously, the Bush certainties: put in a nutshell, as Bob Woodward reported, Bush said of his father that 'he is the wrong father to appeal to in terms of strength. There is a higher father that I appeal to'. They were now Tony's certainties too.

The quickish fall of Baghdad gave both men a lift. Just as he had walked alongside Bill Clinton with the 'college boys eternal' image when both gave delicate, fluttery hand signals, now alongside Bush he was seen as attempting to be the warrior double of the President: chest thrust out, arms swinging with military action, a virile, cocky carriage of the head. There were unfortunate hints of Mr Bean in this. In the shadow of a potential revolt of Labour MPs, Cherie shamelessly canvassed the women MPs to have them on Tony's side. Lady Macbeth was screwing up her husband's courage to 'the sticking place'. They would not fail, and Tony waxed confident again, proclaiming proudly that the Iraq war was the most important event for a generation and that in twenty years' time it would prove his reputation in history.

For the war-like leader who had now become, 'not casualty averse, like Clinton', killing a lot of people is not much different from killing one. Large numbers mean nothing. Taking the plunge strengthened Tony and affirmed him as a war leader. Quoted in Anthony Seldon's *Blair*, one insider said, 'He's become much more confident because during the war he had to stand up to the most senior military and security figures in the land. It made him grow up very quickly.' More confident, yes. But was it growing up? Surely, it stopped him growing up. Another insider observed how it 'bonded' him with his team. 'It made us a close family.' But a close family cannot be made on shifting sand.

The eager fourth-former was now strutting by the side of the headmaster, Bush, who saw in Blair an ideal PR for his own agenda towards war with Iraq, in which Blair became the enabler, the authenticator, and with quantitatively smaller, but qualitatively much more professional, armed forces than the United States had, to support this. Both were to an alarming degree helpless puppets of their own times and lack of vision. Governments of democracies in particular had just not worked out how to deal with this new world order. It may seem absurd, but the fundamental interaction and expectations of people in power and their constituencies, local, national or global, had reverted to a form of medievalism. As J. K. Galbraith wrote, 'In such a [medieval] world all politics were embodied in personal affections, or in personal hatreds and jealousies.' Not only in the way that Blair and Bush had, as a means of survival, created medieval courts around themselves, but the ever-intrusiveness of the media meant that politics had in every aspect a human face (albeit sometimes a very distorted or manipulated one), which it had not had for most of the intervening centuries.

*

Over the months after the occupation of Iraq while looting was rife, and the interior security situation went from bad to worse, it soon became clear that for all the costly and frantic search, no WMD were going to be found. This resulted in a hardening of the intellectual and moral case for a just war, paradoxically even from right-wing Catholics such as George Weigel, who knew how vehemently Pope John Paul II was opposed to war as a resolution of any conflict, but who had in writing about him claimed that the Pope told an archbishop prior to the first Gulf War that he hoped the Americans would win, and wanted them to win quickly to limit casualties. Weigel had otherwise criticised John Paul and the Vatican for its exaggerated predictions of the direct effect of military action in the Gulf.

David Kay, in charge of the hunt for WMD, had 946 locations that US intelligence showed as potential sites. But all when investigated on the ground gave the lie to the rhetoric on which the invasion thrived: namely, in Bush's famous words, 'we know for a fact that they were there'. Iraq's scientists, quizzed and requizzed by agents, and offered large bribes to reveal the secret arsenal, came up with nothing, while the scores of talented fabricators were all proved unfounded in their claims.

The terror of US Army units, under-equipped with biological warfare protection, had all been stimulated by the huge hoax on Saddam's part that if Iraq was invaded he would retaliate. Saddam never had WMD but he pretended he had, which is now understood as a tool of intimidation for Kurd nationalists and the majority Shi'ite Muslims in Iraq. Kay concluded that the disease of the intelligence community is this over-focus on current intelligence as opposed to longer-term strategic intelligence. Quite frankly, said Kay, the press does a better job.

35

A chapter without title

What is Cherie Blair like to meet in person?

I visited Downing Street in June 2003. I was writing the life of John Paul II and I asked her for the inside story of her visit to the Vatican in late February, on the eve of the Iraq war. I had never interviewed the wife of a Prime Minister.

My appointment took place at 4 p.m. on Tuesday 10 June; I had been allocated thirty minutes. I cleared the security formalities at the iron-gated end of Downing Street and when I arrived at the front door of No. 10 gave my name and was admitted to a seat in a corridor recess which was quite modest and public. Self-important young women with badges scurried back and forth, and photocopiers chomped and whirred in the background. I can only describe the atmosphere as Dickensian, as when in *Little Dorrit* Clennam waits for an interview in a ministry. A little while later I was conducted by a friendly aide upstairs through a door marked 'private' to the No. 11 flat. At the top of the stairs was a landing littered with building blocks and leftover party balloons; to the left I could see a small, galley-like kitchen; the flat was, to be frank, scruffy and untidy. I was ushered into an empty sitting room to the right of the toy-covered carpet and left alone. Here there was a grand piano and Tony's guitar case propped against a yellow, upholstered chair; the room was very middle class in its furnishings. I sat on a large couch which faced another across the low coffee table; asked by an aide if I wanted something to drink, I requested a glass of water. Cherie kept me waiting a few minutes so I wandered round the room looking at family photographs; one was of Kathryn, in a white communion dress, another was of Nicky at his first communion, I presumed, holding a candle. What did surprise me, considering the general view by now of the Clintons, were two prominently placed pictures of Tony and Cherie with Bill and Hillary, standing in a mutual adoration pose; in another photo Tony was at one end of a sofa, Bill at the other, looking in different directions but talking on the phone. There was a handwritten Clinton joke encapsulated in a cartoon balloon: 'Why not just hang up and talk face to face? Is this what the Third Way means?'

Cherie entered the room swiftly, came straight over, shook hands with me and informally settled down opposite. Dressed in a loose black top and trousers, she was both smaller and quicker in manner and expression than she appears in photographs or on television, and though she did have the deep bags under her eyes which give her that goggle-eyed look, she was quite attractive.

I was impressed, I suppose slightly overawed, by her unexpected informality. She was at pains to let me see her warm, lovely, human side, but there was a kind of labile openness, almost – but not wanting to put it too crudely – a flirty looseness about her which I found quite disconcerting, and which she played on. It would have been more expected, say, in a young actress meeting her director for the first time.

Yet she was polite, engaged, in tune with what I asked. Marie Stubbs, the head of St George's Roman Catholic School in Westminster, where the previous head had been murdered, says, when Cherie visited her school in February 2001, how she related to the staff 'in a warm and friendly way, not at all stuffy, but genuinely interested, accessible'. This was my impression too. For instance, at one point she collected and showed me an album of pictures taken of the family visit to the Vatican to meet John Paul II, including ones of Leo on the Pope's throne. True, I was flattered to be taken into her confidence and privileged as a papal biographer to be extended this intimacy, when I knew that she refused to give interviews. But at the same time I became slightly alarmed at the way she came and squatted down on the floor just in front of me, bending forwards so that I could see into her cleavage, and that she wore no bra. At one point she came up very close to me, almost face to face.

This made me think about a comment Lynda Lee-Potter made in the *Daily Mail* around this time that Cherie was not getting much bedroom attention from Tony, and needed to spice up their sex life. It might well be true, or it might not, but should we be thinking about her in that light? Cherie had changed from an 'austere, uncompromising career woman who hated the limelight' and reinvented herself as 'a paranoid, insecure free-loader, traumatised by her body, [who] can't apply her own lipstick, and has entrenched Catholic guilt about sex' – this was what Lee-Potter at her most extreme had said. The public saw, from the *Marie Claire* article she referred to, pictures of Cherie sitting on the marital bed, holding out her lips to have lipstick applied by Carole Caplin; that she and Tony slept in a garish bedroom of execrable bad taste, on the other side of the hall, which 'looked as though it had been designed for a commercial traveller staying at a Holiday Inn'; and that Cherie had spread about Downing Street her deep litter of children's toys and her own underwear. Lee-Potter went on:

> If she'd wanted to portray herself as Mrs Average, this was a great mistake. The rest of us would have been up at dawn shoving knickers, tights, make-up and bras into any conceivable drawer before running round with the vacuum cleaner. In fact, most of us wouldn't allow a photographer anywhere near our bedroom.

And here I was, in the same locale. I can only describe it as bizarre.

Cherie generously gave me the account of the Vatican visit, which had ended with her saying it was 'the highlight of my time here', and after this she showed me the Pope's gift, an Orthodox icon of the Virgin. I left feeling flattered and fulfilled on the one hand, on the other hand confused and perplexed at how she came over. There was undoubtedly a strong contradiction here. It was perhaps this meeting more than anything else which gave me the purpose of trying to understand the Blairs better, as not to reduce them, but to enrich our way of knowing them, and through them ourselves and our perception of political power.

36

I dreamt tonight that I did feast with Caesar

I dreamt tonight that I did feast with Caesar,
And things unlucky charge my fantasy.

William Shakespeare, *Julius Caesar*

In *Julius Caesar*, when, after repeated stabbings, the dying Caesar turns to Brutus, his friend, his intimate, and just as Brutus is about to thrust the weapon into his heart, Caesar cries out, 'Et tu, Brute'. Later, because of their closeness, Marc Antony shows the dead Caesar's wounds to the crowd gathered in the forum and picks out the one made by Brutus: 'This was the unkindest cut of all.'

From time immemorial this treacherous and brutal stabbing has been the subject of thousands of political cartoons. But more than ever today *Julius Caesar*, in all its aspects of political conspiracy, sacrificial cycles, murder and betrayal – and ultimate civil war nemesis in the media village – serves as a brilliant parallel or sounding board for the ten tragic years of Blair's rule. In Shakespeare's plays the self-destruction of authority in all its forms is fundamentally exposed: he shows power teetering on the edge of its own collapse, and most of the leaders he depicts have a fatal taste for self-dramatisation.

The conspiracy to topple Saddam Hussein had been hatched in secret. Its legality and illegality became disputed endlessly, while the global civil war unleashed by the invasion of Iraq was to have much in common with the conflicts which tore apart the Roman Empire after Caesar's death. As a crowning example of unconscious irony George Bush's statement of 2004 – 'A free Iraq will change the world' – has become only too true, in a way very different from Bush's intention.

Saddam was the sacrificial victim in more ways than one: although by no means an intimate of Bush and Blair, even so he was a mimetic double of the pair. Those hollow yet universally blazed moments of victory when Saddam's statue was torn down, his palaces ransacked, are astutely caught by Shakespeare's camera eye in similar scenes: the reassurances of Brutus are echoed in the many post-war speeches of Blair and Bush.

But there is one short scene, above all, that has always haunted me. This was the murder of Cinna the poet, who is mistaken for Cinna the conspirator. In this scene the savage mob, inflamed by Marc Antony's subtle but vengeful rhetoric of 'Friends, Romans, countrymen, lend me your ears', roams the streets seeking a scapegoat to murder and comes upon the hapless poet Cinna. Because he shares his name with one of the conspirators the Roman mob first torments him, unsure of his identity, but then decides he will do: ''Tis no matter who he is,' says one. 'Tear him to pieces.' Nothing exemplifies more perfectly the fragility, the temporary and precarious nature, of human authority and power. It uncannily resembles also the needless and catastrophic death of an innocent man in 2003.

On Thursday 17 July that year an unassuming civil servant, one year away from retirement, set out on his evening walk to an isolated beauty spot near his home in Oxfordshire. He clambered through woodland thickets to a hidden secluded pocket. He carried with him a small bottle of mineral water, some packets of coproxamol, a painkiller, a mobile phone and a knife. The following morning, after a wide search to find him, he was discovered dead, lying beside a tree.

*

Six weeks earlier, two days after the fall of Baghdad, and in the absence of the disclosure of any weapons of mass destruction, began Stage 1 of the stand-off between Andrew Gilligan, a BBC *Today* reporter, and Alastair Campbell: a defining moment of Blair's reign.

Gilligan reported, 'Baghdad may in theory be free, but its people are passing their first days of liberty in a greater fear than they have ever known before.' The BBC–Downing Street conflict escalated quickly, as Gilligan went on to claim that the first dossier of the previous September, which stated that Iraq was capable of deploying WMD in forty-five minutes, was promulgated even though Blair knew it was 'probably' false. Gilligan stated that his claim had come from one single, uncorroborated source, and that the dossier had been 'sexed up'. Downing Street (with the ungrammatical, double negative imprint of Campbell) issued its denial: 'Not one word of the dossier was not entirely the work of the intelligence agencies.'

The subsequent dispute mounted in intensity and scurrile denunciations from Downing Street of the BBC. The twists and turns of this mini-civil war within the British Establishment have been endlessly trawled, but they led, inexorably, to the need for a scapegoat or sacrificial victim. Here, from his own innocence and unworldliness, Dr David Kelly, as if it was almost predetermined, perfectly fitted the bill.

Just as Cinna had chosen to be out in the streets of Rome just after Caesar's murder at the Capitol, so Dr Kelly had rather naively, while being a distinguished and meticulously objective weapons inspector in Iraq, voiced his opinion to Gilligan – while even supporting the invasion of Iraq – that no WMDs would be found. He then, very foolishly, denied he had said he had doubts about the dossier, and even more foolishly taped for BBC's *Newsnight* the comment:

> The forty-five minutes was a statement that was made and it got out of all proportion. They were desperate for information that could be released. That was one that popped up and it was seized on and it is unfortunate that it was. That is why there is an argument between the intelligence services and No. 10.

Nothing more perfectly demonstrates the cruel need of the political world to attribute blame to bolster up its own power, or how close Blair and Campbell felt to the collapse of their own power, as the desperate, indeed manic, need on both sides – that of the BBC and No. 10 – to find a scapegoat. 'Tear him to pieces' became a need from No. 10 to vindicate its revenge against the revelation of its own cover-up, and equally a need from Gilligan and the BBC to prove they were justified.

Did he kill himself, as a psychiatrist said at the subsequent Hutton inquiry, from a 'severe loss of self-esteem, resulting from a feeling that people had lost trust in him and from his dismay at being exposed to the media'? On his previous appearance at the parliamentary hearing of the Foreign Affairs Committee Andrew MacKinlay MP had called him 'chaff' and told him he had been set up as a fall guy. There were allegations that the Ministry of Defence had hounded him, threatening his reputation and, more importantly, his pension. Downing Street considered him a Walter Mitty character, while Jack Straw, whom he had once accompanied to a function, let it be known he was upset to be accompanied by so junior a figure. In fact the government had gone to extreme lengths to make sure the public knew his name. But was there something more ominous and sinister at work, as when he sent an email on his escape to the West Country to evade publicity before the 'outing' that there were 'dark actors playing games'?

PC Andrew Franklin, who found him on the morning of 18 July, slumped against a tree, with the three-inch pruning knife lying nearby, together with his watch, flat cap and the open bottle of mineral water which he used to help swallow the pills, said: 'He was lying on his back with his right hand to his side and his left hand was sort of inverted with the palm facing down, facing up on his back.' Doubts emerged subsequently as to whether it was suicide, but these were ignored by Lord Hutton, in charge of the later inquiry. A forensic toxicologist disputed the claim that the tablets had contributed to Dr Kelly's death, saying his stomach was virtually empty; the lack of blood from the wrist artery he was alleged to have cut with a blunt gardening knife prompted the ambulance crew who collected his body to say they thought it 'incredibly unlikely' that anyone could have died from the minor wound they saw. Moreover there were conflicting reports over his mood on the fatal day – one of his daughters was due shortly to be married – while search party volunteers who first found the body contradicted the later police testimony by insisting it was slumped against a tree, and none of the three items, the knife, the watch and the water, were in evidence. Many questions posed by Liberal Democrat MP Norman Baker as recently as July 2006 remain unanswered, notably those concerning the discrepancies in the medical evidence suggesting it was no suicide and could have been murder. The subject in the future will no doubt attract further development in the arena of conspiracy theory.

*

The news of the discovery of David Kelly's body hit Blair on a flight to Japan. He phoned Charles Falconer to set in motion at once an inquiry, to be chaired by 75-year-old Brian Hutton, the Northern Irish Law Lord. Announcing this tactic later to a press conference, at which he appeared grim and white faced, he fared badly when Jonathan Oliver of the *Mail on Sunday* asked him, 'Have you got blood on your hands, Prime Minister? Are you going to resign?' He glared silently at his interrogator and left the stage.

The BBC, confirming that Dr Kelly had indeed been Gilligan's source, brought the blood back to his face quickly. But four days later, this time on a flight to Hong Kong, he answered, jabbing his finger, the question 'Why did you authorise the naming of David Kelly?' with 'This is completely untrue', and then denied emphatically he had authorised anyone in Downing Street or the Ministry of Defence to release David Kelly's name.

Six days after Dr Kelly's death, the grief, if ever it was there, had rapidly passed. Cherie had joined Tony in Beijing wearing a Lizard suit, valued at £1,000 but bought at a knock-down price of £500; among an audience of students one piped up, 'Sing us a song. Sing the Beatles,' and while Tony appeared flustered, Cherie took the microphone and sang the first verse of 'When I'm Sixty Four' with Tony sheepishly mouthing the final line, 'birthday greetings, bottle of wine'. Tony was missing his minder, Alastair, who would not have allowed such unseemly behaviour, but friends insisted Cherie was lightening the mood by celebrating her Merseyside roots.

At the Hutton inquiry in August 2004, Tony significantly altered his dramatic mid-air assertion: 'The issuing of that statement authorised by the Prime Minister did give rise to questions by the press as to the identity of the civil servant, and those questions led onto the MoD confirming Dr Kelly's name' (Hutton inquiry report, p. 286). Not only this, but those who listened carefully heard him contradict himself. 'The September dossier [of 2002] was not making the case for war,' he said; its aim was to 'disclose our reasons and the reasons why we felt this issue had to be informed'.

The actor Blair had by now assumed full control of the mimetic repertoire at his command, and for this performance at the inquiry, displaying bronzed wrists after his summer holiday (no echo intended of Dr Kelly's supposed death wound), he gave a stumbling performance of heartfelt sincerity. The prop this time was his glasses, which over and over again came on and off his nose.

The choice of words was revealing. 'This thing was already starting to build as a major story' – the words defined his attitude to what had just passed: namely, that it was a story. The content of the event had already flown; there was only the perception and, as one observer noted when the dry voice was corrected by an adjustment of amplification and rang out more contritely, he could expound from his deferential imitation of Hutton, and 'I'm a big fan of yours' gazes, into his smokescreen of 'as I understand it' and 'as I was informed', and his worldly shrugs of 'hey-what-could-I-do?' once Campbell had got his Rottweiler teeth into Andrew Gilligan. It was of course the press that put the 'booster rockets', as he called them, on the narrative, while more persistent probing from Hutton provoked a barrage of 'frankly', and more expansive hand gesturing.

Aides and gum-chewing bodyguards soon led Blair and the 'whole, scheming, nay-saying chance-caravan' (as Letts wrote later) away to the stuffy inquiry bunker in quest of a new story. Campbell conducted his long-overdue stepping down afterwards with consummate management, announcing the day after Blair gave evidence that he was leaving Downing Street.

Both celebrated the tepid vindication supplied by the publication of the Hutton report and later both Campbell and Cherie signed copies of the report to raise money for charity, which seemed extraordinarily tasteless (Cherie pointedly refused to apologise). Would the tarnish, the stain, of David Kelly's death ever go away, in particular the way his character and skills were denigrated by the spin machine before his death?

That Dr Kelly should have intentioned all this conflict and accepted the role of a fall guy thrust upon him was a sign of his inner vulnerability and sensitivity, for it was evident from his conversion to the Baha'i faith, which he found after visiting the United States in 1999, and from his reading of the Koran that he was almost the reverse image of a Blair or Campbell. As Robin Cook wrote later in *Point of Departure*:

Andrew Gilligan provided No. 10 with the great gift of an opportunity for displacement behaviour. By alleging that ministers knew the claims in the dossier were wrong he enabled them to turn the debate into a question of whether they had acted in good faith without either answering whether they had acted competently.

Indictments of Tony's mendacity over this affair surfaced regularly, in particular in Greg Dyke's account of the events that led to his resignation as BBC director general, published the year after. (Dyke also revealed how Cherie once phoned him in his role as director of Manchester United to ask for a discount on a David Beckham shirt for Euan.) Tony had skilfully distanced himself from Campbell before the latter's departure, by disclaiming responsibility for him and acknowledging that he was 'out of control'. But in this context and many others, Campbell's words about never having acted without Tony's express command and with his knowledge ring true. 'Everything I do,' he said, 'I do because the Prime Minister wants me to.' Tony couldn't acknowledge that the Caliban monster that Campbell had become was largely of his own creation and licensed by him. He would never cut him down to size. Why? Because Campbell unleashed had worked, and delivered the goods.

In 1992 the Tory MP Rupert Allason had taken Campbell and the Mirror Group to court on a charge of malicious falsehood, and in summing up the case the judge, Sir Maurice Drake, described Campbell thus: 'I did not find Mr Campbell by any means a wholly satisfactory or convincing witness . . . less than completely open and frank, he did not impress me as a witness in whom I could feel 100 per cent confident.' 'Every time he lies, he sniffs,' echoed Charlie Whelan, Gordon Brown's trusted aide.

But it was passion, a burning conviction that he was right, which carried the weight in the media-dominated political pond in which Campbell swam as the largest predator. In the libel case against Allason he held a toy duck in his hand (suggested by his lawyer) to release the tension or threat of his ungovernable anger. This displacement activity seemed in a direct line from Humphrey Bogart's Captain Queeg, who when cross-examined in *The Caine Mutiny* gives away his inner condition by rolling ball-bearings in his hand. For his interrogation by Hutton as to whether the British public had been misled over the war, a Downing Street aide offered him an earring: instead he used a sharp pin. When he emerged later there were spots of blood on the papers he placed on his desk; in such gestures, worthy of an Opus Dei extremist like something out of *The Da Vinci Code*, Campbell wielded his secular power driven by greed and *ressentiment* for that power.

In July 2003, at the very height of the David Kelly debacle, Robert Harris wrote:

> Mr Campbell exercises an extraordinary psychological dominance over the Prime Minister. It seems that he can get away with anything. He has called him 'a prat' in front of one witness and has told him to 'get a f . . . . . . move on' when he believes a meeting has gone on too long, and instructed him to concentrate on something else 'because it can f . . . . . . wait'. Watching him once on a mobile phone to Blair, striding up and down and wagging his finger, I felt I was hallucinating; surely here was the Prime Minister issuing orders to an official rather than the other way round.

After leaving No. 10 Campbell claimed he spoke to Tony 'at least twice a week'. As his departure came close in the wake of David Kelly's death and the Hutton inquiry, so Tony, hitherto swept along in Campbell's wake, possibly experiencing pangs of guilt (and a need to atone) formed the 'worthy' intention to put religion right at the centre of government. Yet again did he mix up Caesar and God.

He set up a ministerial working group in August 2003 charged with injecting religious ideas across Whitehall. He had already by this time, in spite of Campbell's assertion that 'we don't do God', solemnly affirmed that for the deaths of British soldiers in Iraq he would answer to 'my Maker' (see Chapter 32). But here was a new twist, supported by other leading Christian members of the Cabinet, Home Secretary David Blunkett (soon to be revealed as a sinning Christian in his behaviour with Kimberley Quinn) and Paul Boateng, Chief Secretary of the Treasury.

It would seem that Dr Kelly's death had played its part in impelling Blair to take further refuge in his faith, to spark as it did at this very moment this new prime ministerial initiative. Now he had proved to be the longest continuously serving Labour Prime Minister perhaps he felt that he could act more from his deeper convictions – or that the anchorage of his gesture-ridden faith would bring him reassurance. It echoed the visit to Pope John Paul II in February.

Whatever happened to this 'inclusive' religious gesture? The National Secular Society raised its hands in horror: 'We feel this is a further example of the government's desire to favour and privilege religious organisations . . . The non-religious feel alienated and excluded from the political processes that help shape our society.' Given that the most commanding and driving influence in Blair's government had been the robustly secular Campbell, one has to wonder on what planet the secularists lived.

Blair and Campbell, while sacrificing David Kelly as their spiritual if not corporeal scapegoat, had, with a little help from the press and the media, who were now their mimetic antagonists, indirectly and in a subtle and complicated way transformed – and not without some of his own naive complicity – Cinna the poet into his double Cinna the conspirator. Everyone wanted a name to fix the blame on. Reality no longer mattered. As the Fourth Plebeian, about to bludgeon the poet to death, dismissively says, 'It is no matter, his name's Cinna. Punch but his name out of his heart, and turn him going.' On his fatal and ill-conceived desire to walk at night at the beginning Cinna had said, 'I dreamt tonight that I did feast with Caesar.' This is exactly, by coming into the spotlight, what Dr Kelly had done. They were united. Cinna and Caesar, both of them, as sacrificial victims, as scapegoats.

37

Parting is such sweet sorrow 3

Could Robin Cook, in his opposition to the Iraq invasion in 2003, have joined forces with Clare Short and other Labour dissenters to cause such a revolt as would have forced Tony to reconsider? It is a moot point.

The sceptic with a coruscatingly sharp mind and wit had held reservations about New Labour. MP for Edinburgh Central, he had been elected in 1974 while Tony had been up at Oxford. He had been Neil Kinnock's campaign manager when Kinnock became leader, and before this a left-wing colleague of Gordon Brown, with whom he had collaborated on the book *Scotland: The Real Divide* in 1983. He and Brown had quarrelled, and the cause of this long-standing antagonism remains unknown to this day, except that it was an antique and trivial dispute ('they say') about power and influence in Scotland.

Brown's authority was paramount in keeping Cook out of domestic social politics ('Mr Brown is especially good at nursing his wrath to keep it warm,' an aide quoted from *Tam o' Shanter*). Cook did not want the foreign affairs portfolio Blair foisted on him in 1994, and later Blair held his principled ideas such as tightening the number of arms-controlled exports in some contempt. Cook made his mark in 1996 by attacking John Major's government in the arms-for-Iraq scandal.

In the jostling 'girls' high school' atmosphere and clash of the leaders, Cook resented spin and belonged to no particular faction, but championed passionately the rights of Parliament and its belief in democracy. As he wrote in his diary on 17 July 2001, 'I am a tribal politician of the old school' and 'I'm not good-looking enough to be party leader.' The scandal of his affair with his secretary, Gaynor Regan, and the ensuing break-up of his marriage robbed him of some of his political coherence and tarnished his moral credibility, while in 2001 Blair, in spite of Cook's impressive showing there, removed him from his post as Foreign Secretary and appointed him Leader of the Commons, a position, as Brown said at Cook's funeral in 2005 (to which Blair refused to go), he neither sought nor contemplated, and for which he certainly had not volunteered.

While he could applaud as he did in November 2001 that Tony was 'rare among the leaders I have known, in that his speeches have got better, not worse, with the cares of office', he also accurately assessed that, by Labour's fifth year in power, the 'growing perception' was that 'politics is something top people do within that curiously introverted and gossipy Westminster village' and 'the elector is reduced to being a spectator rather than the owner of the [political] process . . . Our present culture is destroying trust not just in government but in our democratic process.' He noted that the public wanted more 'MPs with whom they can feel some psychological empathy'.

'What oft was thought, but ne'er so well expressed', as Alexander Pope put it: Cook shows this in his journal of events of 15 August 2002 and 17 March 2003. After writing how absurd the government claim was that Saddam Hussein could produce a nuclear weapon in between one and two years – 'the language is frightening. But as evidence that Iraq was a threat it is pathetic and the authors must have known it' – he goes on to observe: 'Intelligence is supposed to be the evidence on which ministers reach decisions on foreign and defence policy. It is not meant to be the propaganda by which ministers sell a policy to a sceptical public.'

On the 'sexed up', unfairly one-sided, dossier he also passes judgement:

> The intelligence was wrong and ministers who had applied a sceptical mind could have seen that it was too thin to be a reliable basis for war. No. 10 believed in the intelligence because they desperately wanted it to be true. Their sin was not one of bad faith but of evangelical certainty.

Cook felt sharply in his own compromised awkwardness the dilemma of the loyalist when the Tories tried to get him to admit he had ministerial responsibility 'for the crushingly embarrassing government dossier that turned out to be a plagiarised PhD thesis of a decade ago'.

A little later he meets the confident protagonist of strife, who is quite oblivious:

I saw Tony privately shortly after we left the chamber. He remains in surprisingly good humour despite the disaster that is staring him in the face. He even began with a joke: 'They gave me a whole briefing on what to say if asked about the extermination of the ruddy duck. I said what I'm worried about is the ruddy French.'

Then Cook resigned. In August 2005 he collapsed and died while walking with Gaynor, now his wife, on Ben Stack, a mountain in the Western Highlands of Scotland, 300 yards from the peak.

Tony and Cherie came in for a lot of stick from Scots newspapers for their absence from the funeral. They were on holiday at an unspecified location. One could imagine that Cherie's response to Brown's eulogy would have been similar to her response to his Labour conference speech in 2006. Tony, of course, would have just smiled and nodded approvingly.

'The worst political scandals do not come', wrote Cook in *Point of Departure*, 'from an initial mistake but from the subsequent attempts to deny that anything was wrong and to cover up any evidence to the contrary.' Tony should have listened. If that was not enough, the following statement should have driven Tony to don sackcloth and ashes and embark on a pilgrimage of atonement to the Holy Land: 'There were no international terrorists in Iraq until we went in.'

And Cherie? Had she, during this, 'dwindled', in the word of Millicent in Congreve's *The Way of the World*, into a wife of someone? She is not much in evidence during these months. But it is perhaps not Cook who should have the last word on Cherie's role in 2003, but his jilted wife. Was Cherie, asked Margaret Cook, 'far from easy with herself, wrestling with demons, totally unaware that the modern feminist is gradually losing the tug-of-war to the ancient alpha female, who has no choice but to walk behind, biddable and subservient, in the shadow of her man'?

Not long after the Hutton inquiry was over, Tony felt unwell, which was not surprising. On a Sunday at the end of October when he and Cherie were at Chequers his face went red and he doubled up with pain. They rushed him to Stoke Mandeville Hospital, where they found he was suffering from atrial fibrillation, in which the heart beats so fast it quivers. This may lead to a blood clot, which in turn may cause a stroke. Tony had a history of this, going as far back as when John Smith suffered his first stroke. The accelerated heartbeat awoke an ancient tribal wound and fear, that of his father's debilitating stroke when Tony was eleven and Leo forty. He was transferred at once from Stoke Mandeville to the heart unit at Hammersmith Hospital, where he was anaesthetised for twenty minutes and doctors administered electric shock treatment to slow the heartbeat, which rises in such cases to between 300 and 500 beats a minute. Later they made light of the whole affair; it was spun as 'relatively common', but panic had struck Chequers and Cherie at first, and she had even called in a priest.

Subsequently Cherie became fixated that endless cups of coffee had been the cause, and a ban on drinking coffee was imposed on and around him (colleagues were forbidden to drink it in his sight). Carole Caplin and Peter Mandelson endorsed this. Later Cherie took him away to Sharm el-Sheikh on the Red Sea to recuperate and as Carole was no longer in favour to give him back massage, Cherie spent £3,000 on a Keyton Concept massage chair for 'an automated back rub'.

The price they now paid in their lampooned images had augmented. Dave Brown, cartoonist of the *Independent*, relished drawing Tony's 'split personalities', as he called them, 'the one staring, glinting eye over the one closed, slightly crinkled eye', while Matt Buck, whose work frequently appears in the *Guardian* and *Tribune*, said his teeth 'had got more battered and disorganised' since Dr Kelly's death.

Cherie also had her fair share of being lampooned, revealing something in her she wanted to hide: her wide-eyed stare with the whites visible above and below the iris. This was, according to David Hockney, an eye condition called *sanpaku*. She shared the condition with John Lennon, John F. Kennedy and Princess Diana.

Part V

2004–2007

38

Nemesis

The strongest poison ever known,
Came from Caesar's laurel crown.

William Blake, Auguries of Innocence

Children survive in spite of their parents.

We again have to go back a bit here. Ann Widdecombe recalls the time when both she and Tony Blair were backbench MPs. It was during the 1989–90 session, and she and Tony, picked from opposite sides, were asked to a taxation seminar in Gleneagles, hosted by a giant petroleum corporation. The other participants at the seminar, who had all come alone, could not believe it when Tony arrived with Cherie, their three children and Gale, Cherie's mother: their hosts backed away, wide eyed with embarrassment – an early sign, possibly, as Widdecombe put it, of the 'inveterate scrounger'. But it was more than this; it was an early indication that 'like it or lump it', the political world had to accept the Blairs as a package driven mainly by Cherie in which the children were pushed to the front. But even the children as they grew older were to be excluded from the narcissistic bonding of the pair.

Early in his leadership Tony spoke volubly to *Woman* magazine of the three women in his life in a way that validated their independence of his own political ambition. He started with Cherie, but then went on:

> My daughter Kathryn has my mother's red hair and her second name is Hazel after my mum. She's a gorgeous girl with a great personality – sweet and strong willed. We've always tried to treat her the same as the boys but she's so

different and has always been completely uninterested in their passion for football. She went straight for the dolls. I think all fathers dote on their daughters and it's lovely to have a girl in the house.

Together with this *Woman* printed six pictures showing Kathryn as a toddler, the Blairs with their children and Kathryn as an older child with Cherie and Gale.

But Tony and Cherie, linked in their capsule of self-regard in their rise to power, all too soon began to see their children as extensions of themselves, in spite of their earnest intentions and protestations. No greater example of this is there than the letter Tony wrote in early 1996 when, as Labour leader, he addressed his vision to Kathryn.

'Dear Kathy,' he wrote in the *Daily Express* on 3 January, just weeks before her eighth birthday – blithely ignoring the fact that his words would hardly be understood at that age, 'Britain is a great country [but] at times we seem to be a nation that has become tired, resentful . . . Relying on our past as a great nation . . .'

The fulsome dream of the future Prime Minister of active, dynamic youth listed his aspirations:

> I want a Britain where the NHS is once again a pillar of security . . . I dream of a nation where as a parent I am less worried about you going out on your own, where crime does not breed insecurity and fear . . .
>
> I want a Britain where *every* [my italics] child has the chance to go to a good school . . . where they learn to think and use their imagination . . . I want a Britain where people have faith once again in politics . . . I want Britain to be leading in Europe so that we can shape Europe to British interests rather than being sidelined and humiliated . . .

Tacked almost onto the end of this litany of aspirations for a seven-year-old he proclaimed, 'There is no greater responsibility than that which a parent has to a child. My duties as a father come first.' But yet another barnstorming punchline followed: 'But it is to help build that better Britain and that united society that I came into politics. Love Dad' (in his own hand).

What could Tony be thinking of? What could this mean to a little girl?

*

Sarah Smith, daughter of John, once asked her father, 'Why can't you come and see me in the school play?' to be met with the answer, 'Don't you know there are people in Airdrie without a roof over their heads?' David Steel called himself the 'classic absentee father. I've always felt guilty about that.' Richard Crossman, in his much-praised diary, tragically foreshadowed the suicide of his son Patrick, who at the age of seventeen hanged himself with his judo belt in the kitchen of their Oxfordshire farmhouse. On Patrick's ninth birthday Richard and Anne Crossman had been at the Labour Party conference in Brighton. Richard wrote:

> We telephoned him. Poor boy, he was born on the Friday of the Brighton conference 1957 and the next time we came to Brighton was for the conference five years later when Nanny brought the children. There we are, away again on his birthday. It's no fun to be the son of two politicians.

Lucille Iremonger, married to a Tory MP, in *And His Charming Lady* (1961) pointed out there were four different orbits in which an MP's wife spun: 'in the constituency, in the home, in the House and in the public eye'. Just to complicate matters, Cherie had a fifth orbit, in the Inns of Court as Cherie Booth QC.

The year after Tony's letter to Kathryn, he and Cherie put their family on display by walking with all three children across the green to Trimdon Colliery to cast their vote in the 1997 election. The children looked uncomfortable, Nicky and Euan with heads bowed, Kathryn clasping Cherie's hand for reassurance. They had to walk towards a makeshift gantry crammed with cameramen. Did the children have a vote? No. So why were they there? For the image. They were there for Tony and Cherie to use for political capital.

Having not received the message, Tony and Cherie repeated the performance at the 2001 election, this time under the banner headline 'Blair's second chance'. The whole family again advanced on the photographers with right arms raised as a choreographed photograph, in a deliberate stunt to copy the von Trapp family in *The Sound of Music*. This time only Kathryn declined, dressed in pedal pushers and bulky top instead of the earlier, elegant long-sleeved smock dress. She refused to raise her hand, and clasped her father's left hand with her right.

247

No mother concerned with her child's own developing self-esteem would ever have let her dress like that. Even so a source close to them said, 'Kathryn has the same kind of awkwardness as Cherie, and will go out of her way to be helpful; Cherie and Kathryn are very close.' But why did they take the children to the polling booth if not for the photo opportunity – in other words, to exploit them?

But it was not all manipulation and political egotism; there was another side before Tony became PM, the artless, accident-prone informality about the way they carried on that would, and did, continue to endear the Blair family to the public at a soap opera level. A documentary film-maker had shot footage of the student-like domestic chaos in which the family lived in Richmond Terrace. A close neighbour remembers seeing Cherie driving about in the family's beaten-up old Mini, biting her nails when stuck in traffic jams. Tony teased Cherie about how often it needed its bodywork rearranging, and an aide who drove the children to school complained that Cherie kept it so low in fuel that it ran on gas fumes. This was before they switched to a Ford Galaxy people carrier.

In Islington Tony and Cherie decided to send Euan to the London Oratory School, a Catholic school in Fulham, halfway across London, with strong links to the Brompton Oratory in Knightsbridge. 'You can't fucking do that!' Alastair Campbell told Tony, and threatened to resign. When in 1994 Tony announced his and Cherie's decision, Labour worthies such as Roy Hattersley accused him of following the hypocritical path of middle-class free choice – or, in other words, freedom to talk your way into unfair advantage.

Hattersley recalls a lunch with *Daily Mail* executives when Tony was leader of the opposition. Asked why he and Cherie did not send their children to the local comprehensive, and assuming wherever they went they would go to university, Tony answered that he wasn't so sure. 'It didn't work for Harold Wilson,' he snapped back. The questioner then pointed out that Wilson's children, Giles and Robin, had carved out decent paths for themselves: Giles, while somewhat of an eccentric who collected veteran locomotive engines, had been a headmaster; Robin (the present writer's neighbour in north Oxford for fifteen years) lectured for the Open University. Tony retorted contemptuously, saying, 'I hope my kids do better than that!'

Blair and Campbell had always differed violently on this issue and here Campbell showed both consistency and integrity. He and Fiona Millar believed passionately not only that the children of Labour leaders or sympathisers should attend non-selective comprehensives, but that they should, regardless of quality, go to the nearest school to where they lived. Campbell's progeny accordingly attended their local comprehensive in Hampstead, but Andrew Marr, the high-profile left-wing journalist and a neighbour, whose children were chums with Campbell and Millar's, and his wife, Jackie Ashley, a *Guardian* columnist, opted for the private sector. Thereupon the two families fell out, and Millar, well known like her partner to speak her mind, not only cut Ashley dead in the street but also berated other Labour leaders for their hypocrisy. What they did with their children they expected others to do. Invitations to dine with them were rapidly declined. On this occasion even Campbell was on the side of the hated *Mail*. Millar attacked Ruth Kelly over the same issue in 2007.

Campbell also reacted angrily over potential 'streaming', but Blair gave way; and when John McIntosh, the Oratory's headmaster, introduced a parental subsidy for his pupils of £30 (£15 for a second child), Campbell harangued him, saying, 'Just remember that if it wasn't for the Blair children your school would be nothing.' This of course was rubbish, but the Campbell household deserved credit for implementing their strong beliefs, with Millar joining as a school governor of her children's comprehensive, campaigning to improve it, and ultimately forcing out a hapless headmaster. The Campbell–Millars' problem was that they still had a streak of unreconstructed socialism.

The two Blair boys had a compact and supported each other at the Oratory School, although John McIntosh attacked Tony's education agenda, while Tony and in particular Cherie disliked some of the ways the school tackled various incidents involving Euan and Nicky.

In January 1999, when Blair was at the peak of popularity, the *Mail on Sunday* launched an assault on him, or rather his wife, for organising for Kathryn, then ten years old, a much sought-after place at a Catholic comprehensive in Hammersmith, six miles away from Downing Street. Local Catholic girls were denied places at the Sacred Heart, and the *Mail* mercilessly scrutinised this double standard of Tony and Cherie. Tony made a complaint about the *Mail*'s intrusion into their daughter's life.

The *Mail*'s scathing attack on the Blair's 'giant hypocrisy', which also marshalled eleven disappointed children from the local feeder primary, must have been embarrassing, but to bring a complaint to the Press Complaints Commission over intrusion of privacy (Cherie's initiative very evident here) compounded the embarrassment for Kathryn, who now would arrive at the new school tagged with favouritism, as well as the stigma of chauffeur-driven transport and private detectives. Lord Wakeham, chairman of the PCC, upheld the Blairs' complaint, but this can only have acted to accelerate Kathryn's becoming a target for taunts.

One source close to Cherie and Tony suggests a solution to these problems would have been to send all the children quite unashamedly to private boarding schools. (They were said to be supplementing the Oratory with private tuition for Euan by courtesy of teachers from Westminster School.) Tony could then with honesty have claimed that he was the product of private education, and so felt it appropriate that his children should have the same. He would also by virtue of his privileged position be freeing up places at good state schools for other children. This would have assured his children their privacy, at the same time making his position clear and unequivocal to a party that loved him and had appointed him its leader. His children would also have mixed from the start with the children of the celebrities they met on holidays.

Defending the Blairs' action, Polly Toynbee, at that time the Islington's high priestess or celebrant of Tony's popularity, laying into the *Mail on Sunday*, wrote, 'A politician who sacrifices his child to suit his own political career is rather more despicable a disgrace than one using a little mild hypocrisy,' while – quite naturally for her – saying it was a disgrace anyway that one third of all schools in this irreligious non-church-attending land were church run. They were immensely popular for the wonderful spurious reason Toynbee gave: because they got away with back-door selection (and not because they had moral and ethical standards). In her next breath, Toynbee praised the Blairs for being 'sincerely religious, unlike a great many parents'. (But she changed her tune by April 2005, when she railed in the *Guardian* against Tony's kneeling in respect to pay homage to the deceased

Pope John Paul II: 'How dare Tony Blair genuflect', she wrote at the funeral, 'at the corpse of a man whose edicts killed millions?')

In April 1999 Kathryn suffered a jet scare; unusual night turbulence caused the British Airways 747 to drop 300 feet during her return journey from Australia, where she had already been thrown into the water from a speedboat, both of which must have been very scaring (she was still only eleven), a short time after starting at the Hammersmith school.

This confusion of lifestyle, of role, and of identities, not only increased but intensified pressure on the family in Downing Street. While Euan, with his highly publicised late-night escapade in Leicester Square, his arrest and release, was no stranger to headlines, his younger sister was thrust by her mother, in her Scouse, no-nonsense way, into the newspapers. Only days after Iain Duncan Smith attacked the Blairs for exploiting their children for political advantage ('once you open your doors to your children it just gives the press an excuse for intrusion'), Cherie used Kathryn in a political attack against sexism and the way law firms treated women. In emails sent in 2002 to Marina Wheeler, a *Telegraph* journalist who had questioned Mrs Blair about her views, Cherie bluntly replied the law was a 'very family-unfriendly profession' and then brought Kathryn into the discussion, saying she would recommend her daughter, if interested in a legal career, to choose to become a barrister rather than a solicitor because 'you have more control of your life'.

But who has that control? In September 2002, accompanied by a photograph of himself cuddling Leo and asserting how keen he was to be an ordinary father to boost his image as a family man, Tony said, 'When I cook the children go on strike, although Cherie says I do a good roast chicken.'

Cherie took the children with her on a paid trip to attend a legal conference in Australia during the April 2003 school holidays. Invited by the management of Globe International, a designer clothes showroom in Melbourne, to visit the store and choose a 'few free gifts', Cherie brought Euan, Kathryn and Nicky along with her; they spirited sixty-eight items away with them, as revealed by the *Sydney Morning Herald*, which included fourteen pairs of stone-coloured trousers and large 'outsize' Julius pyjamas, presumably for Tony because the designer Paul Frank described his Julius, the cheeky monkey, as an 'all-round great guy. He stands as the voice of reason in a world of chaos.' It must have reminded Cherie of what Tony said about his friend Bill Clinton.

*

Like her mother, who felt badly bruised by unflattering pictures of her on holiday in the Seychelles and the woeful under-performance of her Flowtron leggings in disguising her orange-peel thighs, Kathryn had a tendency to put on weight. This was evident in the family Christmas card of 2003, published in the *Evening Standard*: yet again, they complained about intrusion into their family privacy, but then encouraged it. The children must have often felt from an early age that they were political props, while the intense pressure now heaped on their father when he became PM meant they saw less of him, and when he was there he was mainly preoccupied, while Cherie maintained her high profile in the 'family-unfriendly' legal profession, taking on legal briefs as a QC, having Leo, who was born when Kathryn was twelve. Cherie also made it clear on some occasions, when she ran seminars at No. 10 on topics such as crime, transport, wealth creation and art and culture, that she was a central player in Tony's government, the First Lady in the style of Hillary Clinton.

By April 2003 Tony had been branded a 'warmonger' by many of his children's generation, and if that wasn't enough, they suffered the humiliation and fuss, with their grandmother Gale, of Carole Caplin and her 67-year-old mother being seen in tiny G-string bikini bottoms at the holiday pool. If that was not bad enough, when Peter Foster appeared on the scene he cooked up a national scheme to make children aware of the risk of obesity and promote his own slimming products. Foster had arranged a meeting with Euan, but Euan, who over-slept, did not turn up. Foster also planned, he said, to put Kathryn on his slimming diet.

Where was the authority of the leader and paternal figure during all this? Nowhere. The children's feelings were ignored, or embraced in lavish, over-compensatory displays of affection. In *Iron John* Robert Bly writes, 'Each child lives deep inside his or her psychic house, or soul castle, and the child deserves the right of sovereignty inside that house.' How, by any stretch of the imagination, could that house, for the Blair children, ever be the flat above 11 Downing Street? Bly continues, 'Whenever a parent ignores the child's sovereignty, and invades, the child feels not only anger, but the child concludes that if it has no sovereignty it must be worthless.'

The Blairs would have it that it was the press that stole their family's sovereignty. But in the drama of their lives the press was the antagonist, as well as the object of indirect aggression, stemming from their desire to find a scapegoat for the way they themselves had intruded on their own children's sovereignty by making them swim in an over-heated fish-tank where everything they did was visible. This is not to say they did not love their children passionately, but they failed to apply basic common sense to the situation and give them the essential requirements of growth, space and, above all, anonymity.

A lavish treat was laid on for Kathryn's sixteenth birthday at Chequers on 26 March 2004. Children, especially those in their teens, are always deeply sensitive to how their parents treat their servants, and they must have been aware of Cherie's dominatrix personality. The security man, who used to be a policeman, has said that compared to earlier incumbents at Chequers, such as the Thatchers and the Majors, the Blairs were 'grasping and greedy'.

> They put down every expense and treated the staff in a superior, unpleasant way . . . They took no interest in the food prepared there for themselves or guests – unlike Norma Major, who used to go down to the kitchen to help or work out menus, or Mrs Thatcher, who was gracious and generous over expenses.

The curious feature of this birthday party was that each invitee, says a girl from Kathryn's class, was invited to bring a girlfriend, and then both girls could each bring a boyfriend, and a coach was laid on to pick up this crowd, many little known to Kathryn, outside the school in Hammersmith. They were then driven to Chequers, fed, watered and entertained by performers; they danced and had a great time. But it was far away from most parents' experience of their adolescent children's birthday parties, as in the usual strict and possessive vetting by the host of everyone who came, and the creation of a complete exclusion zone as far as any parents and their friends were concerned.

Less than two months later, on 13 May, Cherie and Tony suffered a crisis and Tony came near to resigning as Prime Minister. There was a complete blackout of news about this: Downing Street asked editors not to report the story, and they out of respect and sensitivity towards the Blairs kept any mention of this potentially sensational event out of the media until such time as Tony and Cherie took the lead in sanctioning it. Even the *New York Post* and the *Australian*, which had prepared stories, withdrew them on the order of Rupert Murdoch, their proprietor.

The children were being taunted at school for their dad being a warmonger, and for his lying. In one poignant exchange reported, Euan was asked to defend his parents. He said his dad 'can't have lied over Iraq because that would mean he lied to my mum'. A friend close to both confirmed that the 'kids at school could be very hurtful', and that while Euan and Nicky had gone to the same school, Kathryn was on her own. Many on the internet clamoured that Tony and Cherie were both professional moralisers, who had at every point of their lives offered, often more than offered, flaunted and imposed, themselves and their family as exemplars of a good family who could both control and command and lead a normal, ordinary life.

It was Melvyn Bragg, whose wife Cate Haste was at that time promoting *The Goldfish Bowl* with Cherie, who talked about Tony's 'wobble'. Bragg presumably believed what he said, and without going into details he revealed on 16 September 2004 in the *Guardian* that Tony was close to quitting as PM during this time.

Bragg had been at Cherie's fiftieth birthday party at Chequers only the week before, held on the third anniversary of 9/11. Naked pro-hunting demonstrators held up arrivals in Chequers car park; the guests who finally made it did not include Fiona Millar and Alastair Campbell, although Carole Caplin attended. They watched a kaleidoscope of Cherie's life, heard Kathryn say what a wonderful mother Cherie was, ate an Indian buffet and watched Tony join the band with his guitar to perform 'Blue Suede Shoes'. Bragg said, 'I think he was under tremendous stress', and, he went on, 'He was being hammered in the press . . . But in my view the real stress was personal and family, which matters most to him. And my guess is that the considerations of his family became very pressing.'

These were the revealing words. Bragg emphasised that the domestic problem was 'not in any sense about him and Cherie. I have never seen a couple get on as these two, it's not that . . . People seem to forget how very, very strong he is. And how very determined he is to make his country a better place.' In other words, echoed by others who knew Blair, 'He would never really resign.'

No more honeyed words than those of Melvyn Bragg could be imagined. He knew that Gordon Brown, aware that the honourable, domestic exit strategy was at hand, was waiting in the wings. The loyalists rallied round.

So why didn't Blair, some asked, as Alan Milburn had already done, resign for family reasons? The simple answer: Cherie was determined he should go 'on and on and on'; 'I don't think I'm hankering after a bungalow just yet,' was how she put it. A close friend, hearing of the crisis at Downing Street, raised the matter in a very roundabout and tactful way in order to express sympathy. Cherie, he said, 'went through the roof', saying the rumours were all 'complete lies'.

Cherie boiled with rage at Bragg's somewhat perplexing admission, telling him off in uninhibited and blisteringly profane terms for revealing them in public. Bragg, duly mortified, apologised abjectly, while Cate Haste told Cherie that he was hopeless about anything other than his arts programme (did this qualify him to sit in the Upper House?). But Cherie did not forgive, and in her search for revenge went on the *Richard and Judy* show. She told Richard Madeley, in answer to a question she clearly had wanted to be asked (or it would not have been), what she thought of Bragg's comments: 'I don't know where Melvyn got it from, and to be honest I think he's mortified that he said it. We can't always explain what goes on in men's minds – I wish I could.'

'To be honest' is a Tony and Cherie mutual mirror phrase, and to be honest, how could she have gone on screen, in front of millions and brazenly faced questions? She broke the taboo. 'Never, never, absolutely never!' Alastair Campbell had said to Susan Crosland when she requested an interview. But Cherie was on *Richard and Judy* to promote *The Goldfish Bowl*, something of her own. She had a higher purpose.

While no one can blame Cherie for wanting to protect her family and herself, one is not sure exactly what the point of this was, except that the press and friends were respecting the Prime Minister's wishes. Was this once again an incredible piece of joint bungling on the part of this pair, showing a disjointedness and lack of principle which deeply revealed the tragic shortcomings in their self-knowledge and maturity? Or was it perfectly reasonable to behave as they behaved in keeping the matter private?

The family recovered quickly and robustly from the near resignation, but again the strain told on Tony. He had to go into hospital for a 'catheter ablation' to assess and correct the fibrillating condition, which had presumably recurred even though this was denied. The atrial flutter, while it often shows no symptoms, could have indicated long-standing heart disease, and the fact that it had occurred before could be life-threatening and suggested that defibrillation was urgently necessary. Tony said, 'It's not particularly alarming, but it's something you should get fixed.' The marked change in Tony's appearance so as to look almost haggard, as well as the decrease in his body mass, suggest that subsequent medication such as digoxin or beta-blockers, if taken, could have had an effect.

The children have since emerged as stronger, more balanced individuals who will benefit from Cherie and Tony's long-overdue stepping down. Had Tony really meant it when he said, 'My duties as a father come first'? Had he left power then, as perhaps if he felt honour bound to Gordon Brown he should have done (this was still within his second term), the country would not have had to suffer three more years of prolonged, agonising rule in which the catalogue of woes and mismanagement multiplied. Was there some kind of poetic justice in this? Clare Short subsequently reported that Tony had been prepared to step down earlier had Gordon let him join the euro zone. 'He could only do those things that Gordon let him do,' Short said. Armed with this reiterated promise Short lunched with Brown and put to him Blair's proposition, but Brown answered, 'There's nothing Tony can say that I will ever believe.'

The two episodes of Blair's irregular heartbeat, contrasted as they were with Brown's fitness and, in the case of the second, the birth of his son John, urged those who plotted towards conspiracy, which not only had spread in the Brown camp, but now affected Blair loyalists. Over the crucial debate on university top-up fees, which almost brought down the government, Brown withheld his support and the motion in favour passed only by five votes when some Brown supporters voted with Blair.

Later on a holiday in West Bahama, when Tony expressed interest in purchasing property there, Kathryn buoyantly and excitedly described the prospect of the family snapping up a colonial-style mansion. Anthony Head, who plays the fictional Prime Minister in *Little Britain*, reported that Kathryn, according to Tony, 'thinks I was better looking than him, but Blair said it was all down to my make-up!' In August 2005 Kathryn voyaged to Lourdes on pilgrimage. Tony regrets he can't have much philosophical discussion, and their chats came down to 'could she get on with more homework, please'. She moved from her Hammersmith school to the Oratory, and here she followed up her earlier interest in acting by directing the school play. No. 10 – Cherie no doubt, or with Cherie's sanction and encouragement – tipped off the *Sun* that Tessa Jowell would be present on the Monday night to see Kathryn direct. Alongside a photograph of her smiling, as she always does whatever happens, the minister enthused fulsomely, 'It was the Prime Minister's daughter who was the star of tonight.' So there were still signs the children were being used by No. 10 for political advantage, this time to help whitewash yet another ailing Cabinet colleague mired in a sleaze scandal through accusations in an Italian court against her husband.

39

We are acting beyond our competence

You know the old Catholic joke. 'You want to make God laugh? Tell Him your plans.'

Cardinal Cormac Murphy-O'Connor to author, 2003

'We are acting beyond our competence,' Tony said in a rare moment of acute openness to someone close to him. There could be no clearer indication of how he and Cherie had got out of their depth. But neither of them could come to terms with disengagement and leaving it all behind, even though the time had come.

Given that nothing since that ill-judged decision on Iraq had gone right for them, it was surprising, even astonishing, that Tony should be re-elected in 2005, although the electorate showed only a marginally greater interest in voting than in 2001. The continued weakness of the conflict-riven opposition played its part, and in spite of a robust, well-fought campaign by Michael Howard, the trust of the electorate eluded the Tories. So Prime Minister by default was certainly one explanation. Another, crucially overlooked by most commentators, needs to be emphasised: the part paid by the Catholic vote, as shown in the MORI poll analysis (see Chapter 25).

*

Harold Wilson said that a week is a long time in politics, but in the five years from the election of 2001 to the summer of 2006, poor leadership in the Western world, particularly in the United States and the UK, led to a haemorrhaging of influence over the direction the world was taking. By 2005, the world order had changed significantly, with above all the limits of the American military now brutally exposed. The millennium seemed, in its sunny halcyon glow, to belong to some former distant age when terrorism hardly existed, there was no energy crisis, no stand-off between nascent nuclear powers and the West.

George W. Bush had pinned above his desk in the Oval office Colonel Tim Collins's rousing exhortation to his troops on the eve of the Iraqi invasion, and there would be no going back.

> We go to liberate, not to conquer.
> We will not fly our flags in their country.
> We are entering Iraq to free a people and the only flag which will be flown in that ancient land is their own . . .

Collins pointed out that Iraq was the site of the Garden of Eden, the Great Flood and the birthplace of Abraham. 'Tread lightly there,' he said.

By 2005 or 2006 Bush would have done as well if not better to have taken to heart the exhortations of General Robert Scales, for example, who said that to win what he called an 'asymmetric war' (meaning the weapons and manpower were ill matched) against a dispersed enemy who communicate by word of mouth and back-alley messengers requires the skill of 'creating alliances, leveraging non-military advantages, reading intentions, converting opinions and managing perceptions' – all tasks that demand an exceptional ability to understand people, their culture and their motivation.

But Bush and Blair were big-picture people, with their 'shock-and-awe mentality' and their 'technological integration', while in the UK it had become politically incorrect to apply common sense to just about any situation. Lord Falconer had even gone so far as issuing a directive to the 26,000 magistrates in the country *not* to use common sense in an evaluation of cases before them. Some critics go further and believe that it was due to his unconscious aggression and his own fear of it, which is a perversion akin to that of his friend Bill Clinton, who suffered from sexual incontinence, that Blair surrendered or lost control of the flow of his aggression over the invasion of Iraq.

Great secularists such as Sigmund Freud (and to a lesser degree, Carl Gustav Jung) believed that organised belief in God protects someone from having to face his or her fears, both inner and outer. Leaders who refer their uncertainties to God are using God as the prime anxiety management tool, and rightly Freud further argued that the practice of religion could undermine intellectual and psychological development – not that it necessarily did. Unfortunately it was the narrowing impact of religion that was deeply embedded in the minds of Bush and Blair.

Visiting Sedgefield in 2003, George stepped out of his helicopter, grinning broadly at Cherie and Tony. He called out, 'Blair!' and then added, 'You're my boy!' Informality could so easily become mockery. Then at the G8 summit in Washington in June 2004 Bush, in front of other world leaders, teased Blair as he arrived last and threw his coat over a chair. 'We haven't even started and you're half asleep!' 'Must be a big day,' he smirked another time, 'got a lot to work on.' Tony smiled and each time swallowed the condescension.

Like Tony, George remained a sucker to the illusion of his inner goodness in the holy war against terror he began after 9/11. But then slowly it began to rebound on him, or, as he said on 11 August 2004, with unconscious irony, 'Terrorists never stop thinking of ways to hurt the American people and neither do we.'

The channelling of aggression into the 'war on terror', the redirection of those different strains, those constituents of personality that made Blair line up behind Bush – or more, as some have argued with convincing force, to be as certain as Bush was himself – in the invasion of Iraq, was a legitimate outlet to that redirected aggression and continued to the very end of his rule to assert the legitimacy of going to war. But 'a definite or self-contained function of an organism, such as feeding, copulation or self-preservation, is never the result of a single drive', according to Konrad Lorenz in *On Aggression*. 'The explanatory value of a concept such as "reproductive instinct" or "instinct of self-preservation" is as null as the concept of an "automobile force" which I could use just as legitimately to explain the fact that my ancient car still goes.' Blair failed to tune into this own inner parliament of instincts, in Lorenz's famous phrase, just as he severed (or never had in the first place) accountability to the Parliament he was elected to lead. He maintained the claim of a legitimate cause even to the extent of lying, as he did on 25 September 2006 in his Labour Party conference speech, that the British presence in Iraq had 'a full UN mandate'.

'The love that dare not speak its name' applied chillingly and particularly to Blair's omission of George W. Bush's name during that conference speech. It seemed it was over. It was not a holy, idealised love such as one might feel for a spiritual mentor. But it had gone to the very core of a psychological need to find authentication in a father figure or fellow conspirator, for a long-repressed release of aggression. This defence of the duty to the father, the weaker to the stronger, may have been on Tony's side part of the free-and-easy style he allowed his entourage in sharp contrast to Bush's senior advisers, who never swore in front of the President, and certainly never ribbed him. He was respected as the carrier of this high office. Not so Blair.

Iraq, as it existed as a single autonomous state, had by then already been destroyed; it remained only for Tony, who with Cherie at his side never had the skill or self-knowledge to direct the aggression and power he possessed to good, to turn it, as malfunctions of an instinct that was essentially life-preserving and had brought him and the Labour Party to power three times, to effect his own self-destruction.

'We did the right thing.' Equally his transatlantic partner clung to the same refrain while one US governor of Iraq after another (four in three years), one insider after another, and one general after another, unravelled his credibility.

*

> *Bush:* Yo, Blair! How are ya doing?
>
> *Blair:* I'm just . . .
>
> *Bush:* You're leaving?
>
> *Blair:* No, no, not yet . . . On this trade thingy . . . [inaudible]
>
> *Bush:* Thanks for the sweater.
>
> *Blair:* It's a pleasure.
>
> *Bush:* I know you picked it out yourself.
>
> *Blair:* Oh, absolutely. In fact . . . [inaudible]

The lunchtime conversation at the G8 summit in July 2006, this time in St Petersburg, offered the best glimpse as to how, in Tony's last year in power, George's condescension towards him had sunk to the lowest level of affectionate contempt. The pictures published at the same time showed Tony, arm on George's chair, leaning over him in a hunched, subservient posture, with his white tie dangling loosely outside his coat. They both were caught with the microphone open: Israel had just invaded Lebanon in retaliation for Hezbollah rocket attacks.

They hoped there might be a ceasefire in Lebanon:

> *Bush:* I think Condi is going to go pretty soon.
> *Blair:* But that's, that's, that's all that matters. But if you . . . you see it will take some time to get that together.
> *Bush:* Yeah, yeah.
> *Blair:* But at least it gives people . . .
> *Bush:* It's a process, I agree. I told her your offer to . . .
> *Blair:* Well . . . it's only if, I mean . . . You know, she's got a . . . or if she needs the ground prepared, as it were . . . Because obviously, if she goes out, she's got to succeed, if it were, whereas I can go out and just talk.

Tony had increasingly come to mirror George in his defensive use of language, but while he tried hard didn't quite attain the positive energy George emanates. The undoctored G8 exchange, which had something about it of the slangy complicity of two sixth-formers at similar privileged schools, contained no mention of Israel. Did either leader ask if the Israeli bombing was not savage and disproportionate, and if Israel should have more of a privileged position to retaliate than the British had in Ireland when the IRA rocketed military barracks – or indeed the British had when Britain ruled Palestine between 1945 and 1948? Then, Irgun terrorists and the Stern gang conducted a guerrilla campaign against the British army, murdering Lord Moyne, the Colonial Secretary, in Cairo, and in August 1946 blowing up part of the King David Hotel in Jerusalem, which was the British headquarters, killing ninety-one people. At a later time they demolished the Officers Club in Jerusalem, killing many, and also kidnapped and later hanged two British Intelligence Corps sergeants they had abducted (just as

Hezbollah abducted two Israeli soldiers). But the Attlee government did not order the RAF to bomb Tel Aviv, or the Royal Artillery to raze Jewish settlements which harboured the terrorists. There was a further lesson here for the two leaders in relation to Iraq (some of these points were raised in the House of Commons debate in the week following the summit). Britain refused to impose a political settlement with force on the mandated territory, even though such an action was endorsed by the United Nations. As events subsequently showed, instead of Great Britain being the favoured ally, it often became merely the flavour of the month – as seen in how France and the United States sidelined the UK in brokering peace in the Hezbollah–Israeli war of 2006. What Tony saw in George, and the reason he was therefore drawn into his religious force field, was that George, although not a churchgoer, as a born-again Christian was a fundamentalist of such powerful animus, linked as it was to his 'phallic narcissism' – in other words his need to prove he was more a man than his father – that his (Tony's) own faith, sincere as it was, could never give him the protection that George gained from his. Here was something, with his eager, mimetic envy, he needed to acquire to use himself.

Blair's weakness was in being overawed by the Bush certainty of manner and resolve, not being able to see that it came from compensating for and concealing an inner weakness and flaw. He could not see it because he identified with that damaged element he saw to imitate the same way of dealing with it, although with more circumspection and caution.

Bush had him in thrall because Blair's muddled and misguided Anglican/Catholic faith had as yet no power of granting him such certainties. The need, as he insisted on remaining in power, to find a sustaining inner strategy (which had nothing to do with his skills in getting elected) was paramount, impelling him to imitate Bush. For example, Bush, like Blair, believed the lies Blair now told him with increasing certainty ('What I believe is the truth') because, like Blair, he was cognitively impaired – he didn't know he was lying. But here the worst factor of Blair's admiration for Bush came into being: the outer spin on which the Blair government rode (superbly managed as it was as a means of dealing with the media and public and even the Labour Party) had begun by Blair to become internalised. Now he was his own man, protected by the shell others had shown him how to build, just as Cherie was.

263

This had evidently happened earlier to Bush, who, it was clear to even the most rudimentary of witnesses, constantly changed his take on events according to his *internal* spin system; if this failed, he changed the rules by which what is real was actually defined.

The Labour Party in September 2006 had a final chance to confront the truth about Iraq at its conference. But once again it yielded to the brilliant stage management and performance of Tony; by now so accustomed to and trained in its Pavlovian reflexes, the party once again fell under his histrionic spell. But by then the majority of people in the country had realised how abjectly stupid and undesirable the behaviour of the Labour Party it had elected to power actually had become. Tony, using the language of the old stage trouper, had also become, supported by Cherie, captive to his own cynicism, believing he could abdicate at a time of his own choosing, once he had had time to shape his legacy – if only through Stormont reopening in Northern Ireland, to show he had brought peace there. 'They will love me again, surely,' he was saying to himself, 'and they will see that in twenty years, before history, I will be justified.'

40

The sirens of Baghdad

Fiction is history which *might* have taken place, and history fiction which *has* taken place.

André Gide, *The Vatican Cellars*

In their zeal, their puppy-like eagerness to embrace the American spirit, to become honorary Americans, and their short-sighted dismissal of Europe and traditional British values, Tony and Cherie failed to understand that there could be, and actually should be, a vital difference between the British attitude to terrorism and the American one.

Forging the enemy, their inner demons, into a cohesive, well-integrated worldwide force of terror may well be the main legacy both Bush and Blair leave their countries. Yet here is the paradox. Tony by nature is inclusive, a concession-maker, one who is at his best in calming people down (a much-needed skill in marriage and family life), or coaxing and winning over people to persuade them to support a plan or issue. If he had simply stuck to his brief of promoting world peace, alleviating Third World hunger and reducing global warming, the record could have been different. But as it was he went on from his upending of the evil dictator to join in the war on the abstract, delusional and all-embracing notion: TERROR.

Terror was what the Irgun terrorists of Israel used, transforming themselves under their leader Menachem Begin, to come to power in Israel. Their bloodthirsty proclamations against the 'British criminal terrorist army' could have been posted on the internet by Al Qaeda: 'We shall revenge the blood of the prisoners of war who have been murdered by actions of war against the enemy, by blows which we shall inflict on his head.' Tony the politician

265

politicised terror, just as he had sex and religion, culminating in the Terrorism Bill of February 2006, which allows arrest and detention of suspects for up to twenty-eight days (he had pressed for ninety days). Perhaps it is the only way forward for a politician who has never evolved or matured into a statesman or a leader, or even a competent manager, that he should seek to politicise everything, even his own belief in God.

Again, we must look to the inner man – and his woman. Desperation was increasingly at work inside the siege mentality of Tony (and alongside him Cherie, increasingly at odds with life in No. 10) that now protected the pair. The siege mentality is a recidivistic Irish trait, stemming from long occupation by a foreign power, so here again the 'heritage of emotion' had kicked in. The Terrorism Bill, therefore, was not the result of cross-party consensus, for Tony kept to the idea of his two previous governments that his majority was the same as it had always been. Fuelled by anxiety over the July 2005 London Underground atrocities, which affected everyone, not just Labour supporters, and in spite of again rising to the occasion in his expression of national grief, he drove home a partisan, political answer which alienated more than it unified. It was again the very personal act of a man with a mission. The reason, once more, was not only lack of intelligence based on misinterpretation through absence of self-knowledge, but also a failure in a wider sense in the intelligence services. They had too, mirroring the government, been wracked by internal division, the miasma of political correctness and sheer incompetence throughout, often because of tokenism in the recruitment of staff.

The Channel 4 documentary *Spinning Terror*, broadcast on 20 February 2006, showed how the various publicly touted 'triggers' for the new anti-terror Bill, including the right to detain suspects without charge (in effect the abolition of the ancient writ of habeas corpus) and the muddled banning of the 'glorification' of terrorism, were based on 'narratives', what essentially were fictions. These included the 'discovery' of the deadly poison ricin in a north London flat in January 2003 – the connection to an Al Qaeda poison camp in Iraq even cited by Colin Powell to the UN Security Council – and the equally disturbing panic over the alleged Old Trafford stadium attack – both of which led to fiasco trials which engendered anti-Islamic prejudice and blackened the lives of suspects who were innocent. The over-reaction of calling in tanks and military forces to Heathrow airport over a suspected bomb plot was another case in point. It even enraged the Home Secretary, David Blunkett, who later claimed in the *Blunkett Tapes* that their bungled security move was quite out of proportion to the threat.

Consider the moment in the 2003 State of the Union address when George W. Bush suddenly leaned over the lectern and almost whispered:

> Imagine those nineteen hijackers with other weapons and other plans – this time armed by Saddam Hussein. It would take one vial, one canister, one crate slipped into this country to bring a day of horror like none we have ever known . . . All told, more than 3,000 suspected terrorists have been arrested in many countries. Many others have met a different fate. Let's put it this way – they are no longer a problem to the United States and to our friends and allies.

Such cold-blooded, sadistic statements as Bush has made, and the continuing Guantánamo Bay outrage of holding suspects without trial, betray a total US government malfunction, as reported top down in substantial and repeated detail by Bob Woodward in *State of Denial* – people in high office shouting, hugging, scheming, doubting, bullying, telling lies, shirking blame, fearing dismissal. This mirrors a cognitive failure of universal yet simple proportions – a failure to understand terrorism and the nature of the terrorist. Quoting Lord Chatham on the Americans fighting in their War of Independence, General Sir Michael Rose, the former UN commander in Bosnia, said in April 2007, ' "If I was an American, as I am an Englishman, as long as one Englishman remained on American native soil, I would never, never, never lay down my arms." The Iraqi insurgents feel exactly the same way.'

But if terror is misunderstood on the basic human level (and Cherie did almost unconsciously refer to how the young Palestinian suicide bomber might feel in September 2003, saying, 'As long as young people feel they have got no hope but to blow themselves up, you are never going to make progress'), the means of touching its ideological base and justification in Muslim law and in the Koran was also completely intellectually misguided. The evangelical Christian zeal of Blair and Bush, in their war on terror, had nothing to do with the sacred identity of man, and had the very opposite effect to what they intended. Iraq's 1.2 million Christians were now persecuted as they never had been in the days of Saddam's tyranny. Christian communities in Lebanon were physically destroyed by indiscriminate Israeli bombing; many Christians, out openly on the streets of Beirut in early 2007, support Hezbollah. The Islamic fundamentalists who use force rather than peace and love of Allah to spread their religion had benefited enormously from the clumsy, cack-handed, unimaginative way the two leaders dealt with terror. Had Blair dealt with it differently and really brought his acting skills and persuasive charm to bear on it, he might yet have effected a change in the attitudes of many millions, other governments, and even Bush himself. And instead of lecturing and hectoring on human rights, why had Cherie not used her position to promote peace and understanding between religions, say between Muslims and Jews?

Ill-judged violent response to violence makes antagonists identical to one another. The revelations and graphic brutal images of American soldiers torturing Iraqi prisoners (and especially those of a woman soldier, which would seem to make the contrast of the Muslim women's veil with the female soldiers' battle fatigues only more poignant) and, later, of the British forces' alleged and dismissed descent into barbarous treatment put the occupying forces in terms of propaganda on the same level as the tyrannies they were supposed to eradicate. The sale of rigged pictures of abuse to the *Daily Mirror*, which led when exposed as fakes to the sacking of Piers Morgan, gave the truth-versus-fabrication theme a Pirandellesque twist, for it was revealed in other incidents and in time that the faked events had a basis in truth. As the former US Secretary of State Madeleine Albright, says, proclaiming liberty, as Bush did in his 2005 presidential address ('Freedom is God's gift to everybody in the world'), is far simpler than building genuine democracy.

'What I think is really interesting, the best bit, is what Saddam Hussein does,' said Bush to Blair in another overheard snatch of conversation on 23 July 2006. By then Saddam, caged and behind bars after being hunted down and found in a muddy hole, had shown he was every bit as good a showman and media manipulator as Tony Blair. He always was, but in the televised images shown throughout 2006 of the trial, which was supposed to 'destroy him', to some sections of the Arab world he stole the show, and, rehabilitated by his captors, even showed mimetic rivalry of their dapper and slim figures, carefully cultured hairlines and Western designer clothes. The clearly visible label of his tailor, Recep Cesur, had more than a Shakespearean ring about it ('Ave Caesar!'), while the slaughter of 148 Shia Muslims in the village of Dujail after the 1982 assassination attempt, however horrific, hardly impressed beside the number of Iraqi civilians killed since the 2003 invasion. Even the casualties, most of them innocent, as Colonel Tim Collins pointed out, of the United States' revenge air attack after discovering a potential attempt on the life of George Bush senior on a visit to Kuwait were far greater than those in Dujail. A former member of the Mukhabarat, the feared secret police, assessed for Collins the charge on which Saddam was being tried: 'Right man, wrong charge; not a good idea.'

'Three years in Iraq and the only winner is . . . Saddam,' proclaimed a Western newspaper. In January 2007 the Iraqi government hanged him. What is still extraordinary is that both Blair and Bush, who operated very similar empires of manipulation and obfuscation, should have fallen so naively for the lies Saddam pitched so grandiloquently about his military might and the WMD. But did they really? There are two kinds of liar: the fantasist liar and the realist. The second will always have the advantage over the first, so now we definitely know who has won.

41

Parting is such sweet sorrow 4

A first person account is, after all, a confession; and the one who has something to confess has something to hide. And the one who has the word 'I' at his or her disposal has the quickest device for concealing himself.

Stanley Cavell, *Disowning Knowledge*

As David Blunkett pointed out in *The Blunkett Tapes*, his substantial auto-biography, the informality introduced by Blair in his day-to-day dealings with ministerial colleagues and aides – 'Call me Tony' – did not at all facilitate creative discussion and interchange. While a temporary, pleasing novelty, again an aping of Bill Clinton's procedure in Washington, it had been firmly reversed by George W. Bush, who reintroduced strict formality, no swearing and rigid teetotalism. But as Blunkett makes clear, the lingua franca of this sofa Cabinet meant ministers had from the start adopted a style more appropriate to theatre rehearsals or a film set, with members arriving with bottles of wine, comments on whether it was vintage or plonk, fevered calls of congratulations or condolence, much – of course – obligatory hugging, and an overspill of personal crisis into public crisis (they were legion), as if government was an endless first night and post-performance party. With all this came the overriding anxiety of the next day in the performance and art world: 'Will the reviews be good?'

The press joined in delightedly, and a unique situation now existed in which you had an ongoing tug or dramatic conflict between press and government, itself a colourful narrative in many ways better than anything fiction scriptwriters could dream up. As Blunkett said about leaks, which are the visible signs, the diseased pox or gout, of incompetent government, 'It's just hopeless. You can't have a conversation, you can't float an idea. You can't do anything without it being leaked.'

The historian Norman Davies comments:

> Not surprisingly the Blair government's Freedom of Information Bill as presented in May 1999 failed to meet campaigners' expectations. It threatened to confirm the famous obituary: Here lies a civil servant. He was civil to everyone, and servant to the devil. . . . Ten thousand men and women working at Bletchley Park in wartime did not spill a bean at the time or for thirty years afterwards. And now British intelligence officers were routinely circulating their complaints on the internet. Greed accompanied indiscretion.

Government became one vast, ever-rolling entertainment with 'highs' and 'lows', an X-Factor talent show with hearts broken, tears shed, hugs and smiles, and behind the curtain backstage crises. 'Take but degree away, untune that string, and hark, what discord follows.' Here was a medieval or Renaissance court in full flood of delicious intrigue, suspicion and drama. Here were whispered conspiracies, paranoia in full cry. It was of course based on the American model, but it had run amok.

Libby Purves wrote of Judas Iscariot, if he returned to earth:

> He wouldn't have to settle for forty miserable pieces of silver. He'd have a book deal, a panel spot on *Have I Got News for You*, and an opportunity to unburden himself to Lynn Barber and Gyles Brandreth about his difficult childhood, problems of sexual orientation, and abusive codependent relationships with other disciples.

Substitute 'Cabinet colleagues' for disciples, 'betraying mistresses and girlfriends' and 'uncovered secret donors to Labour' (still being unearthed by the police as this goes to press) for 'problems of sexual orientation' and 'blindness' for 'difficult childhood' and you have exactly how David Blunkett settled for £200,000 for his *Tapes*, published in 2006 by Bloomsbury. In so doing, Blunkett turned himself into the perfect icon of the victim society. The self-generated oversight and negligence scandals that wrecked his career not once but three times, while Tony sought out of pity and therapeutic gesture (and codependence) to reinstate him each time, are well known. But if ever there was a man sadly promoted out of his depth, and for the wrong reasons, as well as prey to the rampant priapism that accompanies power, it was this former leader of Sheffield Council, whose man management skills peaked in that role.

Blunkett had already been notoriously indiscreet to his biographer about his Cabinet colleagues (Jack Straw: 'about as imaginative as a dead frog'; Tessa Jowell: 'like the internet. Tell her a secret and it's out immediately'; Tony: 'he wanted to move Brown but was too tired'), for which he then abjectly apologised to those concerned (although the comments ring true) and then made his apology public. But in his *Tapes*, 'a great mountain of mealy-mouthed junk' according to one eminent critic, he commits the ultimate 'don't blame me' of all political autobiography.

Of all Tony's close colleagues (and it is hard not to believe an important element in his promotion was Tony and Cherie's admiration for his courage in face of his adversity, as well as a customary bluntness of expression), Blunkett came nearest to Cherie in her obsession with the media 'intrusion' on her privacy. 'They are', he writes, 'the equivalent of the Stasi in East Germany.' When he is in the lowest of depths over his tormented adolescent passion for his girlfriend, 'Cherie phones me twice a week', once at 11 p.m. when 'my job is to hide the hurt that is churning my guts out'. But does he hide it? No. Tony tells him, when he is at his most depressed between Cabinet jobs, that he needs to be at peace with himself and ready to get 'embroiled' again in running a great office of state. 'He said that being embroiled would help me to get refocused and get my head straightened out. It was clear that he really understood.'

The endlessly forgiving Tony, the ever-waterproof duck's back in a now deluged but just as quickly emptied pond full of leaks, on one ministerial reinstatement 'tells me to avoid avoidable publicity'. Both should be made to eat every one of his 896 pages: as P. J. O'Rourke points out, 'Being gloomier is easier than being cheerful. Anybody can say "I've got cancer" and get a rise out of a crowd. But how many of us can do five minutes of good stand-up comedy?' He adds, 'We used to be shunned for weeping in our beer.'

What Blunkett's sad progress through his own vale of tears does prove conclusively is that invading your own privacy is an ultimate folly, way beyond adultery, fast-tracking passport applications or the venal failure to declare financial perks. The fantasy of soft curves attached to a sensual, empathetic voice might soften a blind man, as Blunkett says himself, into 'a sucker', but his self-indulgence had turned the old French proverb '*Qui s'excuse, s'accuse*' – 'he who excuses himself, accuses himself' – on its head. It was now '*Qui s'accuse, s'excuse*'.

42

The triumph of 'undifferentiationism'

It will be a great contest, with a lot of talented people.

> Hillary Clinton, on the Democratic presidential race,
> 22 January 2007

The other Blair was an atheist. 'This is a political age,' wrote Eric Arthur Blair, who took the pen name George Orwell, in 1954. Eric Arthur Blair came to know that political world inside out, all the lies and deceptions, and although he was a committed socialist, he viewed the world with a clear and cold eye, writing that it 'is tormented by enormous delusions and hatreds which cut across one another in an extremely complex way' ('Notes on Nationalism', 1945).

This sums up the last year of Tony's rule, by which time, between him and Cherie, mirror imaging had gone too far, and mimetic rivalry had escalated far beyond the point where it could have a positive effect. For herself and for the sake of her family, Cherie had apparently settled for silence and retreat after the blows suffered, and so she abandoned her earlier imitation of other role models. Anybody could have seen, as by now she must have done, that if mimetic rivalry goes beyond a certain point, as it did for instance with Charles and Diana, or Laurence Olivier and Vivien Leigh, it leads to endless conflict.

And here were new rivals to take over and capture the media scene and glut the public eye: Heather Mills and Paul McCartney, the latter in Tony's eyes 'a great guy' and one of his idols. The two heads together, while the world passed, were no longer to be seen. Tony, alone, was now, it seemed, at the centre the sole conductor and overseer of his last year in office, 'master of all I survey' in Alexander Pope's words – which was a government in full and utter disarray. There were now upwards of 1,700 petitions on the No. 10 website against the hundreds of petty restrictions now hampering freedom of action and expression. It showed in Tony's photographs that, in spite of being outwardly 'tanned and looking beautiful' – the one who would compete in exposure to the sun with his children's nannies – there was a faltering in his gaze, an occasional shifty and downcast glance. 'I despair for him', said the loyal David Blunkett, while Cliff Richard had in 2003 seen him looking so 'gaunt and destroying himself' he had lent him his holiday home in Barbados for recuperation. It had not helped much, for a fortnight after his return he was rushed into hospital with heart trouble. Blackpool might have been better.

But he 'stuck to his guns' increasingly about the recommitment to the 'pacification' of Afghanistan's Taliban, which escalated the casualties. Small improvements in Iraq, or minor military successes, as in all faltering campaigns, were spun eagerly in every direction, but the sad self-deception remained firmly entrenched. 'Victory is the only option left' is the cry of the defeated. Historical knowledge remained at nil: on a visit to the United Arab Emirates in December 2006 a young woman asked him if Iraq was heading towards another Sykes–Picot agreement, in other words the drawing up of new national boundaries. This treaty in 1916 had effectively created Iraq (then Mesopotamia), Syria, Lebanon and Palestine. Blair didn't know what it was, and evaded the question. Again that other Blair, fifty years earlier, had expressed perfectly what was to happen to his namesake: 'A known fact may be so unbearable that it is habitually pushed aside and not allowed to enter into logical processes, or on the other hand it may enter into every calculation and yet never be admitted as a fact, even in one's own mind' ('Notes on Nationalism'). The few loyal followers he had left suffered mimetic contagion.

Tony had dismissed Jack Straw as Foreign Secretary because George W. Bush no longer approved of him; when he appointed Margaret Beckett in his place, she replied with one word: 'Fuck!' ('the first and last time she spoke for the nation,' cracked one wit). She told John Humphrys in an interview before Christmas 2006 that 'ministers never suggested Saddam Hussein posed a threat to Britain'. They realised also, she said, that the central claim that Saddam could have WMD ready within forty-five minutes may have been wrong. When pressed to answer why the claims were not discounted then, she said, 'Oh, come on – nobody thought it was relevant. Nobody thought it was a big sweeping statement.'

*

The rest of the New Labour government, those that weren't being switched around, skulked in their ministerially cosseted tents, bickering and bitching in their putative memoirs, to be sold in the future at inflated prices without relation to sales or quality – and in their leaks to journalists. Like the Greeks at the siege of Troy the Labour Party had lost any sense at all as to why it had travelled all the way there. A question of wife-stealing, was it? Infighting in the most savage terms became the order of the day, and the cynical commentators grew fat and rich in their pickings, as the all-too-readily whining ministers and their minions ran to them with their woes. Inside knowledge had been turned out; virtually everything had been leaked and, more than this, added to, embellished. It was truly an unbelievable situation.

*

Tony had no real sense of how business was run, nor did Cherie, and the alignment of government, of statecraft, of rule, of morality, not exactly with management attitudes, but with the endless tracts of self-improvement, self-assertiveness and 'doing your own thing', the shibboleths of New Labour – modernising and meeting targets – was now almost complete. There was no distinction in Tony's mind between a wealthy man, a man or woman who had made a lot of money, and someone fit to hold and exercise authority: he identified one with the other. Yet at bottom 'he never really knew how to run an investment company; worse, he didn't care that he didn't know,' says a banker.

Yet management gurus had been the true Tony apostles and in his attitude to government prevailed their cavalier, entrepreneurial attitudes of rebellion to all the bureaucratic civil service structures, all the paraphernalia of meetings and minutes and consulting. According to Tony, we should do everything like the business leaders we admire – on the hoof, in our shirtsleeves, on the sofa, latte in one hand and mobile phone in the other. Run UK plc as though it were a City investment company. Get by on management jargon. Think the unthinkable – as Blair told Frank Field when he appointed him to look at welfare reforms. (Field did as he was told, but it turned out to be the wrong kind of unthinkable, so Blair fired him.)

Blair's former Cabinet secretary, Sir Robin Butler, watched horrified as the structure of Cabinet government was pulled down about his ears. 'Blair is a good chairman of Cabinet,' one senior former Cabinet minister told us. 'He is relaxed, permissive, lets colleagues speak. But it is not part of a decision-making process.' Butler once told Blair: 'You didn't manage it, you led it. That's different.'

Business gurus such as Charles Handy and John Birt (another Liverpool leveller) advocated an enterprise culture which was not only immoral but actually abolished the need for any difference of opinion, the only criterion being 'does it work?'. As a BBC executive said of Birt, when he became director general, 'All the currently fashionable management devices were tried, all at once, in a hurry.'

Tony believed his great achievement, in three words, was 'to abolish ideology', whether it was in religion or politics, but in effect what he did, in law after law, was to abolish difference in the name of an all-levelling, vague embrace of 'diversity'. To be a Muslim was, in his eyes, the same as being a Roman Catholic, or a Protestant, or a Jew. To be a Labour supporter was essentially to vote for the same policies as a Conservative. The hierarchy of traditional Scottish regiments, the red coats of the masters of the hunt, were relegated to the same trash bin as traditional marriage and Christmas celebrations. To be a man was the same as to be a woman. If two men married, or two women, it was the same as if a man and a woman married. He had abolished difference.

This in essence was what Cherie also did in parallel with her myriad changes in fashion and her way-out health practices: she, in imitation of Tony, reduced all fashion to meaningless shapes, undifferentiated colours and cuts by being seen in virtually everything. The fashion editors shrieked in horror and consternation at her poor clothes sense, her antagonism to her body, her poor poise, her uncouth gestures and ungainly accessories. None of them had really got the point and the point was, like John Lennon, she didn't really care. She felt superior to it all. By refusing to refine, to be consistent, to embrace the difficult demands of integration, to develop real taste and discrimination, she was in effect showing her contempt, her rebelliousness against the fashion and all other worlds. 'I'll try everything,' is the cry of the provocative person who, ultimately and inside, does not care and believes their inflated position grants them licence to call the shots. Here Cherie's 'ethic' has merged with that of the pop idol millionaires.

The same was true of Cherie's lifestyle gurus. Ultimately, because she tried so many, picked them up monthly almost, there was a new roll call of those names 'close to' Cherie – they meant nothing. She had become like sections of the press, daily touting a new lifestyle. Her sincerity, like Tony's, was worn on her sleeve, because the driving need of her personality was for control. There was no sincerity that could outwit her own self-regard.

For all his tense, highly wrought expressions and furrowed play of eyebrows, Tony has a very thick skin. His visible anxiety comes from the intent of not being found out, or caught out, or brought down, rather than the prickings of conscience. But what of their loyal ministers who have survived till the end? They too well and truly joined in the virtual reality show. A good case in point is that of Tessa Jowell's professed 'ignorance' of her husband David Mills's involvement with the dealings of the Berlusconi government, and her denial that she knew of the borrowings and repayments of the mortgage on the house in which she lived. As Ned Sherrin joked in one of his 'news flashes' on the radio show *Loose Ends*, 'Tessa Jowell has just learned for the first time that she separated six weeks ago from her husband David Mills'.

43

More glassy essences

Vice is a monster of so frightful mien,
As to be hated, needs but to be seen;
Yet seen too often, familiar with her face,
We first endure, then pity, then embrace.

Alexander Pope, *An Essay on Man*

Tessa Jowell had been a New Labour insider, a Blair court member from the very start. Loyal (and uncritical) supporters of Tony and Cherie, Jowell and David Mills, her husband, again provide an uncanny reflection, a curious twinning of the Tony–Cherie marriage. When both Jowell and Mills left their respective first spouses within a year of one another in 1976–7, and married in 1979, they embarked, in their similar north London domicile on the same division of marital roles and aspirations. There was a difference, however, because it was Jowell, who had no children and was never to have any, who became the political high-flyer, although she had to wait until 1992 to win her Dulwich seat, while Mills, who had three children from his first marriage, took up the Cherie role as the lucratively paid lawyer. Jowell seethed with the New Labour jargon and ideals, in other words seeking power at all costs, and she joined Tony's early team. Mills, a proud, argumentative *bon viveur*, began to weave an intricate web of highly paid international briefs. He had, according to his friends, a huge ego, like that other legal spouse, believing he possessed a towering intellect; unlike Cherie, however, he was known to be 'an aggressive atheist, and whenever he meets someone with religious views, he would just tear them apart'. We have no record that this happened when he dined with Tony and Cherie. But he would constantly demand people 'justify' themselves – as though they have to – and in the tradition of New Labour grandees his favourite word, to describe what others were saying, was 'bollocks'.

Perhaps it was appropriate that he should be married to the Secretary of State for Culture, for this was how modern British culture could aptly be summed up. Jowell had been quickly rewarded for her loyalty in the early, heady days of power with the post of public health minister. Here, while her spouse, representing avarice, acted for Formula One to lobby for exemption from the ban on TV tobacco advertising, magically became the key minister advising on the issue. Tony granted the exemption before his public humiliation of having to withdraw it and confess the irregularity.

Even so, Tessa Jowell's rich lifestyle hardly faltered, although from 1998 onwards her husband gained notoriety through various demands on him to give evidence in Italian courts over work that he was alleged to have carried out for the Italian premier Silvio Berlusconi. The connection between Berlusconi, Mills, Jowell and the Blairs formed what the *Sunday Times* called 'a charmed circle . . . Mills advised the empire of *Il Dottore*, as Berlusconi was known, on setting up offshore companies. And, adding gravitas, Mills's older brother John was married to Dame Barbara Mills, the director of public prosecutions from 1992–1998.'

This all came to something of an untidy end, or at least to a head, in March 2006, when the scandal broke about Mills's alleged Italian pay-off by Berlusconi, during which Blair accused Mills of dragging him into the scandal. Jowell denied knowing her husband had used the money to pay off their jointly secured mortgage on their Kentish Town house, and Jowell and Mills separated to salvage her career as Secretary of State for Culture, Media and Sport. History will pass its own verdict on Jowell's legislation which brought in 24-hour drinking and the casino 'culture', a word which has itself deteriorated from the idea of what was to be nurtured and developed in differential refinement and expressing the soul of a nation to one of opening the floodgates of unbridled and permissive gluttony, self-indulgence and crime – as in 'binge culture' or 'knife culture'.

In the prevailing political culture, meanwhile, no one had done wrong, of course, and no ministerial codes had been broken, 'naturally', so as usual there was no ensuing resignation, but hugs all round, outpourings of sympathy and denunciation of the vicious press. Tessa had proved her outstanding skill as a minister of sliding scales and differing values, but most of all as a dispenser of that universal feelgood buzzword of the therapy culture – empathy. She once said she would throw herself under a bus for Tony – as long as there was a pantomime manhole in the street for her to disappear down! But how could that devout, ethically motivated couple, Tony and Cherie, allow a close friend to sacrifice her marriage – more than allow, oblige her to do so? Surely Tony should have been the first to insist Tessa should resign and attend to her private life. But Cherie was there, too, in this, insisting that her and Tony's political interest came first, and such a protective gesture as Tony's calling on Tessa to resign was firmly overruled; in her support of Tony over the invasion of Iraq, for instance, she had assured him that by standing up for what he believed he would secure his place in history. But secure it as what? A little later, in the summer of 2003, when Alastair Campbell stood down she testified to his 'integrity', although by then 'the Downing Street reputation for integrity and truth-telling [had] collapsed during the six-year period when Alastair Campbell ran its media operation' (Peter Oborne, *The Rise of Political Lying*).

Greed is contagious. This little cameo should set in perspective the change of culture presided over by a minister who has enjoyed Tony and Cherie's whole-hearted support:

> Tony Blair's ability to draw a distinction has certainly been questioned in the past: it was revealed in July last year that the Prime Minister had, so far, received eighteen luxury watches from Mr Berlusconi as well as four necklaces, two bracelets, two sets of earrings, two rings, a clock and a holdall. An enduring, surreal image of Mr Blair's premiership will be that snapshot from 2004, a few weeks after magistrates had interrogated Mr Mills: the Prime Minister and his wife, Cherie, were walking through Sardinian crowds with 68-year-old Mr Berlusconi, who was sporting a beige bandanna. Mr Berlusconi looked like the cat that got the cream; the Blairs looked acutely embarrassed that their jet-set dream had turned out quite so silly. Many are now wondering what mention was made of Mr Mills when the Blairs stayed at Mr Berlusconi's villa that summer. (*Sunday Times*, March 2006)

Mills speaks of £500,000 as 'meagre compensation' for all the visits he has taken. One thing is sure: he was a person, according to the Italian papers, who, married to one of Tony Blair's senior colleagues, 'you could trust completely'.

In the Commons in November 2004 Michael Howard pointed to corruption inside the Department for Culture, whose officials, allegedly, had been wooing American gambling interests. Tony had an outburst of fake outrage, and sprang to his feet to shout, 'It really is ridiculous! It's utterly absurd!' No one was much convinced.

*

Once an ardent left-winger like so many, Patricia Hewitt had converted to an unbounded faith in capitalism when she became Trade Secretary, at the same time taking private jets to conferences on global poverty. 'I went into politics to make the world a better place,' she pronounced, and to do this she wanted to scrap European sugar subsidies and America's 'mad' help for its 'inefficient' cotton subsidies. But did she achieve this? No. Mission unaccomplished, but power intact, she moved on.

But it may be, along with the 'sisterhood' of the other women ministers, Margaret Hodge and Harriet Harman, she was being attacked not so much because she was a woman, but because she adopted early on an attitude that she was the self-appointed Head Girl of the House of Commons, Her loyalty, when Tony had his 'wobble' in 2004, with its highly visible signs of his impending departure, was characteristically upbeat: 'Tony? Look, he is a terrific Prime Minister. There is no sign *whatsoever* that he is going to take early retirement.' When Trade Secretary, she received from Tony, and no doubt with Cherie's endorsement, the extra post of minister for women. Michael Fabricant in early May 2004 pointed out in the Commons that the old Soviet Union, even though 50 per cent of industrial managers were female, had no minister for women. He asked, 'What is the ministry for women for? What is she for?' At this Hewitt completely 'lost it' in her rage.

An ardent feminist, her credentials for this ministry went back to 1990 when she had written with Anna Coote (who became her adviser) and Harriet Harman, in a social policy paper called 'The Family Way': 'It cannot be assumed that men are bound to be an asset to family life, or that the presence of a father in families is necessarily a means to social harmony and cohesion.' Five years later she was quoted as saying, in a book called *Transforming Men*, 'But if we want fathers to play a full role in their children's lives, then we need to bring men into the playgroups and nurseries and the schools. And here, of course, we hit the immediate difficulty of whether we can trust men with children.' Her new social utopia, as Erin Pizzey says, like that of other feminists, including Joan Ruddock, another minister for women, and Harman, now a justice minister, depended upon destroying family life. 'In the new century,' says Pizzey, 'so their credo ran, the family unit will consist of only women and their children. Fathers are dispensable.'

Hewitt is very pro-abortion right up to birth, which is just what Tony must have felt is needed in a health minister, and has resisted pressure and the general consensus to lower the limit on abortions from twenty-four to twenty weeks. Abortions, now costing more than £5 million a year, run at an annual rate of 200,000, up from 180,000 when Labour took control of health and education, and when Tony said (without his use of verbs): 'The health service. Twenty-four hours!' As a travesty figure of power, of power aggrandisement for its own sake, defending her record in the teeth of hollow heckling and contradicting herself constantly, Hewitt claimed in 2006 that the NHS had 'had its best year ever', yet in almost the next breath she said that despite all Labour's investment, productivity in the NHS hadn't improved, jobs were being lost, and many hospital trusts faced meltdown.

But there is a wider question: what does woman want? In presenting herself as an apostle of abortion, is Hewitt also following the path of Tony and Cherie? In September 1995 Mother Teresa offered this message to the World Conference of Women in Beijing: 'Some people are saying that men and women are exactly the same, and are denying the beautiful differences . . . those who want to make men and women the same are in favour of abortion.' To boost her NHS image as a 'sex as commodity' icon the sex chain Ann Summers dispatched Hewitt a 'rampant rabbit' sex toy after using her face and the toy in a cheeky send-up to promote its £28.99 vibrator for National Nurses Week. In their promotion she holds the buzzing vibrator with a speech bubble proclaiming, 'This is the best ever week for the NHS.'

Hewitt has also been accused of spending more on hospitals in Labour marginal seats, and trying to stop a shake-up of the boundaries of her constituency, Leicester West, by complaining it had 'too many whites'. This prompted the comment, 'The use of ethnicity to allocate people to constituencies will be resented by the vast majority of Asians in Leicester – yet again, being used as a political football.'

But it is as a public performer that her power-seeking displays have been most marked: she likes it out there in the blaze of publicity, she relishes the limelight and here she signifies some very deep dislocation of perception that has taken place over Tony and Cherie's ten years in power. Quentin Letts, the outstanding drama critic of the Commons, produced reviews as vivid as any theatre critic of the past, but they were about the stages which have quite overtaken the dying West End scene, now given over to reviving American musicals and long-in-the-tooth playwrights. The truth Letts validated in his parliamentary sketches is that politics as a performance art has become more gripping a spectacle than anything found in the live theatre. There are exceptions, of course, but many of those plays which have a spark, such as Alistair Beaton's *Feelgood* or Peter Morgan's *Frost-Nixon*, as well as the host of television docu-dramas, have been spin-offs from politics.

Hewitt's voice became to Letts in 2004

> quite a work of art . . . slightly antipodean (she's an Aussie) and so level, so free of peaks and blips, so wall-to-wall-carpeted by nannyish concern, that if you sat her in front of a tape recorder dial the needle would barely move off the middle register. Miss Hewitt is an example to all anger management coaches.

By January 2006 something had happened: 'Mother Hewitt's nasal nannying is enough to give anyone raging, acute neuralgia . . . That Hewitt voice . . . Pitying, patronising, posh, pitted with clichés, it oozes into the inner nodules of the mind causing a semi-frozen agony.'

44

Parting is such sweet sorrow 5

The typical phallic-narcissist character is self-confident, often arrogant, vigorous and often impressive.

Wilhelm Reich, *Character Analysis*

It hardly seemed to matter in the last year of Tony and Cherie's rule whether 'Prezza', John 'Two Jags' Prescott, the deputy Prime Minister, should go or stay following the disclosure of his sexual antics with Tracey Temple, his diary secretary, with his official Dorneywood residence as the 'shag pad'. The affair had been going on for two years and was common knowledge in Westminster restaurants, where the waiters recognised the pair as an 'item'. 'In the old days,' said Harold Macmillan, before his resignation in the wake of the Profumo affair in 1963, 'you could be absolutely sure that you could go to a restaurant with your wife and not see a man that you knew having lunch with a tart. It was all kept separate but this does not seem to happen these days . . . Profumo was incapable of keeping the two sides of his life separate.'

But while undifferentiationism was at its Blairistic height, it never meant there was less hypocrisy to try and protect reputations. The Tony–Cherie official line over Prescott's affair decreed that it was a 'private matter', in spite of every denizen of every watering hole in Westminster knowing he had this 'perk on the side' – so much so that the BBC in its news reports virtually ignored the affair, falling in with the Prime Minister's diktat. But was it a private affair? How do we define 'private'?

In terms of privacy, let us be clear. There is only one criterion to be applied to all the behaviour of politicians, ministers, people who are responsible or accountable to the public and enjoy their trust and their remuneration from public funds (and the BBC's are public funds as well). That criterion, or rule of thumb, is particularly applicable to those who set themselves up, as New Labour ministers have done, as standard-bearers or exemplars for both public and private morality. The rule is that what becomes a matter of blatant public comment can no longer be reckoned to be private. It certainly cannot be suppressed, withheld or glossed over out of 'respect' for the privacy of those involved: it has become public knowledge, and inevitably affects one's view of the protagonist and calls in question his or her judgement. It is a very simple rule, so why was there so much confusion?

Prescott had always been embraced by Tony and Cherie as a token or talisman of their old-Labour integrity, their fealty to traditional socialism: he was, as he aged in office, in appearance increasingly like a Phiz cartoon of a Dickensian character, his outlandish words and grumpy behaviour the jewel in the crown of the Liverpudlianisation of Great Britain. His well-documented ministerial incompetence, his short-sightedness, his bungled vocabulary and his ever-present large retinue were so reassuring to the old guard. Like Dick Swiveller in *The Old Curiosity Shop*, the impression he gives, when holding forth on Blair and Brown in Michael Cockerell's documentaries, is that he knows he is absurd and enjoys that fact too.

He was indeed the true old-style Bolshevik minister, with his uninhibited drinking style, his easy body language, schmoozy ballroom clinch (a contrast to the stiff circling of the floor by Tony and Cherie), his blowsy, faithful wife Pauline, his Dorneywood dacha and his mistress. Stalin would have been proud of him and given him a bear hug before having him poisoned off when he got too big for his boots. But in spite of his robust appearance, Prescott was more of a George Brown than an Ernest Bevin or an Arthur Scargill; more of a fishy chauvinist, lifting up young women's skirts, than a trusty bruiser.

The paradox of Prescott was that he should so display his subservience to a 'toff' such as Tony and his imperious first lady while bad-mouthing all other Tory toffs at every opportunity (although he did, as a former cruise steward, once admire Anthony Eden). His morality stemmed from that popular, amoral figure of the 1960s, Alfie, played by Michael Caine in the award-winning film. 'I kisses her,' says Alfie of his many dollies.

It started out as a friendly peck at the side of the cheek. Then it worked round to a full kiss on her lips. And then I thinks to myself, 'What harm can it do?' My trouble is – I ain't ever learned how to refuse something for nothing. Even if I don't want it. But what man has? 'It'll settle her little mind,' I says to myself. 'Harry will never know, and even if he did he's no right to begrudge me – or her, come to that.'

The ultimate mockery of morality and the most basic commonsense lapse was his apology on being found out. Whether or not Prescott told his wife he was sorry or not is one thing (if he genuinely was), but to apologise to the Labour Party and 'the country at large' over Tracy Temple shows some crowning gesture of contempt towards average intelligence. The country at large realised he would never have apologised if he had not been found out (through the 'smearing, nasty muck-rakers of the red-top press'). All the habitués of the eating houses in Westminster will tell you he hardly kept the affair hidden. So what possibly could the abject apology mean to the party and country 'at large'? The public gesture of confession was as if he was being noble and 'owning up', but the virtue in 'owning up' to a misdemeanour comes when you have *not* been found out. Public guilt was the new perk politicians were giving themselves. Again, copying the media celebrities.

Tony clung on to Prescott; he should have resigned, and so should Tony. John Profumo went first, but then Macmillan ultimately resigned over the 1963 Profumo–Keeler scandal; Cecil Parkinson resigned on account of his affair with Sarah Keays. But what Tony sneeringly refers to as 'the politics of deference', and others might call ethical accountability, had vanished beyond recall. Betrayal and complaint were the order of the day, while the internet had become 'the scandal-brain of scandal and indiscretion' (Norman Davies).William Hague pointed out in Deputy Prime Minister's Question Time on 13 December 2006 that the £2 million cost to the public of maintaining Prescott in ministerial splendour could be used to help keep 100 post offices open. 'Wouldn't it be much better value?'

Prescott was the one that got away, for two obvious reasons. Had he gone Tony would have had to go. Tony's refusal to budge was also a bulwark to the tide of allegations in 2006–7 rising alongside police investigations into the cash-for-peerages affair. This resulted, on 15 December 2006, in a high-ranking police officer (whom the spin-doctor on duty refused to name, but who was called Graham McNulty, accompanied by a police sergeant who took notes), visiting No. 10 and questioning Tony for nearly two hours. Downing Street claimed it was a Home Office official who took notes. In spite of the usual denials – as with the visit to the Pope – the police visit had been contrived and carefully scheduled in advance to coincide with the publication of the Stevens report on Princess Diana's death. It echoed the interment-of-bad-news principle of 9/11: just minutes after the suicide planes hit the Manhattan twin towers, the Downing Street official Jo Moore had dispatched an email to officials suggesting that it was 'a good day to get anything bad out we want to bury'. She had then been forced to give her 'piss apology'.

As Tony became the first serving Prime Minister to face questions on a criminal matter he astutely managed to ensure the news was buried on the inside pages. But were he to be charged after he leaves office – he remains fixed in his view that 'nobody has sold honours or sold peerages' – it would be in the interests of his successor to ensure he is exonerated. The received view is he will never be charged because he has so managed to implement the policy that he is above the law. But he may well have understood, as a mimetic magnet of kingship, that the inviolability that hedges a leader soon fades; and as Lady Macbeth demands of her consort, 'Was the hope drunk in which you dressed yourself?' With Tony and Cherie, whether we like it or not, we have these lasting images of clothes, stories about them, pictures of them, in a thousand different outfits and poses, like the one Tony tells himself of being with Clinton on his ranch and having to dress in some outlandish Texan huckster's outfit for a reception. What could be more perfect advice for Tony, with his grotesque obsession with self-image and vanity of appearance?

He should long before have stopped being so indignant in righteousness or in the sense of his own virtue. But he had so vigorously defended all those reflexes of his own temperament, such as Levy, Robinson, Mandelson, Campbell, Clinton and so on, as 'great guys', 'brilliant', 'completely honest' . . . that in his own eyes he must certainly have remained the same himself. As Caithness sees Macbeth in that ever-quoted play, had he not become a man vainly trying to buckle his distempered cause within the belt of rule? The distempered cause or outsize garment was his power and influence, the belt was his integrity.

If Blair were further questioned, cautioned, and ultimately charged, would he ultimately confess, like Prescott, and say he was sorry?

45

Parting is such sweet sorrow 6

'Why are Scots so attracted to the secret world?' says Smiley in John le Carré's *Smiley's People*. 'Ships' engineers, colonial administrators, spies. Their heretical Scottish history drew them to distant churches.' Le Carré might well have added, 'And to Whitehall.' Here they seemed to conglomerate with a disproportionate number entering high office.

If Gordon Brown, aside from his resentment at not being Prime Minister as promised during Tony's second term, is attracted to the secret, arcane world of Treasury figures, with a massive obsessive interest in detail and an equally obsessional need to control everything and everybody – as well as his abrupt, even rude manner – well, none of those details are necessarily bad in a Prime Minister who can appoint the right people and actually run a country.

*

Brown's former spin-doctor Charlie Whelan called for the Labour Party to get rid of Tony Blair after the May 2005 election. With the local election disaster of May 2006, when Labour lost so many seats to the Conservatives, Whelan demanded even more vociferously that Brown should throw caution to the wind and 'move against his former friend'. Brown remained the soul of caution, but in September 2006 sixteen MPs, including one minister, Tom Watson, and seven aides, mainly Brown's followers, inevitably with his connivance, wrote to Blair asking him to step aside. Either this was a clumsy and maladroit attempt to oust Tony from power, unlikely to succeed, or it was an impatient gesture of revolt by minor figures which could play into Gordon's hands by eliciting from Tony a definite timetable to step down. Amid the endless reports of bickering, stand-offs and emotional outbursts between the pair as Tony and Gordon quarrelled (they spent three and a half hours arguing, reports said), the latter supposition proved to be true. Brown was caught on camera smiling as he left Downing Street, and subsequent outpourings of vitriol from the Blair camp and from Cherie, who was still determined to stay in Downing Street as long as she could, suggested that the strategy, if such it was, had worked and he had obtained the pledge he wanted. Gordon displayed a worrying lack of statesman-like quality in simply not falling in gracefully with Tony's exit strategy. Here, inclusively weak as he was in his desire to avoid conflict and his inability to sack Gordon, Tony, the conciliator, was at least able to upstage Gordon in unbegrudging tolerance.

As is well documented, Gordon had received hospitality going way back from Geoffrey Robinson. He was crucial in overseeing all three election campaigns. It is hard to believe, with his Olympian scan of all detail, that he was unaware of the part played by the party donors who were investigated in 2006–7. His press release on 16 December 2006, which denies any knowledge or involvement with the money that bankrolled victory, creates rather than allays suspicion. Anyway the days when Gordon used, as has been alleged by insiders, to scream like a fishwife, rave and rant at Tony and literally foam at the mouth were now over. In these encounters Tony would not shout back, seeing his job as a manager with a tempera-mental star player who needed to be stood by and supported because he delivered exceptional quality. (In one Brown–Blair encounter, with Prescott there as counsellor and mediator, the ITV docu-drama *Confessions of a Diary Secretary* shows dinner cooked and served by Tracey Temple in Prescott's Admiralty Arch flat. Brown complains that his chair is too low at the table; and when given a higher seat than Blair, the latter quips, 'I'm used to Gordon looking down on me.' In his account of the dinner on BBC 2, Prescott confirmed those same words of Blair's joke, but left Temple out of the scene. Prescott's words were 'we had the table laid out' – not, as a friend of mine thought he'd heard, 'I'd just laid Tracey'.)

One of Tony's main achievements is that this astonishing political embrace did last the lifetime of Tony's premiership, as well as the years leading up to it, and their ability together to have created a single personality into which both have merged is perhaps one of the most salient phenomena of recent political history, resulting in sustained economic growth and success. Tony deserves the main credit for sustaining it. Neither alone would have achieved the power they managed to wield and hold together in a codependency that often erupted into ugly scenes as well as constant, obvious examples of rivalry and disharmony. Add to this the tensions within the troika of Cherie, Gordon and Tony, and you wonder how they kept the lid on it.

But the having and holding of power is not quite the same as making the best use of it when you have it. Cherie, pictured lunging a foil at a fencing display in Glasgow, rang key officials to make sure of their support for Tony during the putative coup of September 2006, while Mandelson – wearing only boxer shorts in a Rio de Janeiro hotel (or so he was pictured) – mustered his dark powers to mount an anti-Brown campaign.

The new buzzwords about Gordon that emerged were not only that he was notably 'psychologically flawed', as Alastair Campbell had said, but also that he was 'autistic'. But a journalist who observed him at close quarters said he came across as calm and accomplished.

> The great thing about Gordon Brown is that he is not Tony Blair. His voice does not have that ghastly fakeness of Mister Tony's Mockney. He does not do the Princess Diana drop of the head or the check in the voice. He may, inside, be as knotted as a scatterbrain's hanky, but he comes across, even when telling political fibs, as a chunky, manly proposition.

At least here was a difference. Gordon and Tony worked well as a unit because they were so different from one another. Freud had been proved right.

46

Riding off into the sunset

I have been more sinned against than sinning.

William Shakespeare, *King Lear*

The end of September 2006 saw a new entente in place, and Gordon Brown rose to deliver his famous line at the Labour Party conference that 'it has been a privilege for me to work with and for the most successful ever Labour leader and Labour Prime Minister'. Tony mouthed a 'thank you'. Impressive though the eulogy was, it will never be shown in the future without cutting to the image of Cherie's silent and smirking disbelief. What a showperson she was! Her denunciation of Brown, 'Well, that's a lie', to Carolin Lotter of Bloomberg News was respun by Downing Street, as 'Well, can I get by?' but no one believed it and Cherie went into hiding for seven hours. Tony Booth grinned. 'Good for her,' he said. 'She has a right to speak her mind. There isn't a wife in the country who hasn't embarrassed her husband at some time.' But this was probably not the feminist, iconic judge image Ms Booth wanted just then. Her brazen cover-up was magnificent, much better than all the boring addresses she made, and for which she was paid handsome fees. 'Honestly, guys,' she said to the TV reporters without a glimmer of shame, 'I hate to spoil your story – I didn't say it, and I don't believe it.' She was yet again dangerously over-reacting to situations which reminded her of her conflicts.

In one rousing finale of self-glorification Tony delivered next day his final conference speech. The speech was the perfect embodiment, says Quentin Letts, of his premiership, a 'beautiful, floaty orb . . . shiny, rainbow-tinted, light as air, caught by whichever wind was blowing, all encasing nothing'. He or his speech-writers borrowed dialogue from John Steinbeck's *The Grapes of Wrath* for the peroration: 'I'll be everywhere – wherever you look,' says Joad, who has killed one of a gang of vigilantes while released from jail on parole, and goes out to face the gang who will probably murder him. 'Wherever there's a fight so hungry people can eat, I'll be there. Wherever there's a cop beatin' up a guy, I'll be there . . . an' when our folks eat the stuff they raise an' live in the houses they build – why, I'll be there. See?'

Tony's version hit the mark in its emotional appeal, and showed he had not stood still in learning the tricks of the trade, nor had he gone rusty: the Don Juan of achievement was engaged in his final seduction. 'Whatever you do, I'm always with you. Head and heart. Next year I won't be making this speech. But in the years to come, wherever I am, whatever I do, I'm with you. Wishing you well, wanting you to win.' It should have been booed down, but it was applauded rapturously. What did that say about the party? In 1950 there were upwards of two million members, but now less than two hundred thousand of the faithful. And in another excruciating display, when Tony had ended, in spite of his brilliant joke about her not going off with the bloke next door (which frankly admitted she had made the remark), Cherie, now acting the trophy wife, threw herself on his neck as if he had won the biggest Oscar in Hollywood. It came over, as we watched it, as weird.

*

Tony's frantic last months, stage-managing a legacy which resembled badly made scenery, falling down every time he tried to stick it up, should probably be seen more as displacement atonement: notably, in his last days, he tried to be a mediator between warring factions – Hamas, Israel – in the Middle East in a vain effort to rebuild his credibility. But it merely imitated or echoed Tony's favourite image of Britain as a bridge between America and Europe. A bridge cannot make choices; by definition it remains something that merely joins, something in the middle. You need a sound territorial base on either side of the divide to construct one.

Tony's final atonement was to attempt to repeat elsewhere the limited success he has had in furthering and fulfilling the peace process in Northern Ireland, through endless tours and initiatives for the Middle East to bring peace to the planet. 'We've got the blockade lifted on Lebanon today,' he proclaimed fatuously in the House of Commons September 2006 after the ceasefire in Lebanon. 'It's not a day for soundbites,' he had said years earlier after the Good Friday Agreement. 'I feel the hand of history on our shoulder.' *Plus ça change.*

'*Blairisme*', as the French call it, as a political concept or philosophy, supported as it has been by three electoral wins, has had a huge international influence, but has proved a short-lived experiment to be avoided (as the French showed in May 2007 by electing as President Nicolas Sarkozy, a right-wing leader that they needed rather than wanted). According to an authoritative *Le Monde* article in September 2006 Tony abolished, or at least temporarily blurred, the divisions between right and left in politics. His 'modernisation' extended itself into 'citizens' rights and the devolution of central powers'. Here again it is not hard to detect the personal component. Devolution may have destroyed the Westminster monopoly but, with the election in May 2007 of the Scottish Nationalist Party with one more seat than Labour, it has set the United Kingdom on a slippery track to disintegration. The application of Macmillan's 'wind of change' to the outer empire has been turned onto the inner empire. So every virtuous intention has had its built-in, self-destructive charge, which stems from, and ultimately resides in, personality, in the personal history of the man and his wife.

From the beginning the gap continually widened between the failure to grasp the reality of what people expect from government and Tony's optimistic assertions, yet on re-election in May 2005 he said, 'I think I have a very clear idea of what the British people now expect from this government for a third term.' In measure after measure, pronouncement after pronouncement, these last years confirmed his floundering, that he was unable to grasp what was expected of him. Peter Hyman, who worked in Downing Street for six and a half years, and as a planner and speech-writer for Tony for nine, concluded:

> Perhaps the biggest eye-opener for me . . . has been how the approach I had been part of creating, to deal with 24-hour media and to demonstrate a decisive government, was entirely the wrong one for convincing frontline professionals, or indeed for ensuring successful delivery . . . What the front line

requires is a policy framework and goals, not hundreds of micro-announcements. I am beginning to see how teachers felt like a circus act having random objects hurled at them by a ringmaster, and being expected to catch them all.

It is in the area of being unable to spot the difference that Cherie and Tony seriously misjudged reality: the mid-term American elections of autumn 2006, which altered the balance of American power in favour of the Democrats, showed up Tony's earlier incapacity to grasp that a difference existed between the narrowly-elected Bush in 2000 and the American public (in April 2007 Senate and Congress voted to withdraw US forces from Iraq), while in effacing that difference Tony upset his potential European friends and has isolated the UK as never before.

So what is a '*Blairiste*'? According to Wolfgang Nowak, an adviser of Gerhard Schroeder, the former German Chancellor, 'A *Blairiste* is a social democrat who has confronted the "truth", namely that voters don't live in a "politically correct" world [here he means true to the divisions of left and right]'. But Nowak, like so many others, could not in the end understand Tony:

> All three [Blair, Chirac, Schroeder] knew that Bush was going to embark on the Iraq war, and what could be the price. They saw that one was running into catastrophe and that Europe was no part of it . . . he would have become the great European statesman of the twenty-first century, like de Gaulle, Adenauer and Churchill had been for the twentieth, if he had not participated in that deadly war.

Character without self-knowledge is more than fate, it is disaster, especially if there are different people and different fates in the same person. In 2006 Carole Caplin continued to hold midnight telephone conversations with Tony, whom she calls Toblerone, giving him fashion advice, diet tips and feedback on his television appearances, even while she was no longer on speaking terms with Cherie. According to the *Sunday Times*, 'He is said to have confided in Caplin about disagreements and "heated discussions" about when he should leave office. Cherie Blair is known to be frustrated that her husband has been forced to resign earlier than he wanted and to have blamed Brown for plotting against him.'

To confirm this an insider says that Cherie would have 'killed Tony' (metaphorically, that is) if he left before May 2007. She, the other half of the dyad, remained true to form to the end: she replaced Carole with Martha Greene, an American businesswoman who had helped Tony and Cherie in the acquisition after Tony's 'wobble' of the £3.5 million Connaught Square house in 2004, which, oddly enough, because of its resemblance to No. 10, had been used for the filming of the Alan Clark diaries. But it seems to be in an unhappy location, near the Edgware Road, known as 'downtown Kuwait City', and here again their misjudgement over its letting while they were still in office made it a poor investment, at least for the moment. Cherie became so reliant on Greene that she tried to secure offices for her in Downing Street, a request which was turned down by officials. Cherie then ditched Greene for an Indian guru, this time one preaching sexual continence. In the future there will no doubt be a predictable round of further leaks, confessions, diaries, autobiographies, proving yet again that, as W. B. Yeats put it,

> The best lack all conviction
> While the worst are full of passionate intensity.

But we can't entirely blame Cherie and Tony: it is hard to blame people specifically for the defects in their thinking when the world at large has seemed only too eager to live up to the same delusions. As far back as 1993 Alan Bennett wrote in his diary, 'Mrs Thatcher and her cronies have uncivilised debate and de-natured the nation.' If anything is needed to show more conclusively how the mimetic contagion of politicians has come to possess the public mind, it is that there have been in their ten years in Downing Street no fewer than five Cherie lookalikes employed by agencies, earning good money. Says one of them, 'My favourite job was when we went to Wormwood Scrubs and I had [as Cherie] to dress up in a cowboy outfit and line-dance with Tony Blair, George Bush and Condoleezza Rice lookalikes.'

The outstanding question which historians of the future will have to address is why did the people of one of the most sophisticated democracies on the planet fall for Cherie and Tony and their dual partnership of control not once, but three times? (Notwithstanding the calibre of the leaders of the opposition ranged against Tony.)

One answer may be that Tony and Cherie combined to an unbelievable state of fusion the Peter Pan-itis of the modern pop culture with the Pied Piper of Hamelin, and by this method 'cheated the spellbound children [the electorate] of their adulthood and led them back into the womb-mountain' (Abse). The leadership they provided was one of androgyny, one that infantilised the electorate; its identity was vague, ill defined and free from the burden of adult and gender choice. Many are those who at the end of ten years think that what Tony and Cherie did to the UK has added up to a complete distortion of values, equivalent in some ways to a form of aberrant sexual behaviour, and that it will take years for the country to recover, if it ever does.

A further reflection is, as the *Sunday Times'* Bryan Appleyard reported as long ago as May 1979, 'Saving your skin is the only higher good left in the contemporary world. And nobody seems to mind.' Do we now all inhabit a culture of lies, so that the confident liar wins, because the one rule in a culture of lies is that everybody, all the time, must be telling the truth? Even worse than this, lying has become 'ego syntonic' – meaning that the lies people tell and the harm they inflict on others don't appear to cause them much conscious anxiety, as in the recent case of Lord Browne of Madingley, the boss of British Petroleum, except when they are found out. This never used to be the case, for to some degree lying to promote a higher good by avoiding a lower evil was an accepted aspect of human nature, and people were able to choose, perceive a difference, distinguish truth from falsehood in the sometimes necessary contradictions. Once again undifferentiationism had triumphed: everything is the same; and as a result lies and truth have become the same.

There is no doubt Tony and Cherie have enjoyed and exploited the trappings of power. In France there is a book prominently displayed in the bookshops in 2006 called *Chirac and the Forty Lies*, and it has a cartoon on the jacket of the former French President as Ali Baba, but with a very long nose. Inside there is a catalogue of the same dismal kind of mendacity and double dealing while he was mayor of Paris as has been emerging in this country over the cash-for-honours investigation (unresolved legally in Chirac's case, as is the investigation into Berlusconi's alleged corruption in Italy). Listening to the corrupt but charming ex-premier of Italy, complete with facelift and headpiece, crooning his own songs at his heavily fortified villa in Sardinia, with its underground access tunnels, takes one into the wilder flights of the decline and fall of the Roman Empire. Perhaps this is ultimately what it is, namely that the heart of Western civilisation is rotten at the core, and we cannot, or have no right to, expect leaders better than Tony Blair.

We need to rethink the modern idea which Tony and Cherie and their court have endorsed, which stems from Freud, Marx and Nietzsche, and which dominates present-day thinking, namely that the resources that power has are infinite. But appetite has, in that terrible phrase of Shakespeare's, become the universal wolf, which will then eat up itself. For power ultimately undermines itself and it is only the ever-vigilant leader who can weather this tendency.

*

Tony even so, to the very end of his ten years, persisted in seeing himself as the model leader – flexible, imaginative and humane. He remained convinced in the power of his own moral rectitude to prevail over history.

It is said that no one willingly gives up power and the privileges of office, if they can help it. One privilege Tony added to the others of his office came from his belief, which he shared with Cherie, that no one had the right to judge them: they alone were capable of judging themselves correctly, so with the considerable powers of legal patronage at their beck and call Tony refused, from 1997 onwards, to appoint truly independent assessors of their actions. But *nemo iudex in sua casa* – no one is the judge of his own case – and there will in time be others sitting in judgment that will not spare either of them in the search for truth and objectivity.

Gordon Brown has – at least – one supremely disagreeable trait: his overwhelming hubris, blowing his own trumpet. Doesn't he trust the public, the ordinary voter, to evaluate his record? Much has been made both of Tony and Gordon's feuding, but also of their extraordinary and indivisible closeness, their love–hate sibling bond. But one factor has been omitted:

Brown has for the short-term financial benefit of Britain weakened its economic ties with Europe and placed it more firmly than ever before in the American sphere of influence. And for all his pride in showing how well the British economy is performing under his control, he admires America far too much.

The United States is a one-class, mercantile society, ruled by money. The love of each and every American is the ethos of buying and selling. In all aspects of American life, whether it is marriage, or education, or war, or the hawking of democracy, it is the deal that matters, and the dynamic of production and supply. This has its virtues but also its drawbacks. Over the ten years of Brown's economic hegemony, Americanisation had proceeded so fast and so thoroughly that by 2007 we rivalled, if not surpassed, the United States in all the social ills and family breakdowns. This now distinguishes us as we move further apart from the happily less modernised, less efficient, older European powers. Our poor election turnouts mirror those in the United States, while in France, in April 2007, 85 per cent of the electorate voted in the ballots for President. Blair never wavered from his distaste for the past: 'You can't deal with the levels of sophistication in today's organised crime by traditional methods,' he wrote in an exchange of views published in the *Observer* (April 2006). 'We are trying to fight 21st-century crime by 19th-century means.' Yet violent crime, obesity, a massive rise in divorce rates, single-parent families, drug abuse, media domination and – soon to arrive here – super-casinos had become some of the more salient aspects of New Labour's American culture. Here, in the latest figures, under Gordon's Brown's Chancellorship, we consumed three times as much confectionery and soft drinks as France and Italy.

One particular sinister and threatening aspect was the extent to which vast tracts of manufacturing industry, power and services, including water, fuel and banking, became targets to be taken over by foreign investors. Or, as a banker friend points out, were 'now in the hands of obscure and unaccountable equity investors'. What would happen, as it inevitably will, on the arrival of a new recession? As foreign companies shed their overseas workforces first, would this not inevitably result in an increase in unemployment? No. 10 buys its electricity from EDF Energy (EDF standing for Électricité de France), its water from Thames Water (owned by a consortium led by the European branch of an Australian bank), its gas either from British Gas (Centrica), Powergen (EOW, a German utility) or nPower (RWE, another German utility). As Roy Jenkins averred, the achievement of Chancellors is written in shifting sand. Far from radically changing things for the better, the modernising alliance of Tony and Gordon turned back the clock to a brash, materialistic and historically myopic society, and one without even some of the saving graces of the American people: their openness, their desire to share their wealth and optimistic ideology with the rest of the world.

But the overriding question that Prime Minister Brown must surely answer to win the trust of his electorate will be this: given his universally acknowledged gravitas, sense of tradition and above all grasp of minute detail, what close scrutiny did he give to the intelligence reports on Saddam Hussein and WMD? He must have known that the invasion of Iraq would be a defining moment in British history. So what stopped him? Did he examine the evidence with his usual remorseless and sceptical perusal, and if so, why did he not conclude rationally, like Robin Cook, that there was no case for war? If he had shown the same inattention to detail or examination of financial documents as he showed towards the various dossiers and intelligence reports prior to the invasion, he would not have had such a very good record as Chancellor. Given that democratic government in the UK is supposed to be based on collective Cabinet decisions and responsibility, why had his voice not been heard?

47

Superbia: his enemies were the shadows cast by his brightness

In truth, our future, our very survival, are linked to the image we shall make of man.

Pope John Paul II

The notion of sin, Tony Blair has said, will become of 'increasing importance in politics'. But in the 'modernised' Blair era what do we mean by sin? In *The Parson's Tale*, Chaucer's witty and ironic sermon on the seven deadly sins, envy, the first of the old sins, is defined as the chief and all-embracing shortcoming of mankind's fallen nature. The parson begins with his claim that envy stems from malice, which is of two kinds: hardness of heart, which is 'so blind that he considereth not he is in sin, which is the hardness of the devil', and the second kind, which is 'when a man opposes truth when he knows what truth is'. Envy is 'the worst sin that there is. For soothly, all other sins been sometime against a special virtue, but certainly Envy is against all virtues and against all goodness.' As such envy leads on to all kinds of 'backbiting' and 'detraction'.

Envy, or aggrandisement, but without the malice – wanting it all – defines Cherie Blair's tenure of Downing Street, and at the end of ten years it would seem she harbours deep rancour in her heart at how she has been treated. The press, she said early on, was 'on a mission to destroy us'. She never changed this view. She identified the press as the main antagonist in the drama of Downing Street. In November 2006, at Roehampton University, she launched into a splenetic rant about the lack of morality in journalists (was this from her 'heritage of emotion again'?). She denounced in a superior way journalism as 'not a noble calling'; and stated bluntly that 'journalists have no ethics'. Was this because certain journalists constantly referred to her as 'The Wicked Witch' and called her 'a brazen, grasping harridan' or 'an acquisitive freeloader'? One says, 'Mrs Blair is a woman who would have an argument with the wallpaper in an empty room.' And ever since Tony had summoned Max Hastings, editor of the *Evening Standard* to No. 10, and given him a dressing down over his attack on the Millennium Dome, he, too, blamed much of his troubles on the press. Unfortunately it looked as if the many reproaches heaped on them had struck home, or this animus against their critics would have long since passed. But until the very end both of them still wanted to duel with every commentator who held or expressed a negative view of them.

Likewise, both shared to an alarming degree the strain, the effort, to create a good impression. The handwriting on the many short letters Cherie industriously writes in replies to correspondents is spidery, small, unemphatic, all over the place – and when you relate it to the multifarious activities of the person, it puts you in mind of the spider again, one who weaves, or sits at the centre of many tough and taut filaments of deceptive frailty, which all lead back to her.

A fortnight of persistent questioning has finally dragged out of the authorities the admission that Cherie Blair has paid the VAT and duty on the cut-price pearls she bought in China in 2003.

It is odd in the extreme that it should have taken so long for the Prime Minister's wife, a professional lawyer and an enthusiastic supporter of policies that can be implemented only through high taxation, to confirm that she had fulfilled her plain legal duty.

And it is hard to believe that anyone else would have been dealt with in such a kindly and discreet manner. Compare and contrast the treatment of Colleen McLoughlin, girlfriend of footballer Wayne Rooney, publicly humiliated on her return from a shopping trip to New York when she was handed a demand for £3,000 in VAT and duty.

The grudging, long-delayed official statement fails to tell us exactly when Mrs Blair paid her bill, how much it was, or whether she was in any way officially rebuked for any aspects of her behaviour. Miss McLoughlin had to put up with a Customs officer moralising that 'the girl is only a teenager and full of naivety, but there are still laws in this country about coming back in with handfuls of expensive goodies'.

Mrs Blair is no teenager. Yet, even so, it seems that she is strangely unversed in the more inconvenient ways of the world, especially when it comes to bargains. From her unfortunate dealings with Peter Foster to her over-enthusiastic shopping trips and her speaking tours, a sad pattern emerges.

Is this the end of it? Or as the final chapter of the Blair saga drags to its drawn-out close, are there still more tawdry and embarrassing matters of this kind waiting to emerge? (*Mail on Sunday*, September 2005)

There were many more such embarrassing items to come. Cherie's impervious skin, which in spite of being flawless and milky due to drinking two litres of water a day, and the common view that she has 'a slate missing', emerged in her television promotion of her book about Prime Ministers' wives: in this, wearing a big billowy white suit, she showed people round No. 10, and cut an undignified image compared to predecessors such as Norma Major. 'Don't cackle like that, we're not in a farmyard,' a friend of mine wanted to say about her commentary.

Envy has been such an overriding and powerful emotion all through Cherie's life that she has not been able to rein it in at the most obvious points, and learn from her mistakes. She has complained about 'No. 10' often, but she has also used her official position to protect her, as in this case of not initially paying VAT and duty on the cut-price pearls.

But what about the ordinary public? They applauded with little exception the views they found in the press. Why had Cherie and Tony never trawled the internet for comments which were open and accessible to all? They had clung to the comforting belief that the public, Mr and Mrs Bloggs, or A. N. Other, actually existed as they would have liked them to be – or Tony would not have called himself so often an 'ordinary bloke'. For example, in a brief selection from Google we find:

Congratulations on finally exposing [in a daily paper] Mrs Blair's latest money-grubbing wheeze of jewellery-smuggling. At least it's a bit more ambitious than fare-dodging on the trains.

Married women do not 'acquire' valuable jewellery without their husband's knowledge, which therefore makes Mr Blair an accomplice in this sordid little affair. As usual though, he seems to have slithered off the hook. Would Customs be as kind to us common folk?

At least with Marie Antoinette we proles got to eat cake. With the Blairs it's a case of 'Let them pay tax'. (Douglas Harrison, Ealing, London)

Mrs Blair is a lawyer. Thus she is no doubt sensible of a quotation familiar to students of jurisprudence: Be you never so high, the law is above you. (A. Chambers, London)

Same old thing. One law for the rich and one for the poor. It'll never change. (Roger Wheeler, Puerto Vallarta, Mexico)

Such comments were the tip of the iceberg. It even led by the final year, 2007, to desertion by many of those who initially were Tony's most devoted fans – his own mimetic doubles, the pop idols. 'I think the Labour Party's crowning achievement', said Liam Gallagher of Oasis in 2006, 'is the death of politics. There's nothing left to vote for.' Oasis's 2005 hit album was called *Don't Believe the Truth*, while Paul Weller said, 'I wouldn't support him [Blair] if he were the last person on earth.'

The liberal intellectual class deserted him earlier. 'Blair was much the best Prime Minister of the past fifty years,' said David Hare in 2003, 'but Iraq changed that. Blair has made the greatest mistake in British foreign policy since Suez.' But there is a flaw here, as I have tried to show, for great leaders do not suddenly become terrible leaders. The Iraq 'mistake', and even more its disastrous sequel, originated deep within the leader's personality and that of his wife.

The reverse side of Cherie's envy was an all-devouring status anxiety, shared by both. Now it is quite normal to be concerned about status, but in their puerile concern the Blairs insisted on policing their own status, using up considerable sums of public money to do so. This is an impossible task which in theory ends with the absurd demand they should duel with every adverse comment and critic. The most democratic substance of all, as John

Macmurray, the philosopher beloved by Tony, pointed out, is dust: we are all, as history shows, ultimately insignificant.

One important, perhaps the most important, aspect of Cherie's envy has been omitted, but it was clear in the photos at No. 10. This was her desire to ape Hillary Clinton, which must now be reinforced by Hillary's election as the Democrat Senator for New York, and her intention to run for the Democratic candidacy. The conductor Sir Thomas Beecham said of prima donnas that they should never marry, or if they did, that they should have at the most one child. Hillary has one grown-up child, and she is as politically adept as her husband and beyond child-bearing age. Would Cherie be lining herself up, when she leaves Downing Street, for a Madonna-style reinvention as Hillary Clinton? The lemming-like, mass insanity of the Labour Party would probably endorse her, while Liverpool has for her a very special place in its heart.

The privileges seized from her involvement with the Catholic Church expanded considerably towards the end, for the family no longer went to public mass at Westminster Cathedral, but asked their local priest to come round to celebrate it in that top-floor sitting room of No 11. Priests are servants of their flock and do as they are asked. This privilege reminded me of the El Salvador priest-martyr Archbishop Oscar Romero, who, frowned on by the church for his 'liberation theology', refused the demands of the Salvadorean dictator to celebrate mass in his private palace, insisting instead that the dictator and his family should enjoy the same rights as the rest of the people and attend at the cathedral. Archbishop Romero was gunned down at the altar while celebrating mass in 1982.

In the more genteel surroundings of 10 Downing Street, the Blair family, sitting on those sofas, gathered round the coffee table in rapt devotion to receive the sacrament from the chalice. The priest, who had slipped into 10 Downing Street by the back door, has to move the coasters, George W. Bush's presidential gift to the Prime Minister, with the face and that smirking grin, to make space for the Eucharist. Caesar is put to one side as God takes over.

*

The Latin word for the sin of pride is *superbia*, a feminine noun. The pride Tony exhibits belongs more to the feminine side of his nature than the masculine; it is this side of him which identified strongly with Diana, the 'people's princess'. The phrase rebounded on him, for more than one columnist persisted in calling him 'Princess Tony', while in 2006 listeners of BBC *Sports Talk* voted him in their annual poll 'the most stupid woman of the year'. By the same token *Sports Talk* voted Bush the most stupid man. At one stage, when dangerously close to aping Blair, the Tory leader David Cameron was also referred to as a 'transexualised Diana'.

Chaucer's parson in *The Canterbury Tales* subdivides the sin of pride into headings which include the following: hypocrite – 'he that hideth to show himself such as he is, and showeth him such as he is not'; insolent – 'he that despiseth in his judgment all other folk, as to regard of his value, and of his cunning, and of his speaking, and of his bearing'; presumption – 'when a man undertaketh an enterprise that he ought not to do, or else that he may not do and this is called surquidry [arrogance]'; pertinacity – 'when a man defendeth his folly, and twisteth too much in his own wit'. Examples of this for Tony could be found everywhere – they would fill a book on their own. They add up to, as Chaucer writes, 'a proud desire to be magnified and honoured before the people'.

Bill Clinton claimed he had read *Men Are from Mars, Women Are from Venus* seventeen times but, by the reckoning of that book, Tony was not the male who retreats wordlessly into his cave. For instance (writes John Gray),

> when a woman suggests that her husband follow the advice of some expert, he may be offended. I remember one woman asking me why her husband got so angry at her. She explained to me that she had asked him if he had received his notes by me on the secrets of great sex. She didn't realise this was the ultimate insult to him.

Tony appeared up for every kind of advice, flattery and reassurance, but the *superbia* was not his alone; it was shared, dyadic, combining the power of both of them.

Long-term narcissists, in other words those who advance into middle age without shrugging off the necessary phase of narcissism every child goes through when growing, expect to receive from others recognition of the grandiose persons they conceive themselves to be. They have long succumbed to the habit of thinking of themselves not as 'feeling this' or 'feeling that' but as 'the person they think themselves as'. They have, as Freudians argue, taken on and internalised their mothers' images of themselves, and have made this image their own, to the displacement of their own spontaneous, first-hand, feeling response to what happens around them. Self-belief becomes hermetically sealed against self-knowledge. They have become controllers. As their mothers' image of them was one of admiration, so their self-image is essentially grandiose. In the declining years of his premiership Tony increasingly looked drained, while both of them used every external tool and prop that money or patronage could obtain to bolster their own self-images. In both the inner vitality, which connects above all with truth, with nature and with self-knowledge, had been depleted by their reliance on those images they have of themselves.

Perhaps we shouldn't blame them too much. As Sebastian Moore points out in *The Crucified Is No Stranger*:

> Unfortunately, the narcissistic personality . . . formed in the earliest years is heavily endorsed by our society with its heavy emphasis on *imagining ourselves*. The vast, technically empowered world of advertising, stresses day and night the importance of being with the 'right' people, in the 'right' clothes, in the 'right' car, in the 'right' job, etc. I must be forever improving my image, learning more and more to see myself in the image of the good life.

But Tony's obsession with 'my legacy' teetered on the fence between pure pathos and an absurdity worthy of derision. As far back as 2002, on Tony's first trip to Africa, Clare Short, accompanying him on the plane, noticed this preoccupation with what his legacy would be.

Freud believed that there were two basic kinds of love – the anaclitic and the narcissistic. 'One choice, the anaclitic or attachment option, is governed to a greater or lesser degree by a dependence on images of parental figure.' This is not the path either Tony or Cherie have followed. The second kind, the narcissistic choice of partner, 'operates on the model of the relationship with his own self, with the love-object representing some aspect of himself'. Neither to date has as far as we know ever challenged the other's narcissism, although Cherie has been known to remark that Tony likes the sound of his own voice. Sooner than confront it, which would mean confronting the narcissist in themselves, they withdrew, sometimes hurt and angry, but quickly, far too quickly, ready to forgive in order to repair the surface image and go on gratifying more of it. They both of them found, as we know, and which is all too easy and available to those in power, plenty of scapegoats, victims to sacrifice, to avoid at all costs the painful growth process of self-knowledge.

But it could not, and never would, last forever, because such intense narcissistic bonding, such exclusiveness, closeness – applauded on all sides as it was acted out on the public stage – was bound to lead to an explosion. However close and perfectly matched two people are to be partnered for life – and theirs has been publicly endorsed with thousands and thousands of articles and photographs – they could not continue supported by external events, by the trappings of power without some corresponding insights within that would take them beyond their bonded narcissism. Age makes people more sensitive to their interaction with others, particularly those with whom they share their life and family. Moore writes:

> Each of us is, of his nature, a magnetic field that distorts reality into its pattern. Each of us wants, and has to want, reality to be after the manner of his field. There is an appropriate loss of innocence which comes to see that, while the manipulation of others in its grosser and more cynical forms is to be deplored and cursed, a person-with-others is manipulative by nature. Each of us wants it his way.

With Iraq the narcissist Tony had his own way – and confirmed and imitated his counterpart, George W. Bush. Everyone correctly inferred that Cherie did not want to go along with the invasion, though publicly she supported Tony as a means of bringing justice and equality to Iraq. The tone which stood behind her support – 'have it your own way' – withheld her true feeling, confirmed her own image of herself rather than how she felt, and gave Tony the freedom to release that inner anger.

But, the appearance apart, she actually withheld freedom. Permissive statements – this goes so deep in the way this leadership pair mirror the characteristics of their society – are dismissive statements. She had 'permitted' him his war because, no less, in the touchy-feely, feelgood ambience, he had made the 'concession' over Carole Caplin. He felt guilty, he gave up his force field: a loss of temper, a few damage limitation gestures and a *laissez-faire* to the other force fields around him (Campbell, Mandelson) meant he could turn off the current with the utmost ease, allow the 'gypsy' (as Lord Levy called him), the hippie within, because in him, as in the hippie, there is no disapproval. He gave Cherie the signal 'anything you do will meet with my smile and my love'. It was a hideous cheat.

There were reasons other than Cheriegate – family difficulties, the whole open, ultimately dysfunctional nature of the Blair court – why Tony did not come to see standing apart from the United States as a higher form of courage, leading to a stronger heroic outcome of that need he had to grow up and prove himself.

What Tony and Cherie failed to do, with devastating consequences while straining in their spin and PR to show they were the perfect, loving, adoring couple with an exemplary family, was to achieve a well-grounded and mature relationship. They have shown that is perhaps impossible once you have crossed the threshold of Downing Street. Tony had been prophetic when he told a close aide that 'personality', a word he used on many occasions, would be the means by which his own government would ultimately be 'brought down'. But it was by his own and Cherie's personalities as much as by those of others. The difference between them, the hidden clash of his personality with Cherie's, took a long time in coming to the surface: but weren't these anyway reasons for celebration rather than concealment?

Both asserted as politicians how 'good' a marriage they had. To the world outside this was true. But this marriage still belonged to the fledgling unconscious stage of their relationship in which they had married. In Downing Street it had not developed into something more, which it yet may be able to do when they leave. Being in power had not allowed either of them to gain a more realistic view of love and marriage, and overcome their confusion over their faith and God (in both cases they held a narcissistic view of God). Neither in their ten-year spell of power had grown and changed or been free enough inside to become the right partner for the other, which would have meant a self-understanding still beyond the reach of either.

When asked how he thought Tony would be judged Ken Livingstone answered, 'Tony's most severe judge will be himself.' The cold dawn of a future life without power would break all too soon.

Appendix 1

The faith of Cherie Blair

The twenty-first century will be a century of religion or it will not be at all.

André Malraux

The word 'religion' comes from the Latin *religare*, meaning 'to bind back', and in the present climate, in a society awash with an 'all-pervasive claim to victimhood', and the escalating fear and often reality of violence, a 'binding back' in multiple ways, not least culturally, is needed. While the No. 10 press aides and the protagonists themselves have strenuously tried to keep religion out of politics, and in spite of the notorious British reticence in such matters, it both demands and needs a central place in the new 21st-century world picture or disorder. As for the recent growth of proselytising atheism, who would not rather listen to Albert Einstein, perhaps the greatest scientific mind in history, than diehard secularists such as Richard Dawkins? Einstein wrote in his diary, 'What separates me from most so-called atheists is a feeling of utter humility towards the unattainable secrets of the harmony of the universe . . . The problem involved is too vast for our limited minds.' In declaring his personal creed he states, 'The most beautiful emotion we can experience is the mysterious. It is the fundamental emotion that stands at the cradle of all true art and science. He to whom this emotion is as stranger . . . is as good as dead.' More mundanely, Madeleine Albright, former US Secretary of State, in her timely book *The Mighty and the Almighty* (2006) defined the way her own country ill-advisedly tiptoed round the subject of religion.

Religious arrogance, or identifying oneself with the Messiah, could hardly be excused in Tony Blair, as it was by Dominic Lawson, as 'unwittingly' expressed. Cherie's religious presumption has been of a more complicated and pervasive kind. Because she is a woman, and also an influential role model to other women, her beliefs have been both more invasive and convincing for other women, in particular those who put their gender first and their religion second.

Her revolutionary tenet, not exactly uncommon, and worthy of Lenin, which she holds with undiminished fervour, is that if you want to change an institution you join it and change it from within. In *Why I Am Still a Catholic*, published in June 2006, she averred:

> Of course, like many Catholics in this country, I have doubts about some of the positions taken by the Church as an institution – for example, on contraception, or the role of women. But I am not one of those who believe that the only response is to walk away because you have a different viewpoint. I have been taught that you should stay and try and change things.
>
> It's like the Labour Party in the early 1980s. I wasn't happy with the way it was going so I tried to help change it from within. Thankfully, we won that battle. And though the pace of change in the Catholic Church can seem slow, I believe that there are many people in this country – and not just in the laity – who are convinced of the need for it. That message, however, is not yet fully accepted by the Vatican. But, then, the Church isn't just the Vatican. It is about all of us, the people of God as the Second Vatican Council put it.

Father Beaufort, a priest from York, commented:

> It would be terribly arrogant for any of us to suggest that we were somehow doing the Catholic Church a favour by gracing her with our membership. The idea that the Church is basically a human institution that has to be allowed to evolve to adapt itself to the spirit of the age owes more to Protestantism and to the modernist heresy condemned by Pope Pius X than it does to true Catholicism.
>
> Ms Booth says she has some problems with certain positions taken by the Church 'as an institution', like the ban on contraception. But for Catholics, the

Church is an institution *unlike* any other – a supernatural institution, founded by Christ. As the Mystical Body of Christ, the Church is the extension of His Incarnate Presence on earth, invested with divine authority to teach on matters of faith and morals. Catholics believe that the Pope, as successor of St Peter, is invested with the charism of infallibility. This means that no Pope, however sinful he is, can ever err when he teaches *ex cathedra* on matters of faith and morals.

As a moral issue, contraception is a good example of something that clearly falls under the Church's teaching remit. To reject the Church's clear, consistent and authoritative teaching on such an issue is to really deny the teaching authority of the Church altogether, and to cease to be Catholic.

Ms Booth also admits to difficulties accepting the Church's position on the role of women. She doesn't specify, but could she mean the Church's restriction of the Sacrament of Holy Order to men? John Paul II made it quite clear that not even a Pope has the authority to alter the Church's constant teaching on this matter.

To compare the Catholic Church with the Labour Party seems to miss the point that the Church is a divine institution. Yes, we all have a part to play in building up the Mystical Body of Christ on earth. Certain disciplines can and do change. But as far as doctrine goes, and the basic hierarchical structure of (male) bishops, priests and deacons, the Church's role is simply to hand on what was given by Christ to the Apostles. In this sense, the Church is really defined by tradition. As for reform, we are always called to *re*form ourselves, by *con*forming ourselves to the Gospel of Christ, as handed on in the teaching of the Church.

The Church's teaching on contraception and the priesthood will be substantially the same in 2,000 years' time as it is today. It would be foolhardy to make such a claim for any other institution; but we can say it confidently about the Church because of our faith that she is not just any institution, but a divine one.

[...]

Ms Booth says that the Church is 'all about us, the people of God, as Vatican II put it'. Yes, Christ founded His Church for our salvation. But the role of the 'people of God' is primarily to listen and to learn, so that we can extend the sovereignty of Christ into every level of human activity. Vatican II didn't change the constant doctrine that the teaching Church, or *Ecclesia docens*, is made up of the bishops in union with St Peter's successor, the Pope. As the 'people of God', we have to be open to conversion from our preconceptions.

The election of Cardinal Joseph Ratzinger as Benedict XVI was a blow, not only to the left-wing liberal establishment of the English and Welsh bishops. Benedict sees the Catholic Church as a continuous organic whole, enlivened and united by the constant presence of the Holy Spirit, dismissing the view of the church before Vatican II (1965) as bad and after as good, and calling such 'ecclesiastical schizophrenia' the 'hermeneutic of discontinuity'.

*

On sin, Tony had pronounced that the concept of believing in it was 'simple and important', and that 'this is an area that will become of increasing importance in politics'. Cardinal Cormac Murphy-O'Connor agreed: 'You cannot', he said, 'divorce religion and life.' But through legislation, instead of listening and learning, and by this bringing 'the sovereignty of Christ into every level of human activity', New Labour provided and widened the opportunity for 'sin', in Christian and Catholic terms (if you believe in them) in many aspects of social and personal life.

A longer opportunity for abortions, longer drinking hours, liberalising of cannabis, growth of casinos, wider and more useless sex education of the wrong kind (meaning one thing and one thing only, greater use of contraception and greater numbers of teenage pregnancies). Under the aegis of Tony's espousal of population control the government funded international agencies which supported China's population policies, in particular its cruel and inhuman treatment of women who are forced to abort or become sterilised if they want to breed more than one child. Gordon Brown, before he had children of his own, voted sixteen times in favour of abortion, including three times for abortion up to birth, and for disabled babies; for abortion on demand in early pregnancy; and to suppress information about abortions on disabled babies. He cut the VAT on morning-after pills from 17.5 per cent to 5 per cent. He also in 1990 voted for destructive embryo experimentation.

At the same time, New Labour created secular sins for its atheist followers to feel comfortable in denouncing and outlawing, such as fox-hunting, smoking, the right of Catholic adoption agencies to differentiate foster parents on the basis of belief, and even, some would claim, normal married life. A mass of new laws criminalising what had been seen as ordinary if not entirely appropriate behaviour filled the statute book, while a controlling and bureaucratic surveillance state came into being, in many ways similar to that of the former Communist countries of eastern Europe.

Cherie's views on contraception and women priests did not stop her scurrying off to Rome at the first available opportunity to seek an audience with Pope Benedict XVI. The visit, as Father Seed says, 'has to be seen as a perk of the job'. While Cherie had followed form at the funeral of John Paul II in April 2005 by wearing a black dress and mantilla, in her short audience with Benedict she flouted protocol and wore white. The correct dress code was black: only Queen Sofia of Spain, Queen Paola of Belgium and Josephine Charlotte, the wife of Grand Duke Jean of Luxemburg, as consorts of Catholic royalty, are entitled to wear white. This was deliberate. She would have known what to wear. Would she appear in court as a recorder in jeans and sweatshirt? Even Elizabeth II wore black when she and Prince Philip met John Paul. There is a kind of very English snobbishness, all too prevalent, that the Pope in Rome or anyone else shouldn't presume to tell sophisticated lawyers like Cherie Booth what to believe and how to behave. Graham Greene, who would flout the rules even to the point of taking his mistress out to lunch with Father Philip Caraman, his father confessor (who was most upset), had something of the same attitude. It reinforces the notion that Cherie has a very grand idea of herself, but also that Tony supports and sustains her in her delusion. Ann Widdecombe commented, 'She obviously thinks she is the First Lady. My message to her is that you are not a Catholic queen, my dear, and you never will be.'

It was a long way from those stalwart Catholic women of her Waterloo childhood, gathering in their living room rosary circles to pray together. But Cherie has been determined to keep her Catholic options open, like George Bush, who wooed the seventy-seven million Catholics in the United States by visiting the Pope three times during his first term. But she has kept in too with pro-abortion groups such as Planned Parenthood, and posed before their stand at a Labour conference brandishing a condom. In spring 2006 she delivered a paper at the Vatican Political Academy of Social Sciences, speaking about how children 'are forced to grow up so quickly . . . having to take on the responsibilities of adults' because they were neglected by older people. True in some cases for sure, although the trend in her own country was in rather the opposite direction, with children lamentably slowed down in their educational and maturing process, so that, as a head of department at a major public school observes, pupils of fourteen are five years behind the educational standard of those at a similar age ten years ago. In 2006 Cherie joined the Pontifical Academy of Social Sciences as an adviser on social and legal issues.

*

Tony expressed one of his religious beliefs in the foreword to a pamphlet written by John Smith:

> Christianity is a very tough religion. It may not always be practised as such. But it is . . . It is not utilitarian – though socialism can be explained in those terms. It is judgemental. There is right and wrong. There is good and bad. We all know this, of course, but it has become fashionable to be uncomfortable about such language. But when we look at our world today and how much needs to be done, we should not hesitate to make such judgements. And then follow them with determined action. That would be Christian socialism.

Latterly, though, it had become hard to know what he thought. He would seem to waver, disappointing those who hoped he would respect the Church authority, especially over contraception. Falling in line with Cherie, in 2006 he attacked the Church over what he called a 'blanket ban' on condoms and committed money to spread their use in Africa. The Catholic view is that condoms encourage promiscuity and have therefore only a limited value. To promote condom use is, according to Catholic doctrine, only one degree away from promoting the use of prostitutes, or in other words, using sex as a commodity. Condom use is, however, the soul of the sex industry, which expanded enormously in the UK during Tony's premiership, and now he endorsed this wholeheartedly. Red-light districts had proliferated in every town centre, with brothels their inner citadels of degradation for prostitutes.

A recent example is the town of Ipswich, where in 2006 five such poor women were murdered. Some say the condom culture, or commodity sex, is leading to wholesale population decline: one extreme and even absurd prediction is that by 2900 there will not be a single European left in Europe, but there is truth in the trend. After ten years of the Blairs the UK was judged in a United Nations study to be bottom in the moral league of the twenty-one economically most advanced nations.

Cherie invited Pope Benedict XVI to visit Great Britain in May 2007, twenty-five years after John Paul II visited in 1982. He didn't of course come, but if he had it could have proved a final example of Tony and Cherie's ecclesiastical topsy-turvyism. Would they have taken His Holiness to visit Ipswich? In the event, and as a final theatrical flourish in his world tour before departure on 27 June 2007, Tony took Cherie with him to Rome for an audience with Pope Benedict. But this time there would be no Berlusconi to write in the sky with £20,000 worth of fireworks: 'Viva Tony!'

Appendix 2

The failure to understand Islam

It was irony that led Christ to declare that his 'kingdom is not of this world', not to be achieved through politics.

Roger Scruton

Tony and Cherie's inability to operate successfully in the cultural conflict of today's new world may at least partly be traced to their failure, the same as that of their North American doubles or counterparts, to understand the previous cultural conflict, which still wields enormous influence.

The Blairs, because of their youthful rise, were the first Western leadership couple who, when Tony began to assume as leader of the opposition the shadow mantles of power, rose to power in a wholly post-communist Europe. They appeared never to have had any notion of the degree to which Russian and eastern European communist values, with their narrow utilitarian observances and their social utopianism, both formed and checked the so-called freedoms of Western 'enterprise' society. But these values, however badly and corruptly implemented, undoubtedly did do that: there was always, during the communist hegemony of eastern Europe and Soviet expansionism, at all levels a deadly competition of values, which could never ultimately come to showdown using military action (as was shown in the Cuban missile stand-off of 1962), because nuclear war was too horrible a reality to face.

The unravelling of the 'Evil Empire', so dubbed by President Ronald Reagan, while eagerly celebrated at first, led to other dangers, which few leaders have so far developed a strategy to deal with satisfactorily. Paradoxically the West has jettisoned the moral high ground it held in the

Cold War, which many believe was crucial to communism's collapse, namely spiritual and religious values. These at base were what in the communist era divided East from West: the belief in a very different kind of freedom than that which was wrongly supposed by Blair and Bush to be the 'freedom' of democracy – as opposed to 'evil' terrorist values.

Both Muslims and Christians share spiritual values and a belief in the workings of a divine providence. 'It is God who has won in western Europe,' Pope John Paul II said, but he also commented that communism fell through its own internal contradictions. 'Freedom of conscience, freedom of worship', these were the freedoms exalted by the Pope, while the Soviet leader, Mikhail Gorbachev, recognised that the collective will of many millions of people had been transferred to this one leader, whom he called 'the highest moral authority on earth'. By itself democracy was never enough. Gorbachev, in his own prophetic way, emphasised that 'we also need morality . . . Democracy can bring both good and evil – there is no denying it. You have what you have.'

This had never become imprinted on Tony's mind, nor had the fundamental point later made by John Paul in *Memory and Identity*, namely that western Europe was 'spared' communism because it 'could not have withstood so great a trial'. He had developed that argument, with which the Muslim world would probably agree, that zealous but 'Godless anti-evangelisation' (of the kind, let us say, of Richard Dawkins, Polly Toynbee and today's television and pop culture), supported by the West's great financial resources, was striking at the very foundation of human morality and spreading 'another form of totalitarianism under the appearance of democracy'. He quoted an eminent European politician who told him that 'if Soviet communism comes to the West we will not be able to defend ourselves'.

So is it now the West, not communism, that seems more likely than ever to fall through its own internal contradictions? The West's vulnerability has been transferred towards Islam in place of communism. And why? Because unlike the shifting sands of 'truth' or religious belief in the West, secular theories or ideas of authority have never altered the belief of Muslims that 'the gate of *jihad* is closed', meaning, according to the philosopher Roger Scruton, 'that the divine law, the *Sharia*, can no longer be adjusted or added to, but merely studied for the meaning it contains'. *Jihad* (literally 'effort', from the root *jahada*), the 'struggle on behalf of the faith', may lead to independent judgement, but it must be based on the four roots or pillars of Islam – the Koran, the Sunna, *qujas* ('analogy') and *ijima* ('consensus').

In contrast to individualistic or subjective, or secular ideas of differing authority (the shifting sands of 'freedom') Islamic belief is rooted in submission, while from submission flows peace, security and blameless confidence. The Muslim is one who has surrendered, submitted, and this vision of man and society is about as opposite as can be to the Roman conception of law we inherited and practise, which maintains social order by virtue of political instead of religious jurisdiction, and therefore serves for peoples of all faiths. Blair is a good lawyer in his belief that law is made legitimate by the consent and choice of those who would obey it, although in practice his actions would often have seemed to contradict this.

Islam is not governed by politics but submission to a sacred text which pre-dates and rejects Western technology, Western institutions and Western conceptions of political freedom; here is its great strength morally but its great weakness politically. It is the West, Blair and Bush included, which rejects the idea on which Islam is founded – 'the idea of God's immutable will, revealed once and for all in his Prophet, in the form of an unbreachable and unchangeable code of law'. No occupying force, however benign, remaining on Islamic soil will be tolerated for long, and any Muslim man, woman or child who died as a result of resisting such a force would come to be honoured as a martyr. In continuing to occupy first Afghanistan and then Iraq, the United States, Britain and the other countries who contributed forces sacrificed their high moral ground against terrorism.

*

René Girard, the Stanford University philosopher and literary critic who propounded the mimetic theory, spelt out in an article in *Le Monde* (November 2001) how an understanding of the sacrificial basis of both Islam and Christianity is needed. In this he pointed to the rapid expansion of Islamic belief, which he identified both as a religion of sacrifice, practised by

Muslims with traditions of pride, and a style of individual relations close to feudalism and tribal traditions. Girard said:

> Like Christianity, Islam rehabilitates the innocent victim, but it does this in a militant manner . . . The candidates for the act of suicide are not lacking when terrorism seems to imagine, then, what is happening now when – if I dare say – it has succeeded. It is true that in the Muslim world, the Kamikaze terrorists embody models of saintliness.

This, unfortunately, would be seen later when various terror gangs in Iraq, such as that of Abu Musab al Zarqawi in September 2004, were to claim they were sacrificing life in the name of God.

Girard pointed out that in Christianity the martyr does not die in order to be copied, as does the Muslim suicide bomber, whose manifest aim is to transform the world politically. Girard showed that this reversion of the Islamic terrorist to primitive mechanism stems from the inevitable complicity of religion and violence, a knowledge and understanding of which has been entirely lost in Christianity. This is why Christianity has become so weak in relation to fundamental Islam, in whose name the eruption of sacrificial violence in Iraq is a symptom of a cultural breakdown.

We fear sameness, says Girard – we fear the loss of identity. Girard believes that only a properly understood and practised Christianity can withstand the appeal and spread of the Islamic fascination with sacrifice, as well as live alongside it in peace and harmony. 'Violence is the heart and secret soul of the sacred.' Yet for Girard, again –and this is the hard bit to understand – it is God's sacrifice of Jesus Christ as the redeeming scapegoat for that ancient need for violence which allows God to become the scapegoat and reverse the hidden mechanism, the complicity of religion and violence, thereby saving the world and causing 'Satan', or universal wickedness, to 'fall like lightning'.

This is the secret (and not the trivia of populist writers such as Dan Brown and others), which, says Girard, has been hidden 'since the foundation of the world'. Religious conversion for Girard, the necessary basis for the Christian belief, begins in the recognition, the discovery that 'we are all butchers pretending to be sacrificers'. This places him at a more mundane and comprehensible level, with G. K. Chesterton's famous character Father Brown: 'No man's really good till he knows how bad he is, or might be . . . till he's squeezed out of his soul the last drop of the oil of the Pharisees.' The tirades of Jesus against the scribes and Pharisees, described as 'united sepulchres' and 'unmarked graves', are, Girard points out, a denunciation of religious violence 'for covering up its violence'. That is what bad people do – remain in denial, cover up their violence.

Girard adapted, too, his theory of the mimetic rivalry that he sees as informing all human behaviour – what he calls 'relations of imitation' – to the present world situation. Contradicting all notions of 'evil' Islam, he would agree with many Arab writers, such as Yasmina Khadra or the Egyptian Alaa Al Aswany (*The Yacoubian Building*), who believe that Islam, like the West, is consumed by 'the desire for individual and collective success'. They make, in fact, the leader that is the United States the model of their aspirations while feeling they want to destroy it. 'Under the label of Islam we find a will to rally and mobilise an entire third world of the frustrated and of victims in their relations of mimetic rivalry with the West.' We are, Girard concluded, 'in the middle of mimetic contagion'.

Bibliography

Leo Abse, *Fellatio, Masochism, Politics and Love* (Robson, 2000)

Leo Abse, *Margaret, Daughter of Beatrice: A Politician's Psychobiography of Margaret Thatcher* (Jonathan Cape, 1989)

Leo Abse, *Private Member* (Macdonald, 1973)

Leo Abse, *Tony Blair: The Man Who Lost His Smile* (Robson, 2002)

Bruce Anderson, *John Major: The Making of the Prime Minister* (Fourth Estate, 1991)

Gil Bailie, *Violence Unveiled: Humanity at the Crossroads* (Crossroad, 1995)

Alistair Beaton, *Feelgood* (Methuen, 2001)

Francis Beckett and David Hencke, *The Blairs and Their Court* (Aurum Press, 2004)

Simon Blackburn, *Truth: A Guide for the Perplexed* (Allen Lane, 2005)

Gyles Brandreth, *Breaking the Code: The Westminster Diaries 1992–1997* (Weidenfeld and Nicolson, 1999)

Louann Brizendine, *The Female Brain* (Broadway, 2006)

Michael Brunson, *A Ringside Seat: The Autobiography* (Hodder and Stoughton, 2000)

James Callaghan, *Time and Chance* (Collins, 1987)

Beatrix Campbell, *The Iron Ladies: Why Do Women Vote Tory?* (Virago, 1987)

Elias Canetti, *The Conscience of Words* (André Deutsch, 1986)

Elias Canetti, *Crowds and Power* (Victor Gollancz, 1962)

Stanley Cavell, *Disowning Knowledge in Six Plays of Shakespeare* (Cambridge University Press, 1987)

Peter Chadwick, *Understanding Paranoia: What Causes It, How It Feels and What to Do about It* (Thorsons, 1995)

Bill Clinton, *My Life* (Hutchinson, 2004)

Hillary Rodham Clinton, *Living History* (Headline, 2003)

Robin Cook, *The Point of Departure* (Simon and Schuster, 2003)

Robert Dallek, *Flawed Giant: Lyndon B. Johnson and His Times, 1961–1973* (Oxford University Press, 1998)

Norman Davies, *The Isles: A History* (Papermac, 2000)

Daniel Defoe, *Roxana, the Fortunate Mistress; or, A History of the Life and Vast Variety of Fortunes of Mademoiselle de Beleau: Afterwards Called the Countess de Wintselsheim in Germany: Being the Person Known by the Name of the Lady Roxana in the Time of Charles II* (Oxford University Press, [1724] 1996)

Michael Dobbs, *First Lady* (Hodder and Stoughton, 2006)

Greg Dyke, *Inside Story* (HarperCollins, 2004)

J. C. Flügel, *The Psycho-analytic Study of the Family*, 6th ed. (Hogarth Press, 1939)

E. M. Forster, *Two Cheers for Democracy* (Edward Arnold, 1951)

Justin A. Frank, *Bush on the Couch: Inside the Mind of the US President* (Politico's, 2006)

Sigmund Freud, *Art and Literature* (Pelican, 1985)

Sigmund Freud, *The Interpretation of Dreams* (Pelican, 1985)

Sigmund Freud, *On Metapsychology* (Pelican, 1985)

Sigmund Freud, *On Sexuality* (Pelican, 1985)

Sigmund Freud, *The Origins of Religion* (Pelican, 1985)

David M. Friedman, *A Mind of Its Own: A Cultural History of the Penis* (Robert Hale, 2002)

Stephen R. Gaubard and Gerald Holton, *Excellence and Leadership in a Democracy* (Columbia University Press, 1962)

Michael G. Gelder, Juan L. López-Ibor and Nancy C. Andreasen (eds), *New Oxford Textbook of Psychiatry* (Oxford University Press, 2003)

Anthony Giddens, *The Third Way: The Renewal of Social Democracy* (Polity Press, 1998)

André Gide, *Journals 1889–1949* (Penguin, 1967)

René Girard, *A Theater of Envy* (Oxford University Press, 1991)

René Girard, *Things Hidden since the Foundation of the World* (Stanford University Press, 1987)

Johann Wolfgang von Goethe, *Wisdom and Experience* (Routledge and Kegan Paul, 1949)

Philip Gould, *The Unfinished Revolution: How the Modernisers Saved the Labour Party* (Little, Brown, 1998)

Paul Halloran and Mark Hollingsworth, *Thatcher's Gold: The Life and Times of Mark Thatcher* (Simon and Schuster, 1995)

Anthony Howard, *Basil Hume: The Monk Cardinal* (Headline, 2005)

Aldous Huxley, *Island* (Penguin, 1964)

Peter Hyman, *1 out of 10: From Downing Street Vision to Classroom Reality* (Vintage, 2005)

Bernard Ingham, *Kill the Messenger* (HarperCollins, 1991)

Bernard Ingham, *The Wages of Spin* (John Murray, 2003)

Oliver James, *They F*** You Up: How to Survive Family Life* (Bloomsbury, 2002)

Boris Johnson, *Lend Me Your Ears* (HarperPerennial, 2004)

Carl Gustav Jung, *The Integration of the Personality* (Kegan Paul, 1940)

Carl Gustav Jung, *The Undiscovered Self* (Routledge and Kegan Paul, 1958)

Penny Junor, *The Major Enigma* (Michael Joseph, 1993)

Penny Junor, *Margaret Thatcher: Wife, Mother, Politician* (Sidgwick and Jackson, 1983)

William Keegan, *The Prudence of Mr Gordon Brown* (John Wiley, 2003)

Yasmina Khadra, *Les Sirènes de Bagdad* (Julliard, 2006)

Søren Kierkegaard, *'Crisis in the Life of an Actress' and Other Essays on Drama* (Collins, 1964)

Adam LeBor, *Milosevic: A Biography* (Bloomsbury, 2002)

Michael R. Liebowitz, *The Chemistry of Love* (Little, Brown, 1983)

Konrad Lorenz, *On Aggression* (Methuen, 1966)

Linda McDougall, *Cherie: The Perfect Life of Mrs Blair* (Politico's, 2001)

John Macmurray, *Persons in Relation* (Faber and Faber, 1961)

John Major, *John Major: The Autobiography* (HarperCollins, 1999)

David Marquand, *Decline of the Public: The Hollowing-out of Citizenship* (Polity, 2004)

Christopher Meyer, *DC Confidential: The Controversial Memoirs of Britain's Ambassador at the Time of 9/11 and the Iraq War* (Weidenfeld and Nicolson, 2005)

Ronald Millar, *A View from the Wings: West End, West Coast, Westminster* (Weidenfeld & Nicolson, 1993)

Jean Montaldo, *Chirac et les 40 menteurs . . .* (Albin Michel, 2006)

Sebastian Moore, *Let This Mind Be in You: The Quest for Identity through Oedipus to Christ* (Darton, Longman and Todd, 1985)

Thomas Moore, *Care of the Soul: How to Add Depth and Meaning to Your Everyday Life* (Piatkus, 1992)

Piers Morgan, *The Insider* (Ebury Press, 2005)

John Mortimer, *Character Parts* (Viking, 1987)

Mo Mowlam, *Momentum: The Struggle for Peace, Politics and the People* (Hodder and Stoughton, 2003)

James Naughtie, *The Rivals: The Intimate Story of a Political Marriage* (Fourth Estate, 2001)

Peter Oborne, *The Rise of Political Lying* (Free Press, 2005)

Peter Oborne and Simon Walters, *Alastair Campbell*, rev. ed. (Aurum Press, 2004)

Dagmar O'Connor, *How to Make Love to the Same Person for the Rest of Your Life and Still Love It!* (Doubleday, 1985)

George Orwell, *'Inside the Whale' and Other Essays* (Penguin/Secker and Warburg, [1940] 1966)

Jeremy Paxman, *The Political Animal: an Anatomy* (Michael Joseph, 2002)

Ben Pimlott, *Harold Wilson* (HarperCollins, 1992)

John Rentoul, *Tony Blair: Prime Minister* (Little, Brown, 2001)

Paul Richards (ed.), *Tony Blair: In His Own Words* (Politico's, 2004)

Peter Riddell, *The Unfulfilled Prime Minister: Tony Blair's Quest for a Legacy* (Politico's, 2005)

Anthony Robbins, *Awaken the Giant Within: How to Take Immediate Control of Your Mental, Emotional, Physical & Financial Destiny* (Simon and Schuster, 1992)

Geoffrey Robinson, *The Unconventional Minister: My Life Inside New Labour* (Michael Joseph, 2000)

Simon Rogers (ed.), *The Hutton Inquiry and Its Impact* (Politico's, 2004)

Denis de Rougement, *Talk of the Devil . . .* (Eyre and Spottiswoode, 1945)

Paul Routledge, *Mandy: The Unauthorised Biography of Peter Mandelson* (Simon and Schuster, 1999)

Anthony Sampson, *Who Runs This Place? The Anatomy of Britain in the 21st Century* (John Murray, 2004)

Derek Scott, *Off Whitehall: A View from Downing Street by Tony Blair's Adviser* (I. B. Tauris, 2004)

Paul Scott, *Tony & Cherie: A Special Relationship* (Sidgwick and Jackson, 2005)

Roger Scruton, *The West and the Rest: Globalization and the Terrorist Threat* (Continuum, 2002)

Anthony Seldon, *Blair*, 2nd ed. (Free Press, 2005)

Alexander Solzhenitsyn, *'One Word of Truth . . .': The Nobel Speech on Literature, 1970* (Bodley Head, 1972)

Philip Stephens, *Tony Blair: The Price of Leadership* (Politico's, 2004)

Carol Thatcher, *Below the Parapet: The Biography of Denis Thatcher* (HarperCollins, 1996)

Margaret Thatcher, *The Downing Street Years* (HarperCollins, 1993)

Lionel Trilling, *Sincerity and Authenticity*, rev. ed. (Oxford University Press, 1974)

Francis Wheen, *How Mumbo-Jumbo Conquered the World: A Short History of Modern Delusions* (Fourth Estate, 2004)

Bob Woodward, *State of Denial: Bush at War, Part III* (Simon and Schuster, 2006)

Hugo Young, *One of Us: A Biography of Margaret Thatcher* (Macmillan, 1989)

Index